Love Child

Amanda May Philp

Copyright © 2025 Amanda May Philp

All Rights Reserved. No part of this publication may be reproduced, distributed, or transmitted in any form or by any means—electronic, mechanical, photocopy, recording, or any other—except for brief quotations of the authors or editor.

Although the authors and editor have made every effort to ensure that the information in this book was correct at press time, the authors and editor do not assume and hereby disclaim any liability to any party for any loss, damage, or disruption caused by errors or omissions, whether such errors or omissions result from negligence, accident, or any other cause.

Table of Contents

DEDICATION 5

FOREWORD 6

PROLOGUE 7

CHAPTER ONE 9

CHAPTER TWO 14

CHAPTER THREE 24

CHAPTER FOUR 38

CHAPTER FIVE 48

CHAPTER SIX 55

    BRIMMING WITH COCKTAILS 63

CHAPTER SEVEN 64

CHAPTER EIGHT 74

    ANOTHER NAME 75

    Huffle Me Muffle Me 78

    TIL DEATH DO US PART 79

CHAPTERNINE 80

    MY BITCH 85

    COMMITTED 87

    RUNNING FOR NOTHING 88

    TEARS OF A WOMAN 89

CHAPTER TEN 90

    THINGS I REGRET 99

    UP A TREE 101

    SOMEDAY 102

    GARDEN OF RATIONS 103

CHAPTER ELEVEN 113

CHAPTER TWELVE 127
CHAPTER THIRTEEN 141
CHAPTER FOURTEEN 147
CHAPTER FIFTEEN 157
CHAPTER SIXTEEN 165
CHAPTER SEVENTEEN 170
CHAPTER EIGHTEEN 172
CHAPTER NINETEEN 174
CHAPTER TWENTY 179
CHAPTER TWENTY ONE 185
CHAPTER TWENTY TWO 191
CHAPTER TWENTY THREE 200
CHAPTER TWENTY FOUR 204
CHAPTER TWENTY FIFE 212
CHAPTER TWENTY SIX 223

DEDICATION

Of course, it's interesting how people fight. Some dance, some stick. Some smarm and most ignore. Acknowledgement in the metaverse can be a terrible thing, you know. Most say I am naïve. They sneer at love. Love, the very thing that keeps us breathing... (*Bonnie Raitt*)

For my beloved perfume boys, mymother Wendy; my siblings Sean, Kyla, and Nathan; for Doris, my grandmother, who loved books; and for Jean, my grandmother, who never stood a chance but had a great time. To all of you who rescued mefor no reason. And to the little boy who thought he was just the "leftovers",may your heart be bigger than your wallet to the end of time. Stew peas and rice forever.

Thank you for my love,so I can come home and work again. Welcome to the family. We are Canadian – Quebecois, Irish, Jamaican, Masaii, Ghanese, Spanish, Luxembourgese, Dutch, Jewish, Italian, Sicilian, Greek, American, Ojibwe, Cree, Mexican, Métis, Swedish, German, Persian, Russian, Ukrainian, Japanese, Polish, Czechoslovakian, Australian, New Zealanders, Lithuanian, Argentinean, Chinese, Latvian, Romanian, Slovenian, Haisla, South Afrikan, Inuit, Portuguese, Hungarian, Hawai'ian, Indian, Filipino, English, Scottish, Welsh, French, Brazilian, Swiss, Armenian, Romanian and Islanders. Not in any particular order and not how you think because some of us came by boat.

I amliberal. But I'm also weird (a person's destiny).

FOREWORD

"Do you swear to tell the truth, the whole truth and nothing but the truth, so help you god?" the walrus asked.

"I cannot," she replied, "for god only reveals one layer of the truth to me. It might not be your truth. How can I know the whole truth, for I am but a girl-woman, granted favor by the master creator to roam about meeting other creations and learning from them?"

The walrus dribbled. To pin the butterfly would be a marvelous trophy but he sensed the cost would be high. She was violet, and when she moved, all the colors of the act of creation shimmered. Why would the Grace allow such an emissary to flutter about the realms unfettered, he mused. The Leviathan would not like this, not one iota.

The angels shifted behind her: the light and the dark, the breathtakingly beautiful and the truly terrible. She was unaware of her protectors, or, ... Was she a captor? "Love child" blazed in the walrus's brain for an instant and then dimmed. Love child! The butterfly was the creator's love child.

"Oh dear," the walrus wept, "how free you must be."

"Tis my only gift," the butterfly replied. "I may love whatever I please. I may not, however, keep anything for myself as my love is a battery."

PROLOGUE
__WHERE DO ALL THE HORSES MEN GO?__

Once you love close to the bone
Nothing else will do
Even if it killed you the first time
You still try to go home
Or you will fail too
And you'll go;
Even so, even so, even so, even so...

Where do all the horse's men go?
When it's over
Where do all the horse's men go?
When you don't know
How far out on the limb you can go?
But you'll go;
Even so, even so, even so, even so...

How far out do the horse's men go?
When nothing else will do
Or do they fail too?
Where do all the horse's men go?
When the ride is over
But they'll go;
Even so, even so, even so, even so...

Where do all the horse's men go?
Close to the bone on their way home
Where do all the horse's men go?
And they'll go
Even so, even so, even so, even so...

Where do all the horse's men go?
Where do they hail to?

Amanda May Philp
2021

CHAPTER ONE

My name is Amanda May Philp. For those who like this sort of thing, I am a Red Overtone Moon, Wood Dragon, with Isis on my Cancer ascendant and Lilith on my Capricorn descendant conjunct with my sun. My natal moon conjuncts Uranus, Pluto, and widely Mars in my fourth house of Virgo, although truthfully, my soul chart puts them in Gemini, the intercepted sign in my 12th house and of my north node. My south node conjuncts the Galactic Centre and Mercury in Sagittarius, while Saturn widely conjuncts my mid-heaven in Pisces. Basically, everything in the fourth house opposes Chiron one way or the other, and my Venus is a big square impossible dream, one that sits on the Freemasonry asteroid at five degrees Sagittarius (do you like my eyes). Let the good times roll. My social insurance number adds or reduces to thirty-three. All my life, I have occupied the space between. My uncle says I've always been a bit of a flying saucer, a term I can only attribute to the fact that I surface from time to time and then disappear. I'm told I managed to balance my karma, so I haven't the vaguest idea what I am doing here, but they say twenty-threes are extreme and/or blind, so I come by it, honestly. Oh, Uranus was stationary when I re-entered this world backwards. I'm peculiar. 'Nuff said.

I am a disgraced catholic, Anglican, jew, and Jehovah's Witness; mostly due to my heritage. We also have Baptist and Pentecostal in the family and, if I'm not mistaken, some Hindu outliers. It's not my fault or necessarily my problem, but in my experience, all religions are unforgiving and never do anything but demand fealty in the name of GOD. Perhaps that is the way we feel special or better than the next person. I've never found forgiveness without crawling on broken glass, and by then, it was always too little too late because usually, I had no idea what I was begging for. In the end, they would never tell me the truth or forgive anything. My mother was desperate for it, and my father loved her. He loves God. We all do. We just think we are the only ones who are the chosen people. In the end, they never care for our endless faith, abandoning us the moment we need them to help us; which is why I could never leave my mother or father "out there" just in case. It happened to my Baptist Granma Berle, and she called the Witnesses "Jehovah Wickedness".

To be fair, the Jehovah's Witnesses stayed by my mother's side until the end, but you know, corporate insolence isn't just an ESG faux pas. It's healthcare, too. How much is a life worth? You will never decide this. Your doctor will. Buyers beware. My god-daughter is a surgeon, and she makes those kinds of decisions without you ever knowing if your life is worth saving. The first question ever posed is, "Do you have any money?" Healthcare is NOT free. Don't be a fool. Only the elite are treated seriously, and only if someone releases their money to save them. So if your physician won't look you in the eye or yells at you, RUN! Because your somebody will keep your money and let you die. So you did, or you didn't pay for your children. How much does it cost? And when you are done paying, how much will it cost them to pay the same money for you over and over again at the expense of your grandchildren?

You have to understand that military service was the key to honour in past generations, and if you don't, you will if there is ever another world war. Because you are going to be the next one who will have to fight for your freedom along with everyone else, as it were. Military service and babies.

My blood is Irish (Galway, Cork), English (Manchester), Scottish (Edinburgh), French from the Paris District, and Swedish (2%), in that order. My genomes are Persian (from my father) and American from my mother (Jesse James). Although my first crush was a native Indian boy of my medical blood type in grade eight, and my first love in high school was a close blood match, I lived my life as a fancy girl, refusing to have children since I was too young and it was denied to me for religious reasons and so I did what everybody did; married a Canadian as best I could and endured sniffing for the rest of my life because every man thereafter was nowhere near my blood type. They just looked like it. I loved them all in spite of the objections until my health would give out, and I would end up in the hospital, costing the Canadian government money as I tried to unsuccessfully meet my never-ending obligations to the empire.

I was born into the midst of a blinding snowstorm in St Boniface, Manitoba, the worst recorded in fifty years. My mother, still nineteen years old, thought it a great adventure, she told me, water broken, standing in the middle of the apartment living room, unable to locate her husband, my father, who was out on manoeuvres at the base. When necessity dictated, she finally called her physician to tell him that she could not get a taxi and was promptly dispatched by ambulance to the hospital. I was born twenty minutes later, according to my live birth record, just after the sun fell below the horizon at 4:47pm on December the twenty-third in nineteen hundred and sixty-four. It is unclear when my Dad arrived or whether he showed up at all, but his name was typed in. Mom did have a picture of me in the arms of his father, a year before he met his demise, in a christening gown at the Anglican Chapel at Camp Borden, Ontario, three months later; before they (my parents) converted to become Jehovah's Witnesses when I was two years old.

My mother was a truly beautiful woman; a cross between Snow White and Audrey Hepburn, only with a little more flesh on her hips and the face of an angel that remained unlined until the day she died. Truthfully, her second daughter, my sister, would rival her face and figure, possessing the stuff of Maid Marian and Marilyn Monroe, but Mom had a different kind of beauty than she did, although she took great pains to ensure that my sister never knew she was the stuff of starlets.

Having been conceived six months before my parents engaged in the ceremony of matrimony, I was considered oddly illegitimate, and the name of my mother on my birth certificate would be her maiden name. In actual fact, her married name would be recorded on the live birth record until the following month, when the first name was changed to AMANDA and initiated. Two months later, my true name would be written in my mother's handwriting on a medical record at a Canadian army base, although she would never really own up to giving birth to me, telling me I was her friend rather than her daughter. I never really knew if there was any significance to that and, frankly, didn't much think about it at all until I was well into my fifties, when

I was forced to reconcile the assortment of documentation that had somehow lead me to become lawfully and legally Nathallia Brown.

Shortly after the "christening", we moved to Calgary, Alberta, where there is a black and white picture of me sitting on a wall between them against a backdrop of the Rocky Mountains. Less than six months later, we were ensconced in Ottawa, Ontario, on Vachon Street, in a third-floor walk-up where my legitimate brother was born. We shared a room, with him in his crib and me on a plywood frame with a big piece of soft foam beside him. I used to wake in the night and push the foam against the wall. I must have travelled in my sleep and taken the foam with me because I would wake up in the dark with it hanging over the edge of the bed. My grandmother's white leather bag hung on the bedroom door behind me, full of FullerBrush toys from the FullerBrush man. There might have been some Tupperware in there, too. My brother was a mere thirteen months and three weeks younger than I was, and we used to run up and down the long hallway from the front door to our rooms at the back. My parents were young; twenty and twenty-one.

Somewhere in there, my Dad's father died, and he discovered, to his shock, that HE was illegitimate and that Aunt Helen down the street was actually his father's Canadian wife from Wales. It must have been a real kicker since he had emigrated from England in nineteen forty-eight, a mere four months after everyone had been declared Canadian citizens in nineteen forty-seven; with his mother, who came over as his Dad's wife, having married him in England. Ironically, his racial origin is recorded as Welsh because his mother was sent "off the farm" in England to a hospital in Cardiff, Wales, to bear her husband's fruit, albeit with no Welsh blood at all. She had died at the age of forty-nine in Hamilton, Ontario, Canada, from asthma and had left Dad alone with his father. She is buried in St Catharines, Ontario, although she originally "immigrated" to Saskatchewan from Sweden because her parents were Canadian. It's funny because I usually order "ohcanada" candy to put in stockings and it always arrives with a sale sticker. A shame, really, since she served in the last war. Most of my family committed to military service or became doctors and nurses, surgeons or court-appointed officials. Very English in my opinion, since they are a nation of "councillors" who like to do a lot of hidden paperwork. From all accounts, his father adored him but my Dad was shaken. Helen was supposed to divorce his father but having three children already, two daughters and a "mentally challenged" son, she sensibly and unfortunately reneged. Probably because the boy was her legitimate son instead of his so he bailed for Jeanie and my dad. Stupidest thing he ever did because in the end, he lost them both along with his life and my daddy grieved his mother and still does; because her Canadian parents didn't want to lose their Swedish bloodline from Jean Phillips. And so I came to be.

CHAPTER TWO

<u>CANADA</u>
Amanda May Philp

How many miles would it take
To walk Canada
Cause giving in has nothing to do with love
Does anyone love you?
Not especially
Why do others give up when you don't?
You keep producing
And you understand
But you give no quarter
Once you have forgiven
And they hate you for that
Because then, they would have to love you for real
And nobody does that
Take heart
They don't care about each other either
And so you have your freedom
They'll never forgive you for that either
But they need you to be this way
Because love is the only thing that's free
And they want that most of all
Most of all.

My father was still in the Canadian military but was working for CSIS before CSIS actually formed, as the family lore goes. He was, in fact, a British national who worked as a spy, decoding and translating Russian, all the while believing that he was a Canadian citizen. That fallacy was discovered when he was in HIS fifties, and I was in my twenties, having obtained a British passport with which to travel Europe. He was forced to obtain his Canadian citizenship years after leaving the Canadian military and spending his life working for the Crown, only to retire at the age of fifty-two. He wept in the kitchen. I did not have compassion for him at the time, failing to realize until I was his age that everything he thought he was was untrue or built on sand that had shifted. He was still a Jehovah's Witness, by the way. The whole thing was bizarre, in my opinion, but I was still a snotty kid. My dad loved working, he just loved it. It was only the second time I'd seen him cry (the third was the death of my mother), and now I don't blame him one bit.

I knew my maternal grandmother and grandfather well. She was an elegant English woman who hailed from a prominent family in London, so to speak, and loved books. I grew up on the books she sent me for my birthdays and Christmases. I adored reading. Being raised as one of Jehovah's Witnesses was isolating, to say the least, and I was hungry for anything that expanded the scope of my teeny tiny world. My grandfather was from Glasgow, Scotland, and he adored her. She was thrown over for a "blonde bombshell" by her fiancé during the war, as she tells it, and rather than return spurned to London society, she met and married my grandfather and came to Canada with my mother in tow on the last sailing of the Queen Mary. My grandfather would sit with me after dinner and tell me it was a lovely war because that is when he met my grandmother.

So Grandmummy, as we called her, had three older brothers, and she often said that coming to Canada was the best thing that ever happened to her because, in England, she only played tennis and knew how to boil water for tea. In Canada, she cried with her best friend at the bus stop the first year they were here because they had no money, but she learned to stand on her own two feet. She was very English and quite intolerant of my mother, who wanted to have six children, which, in the end, she almost did, but much to the life-long bitter disappointment of her mother. Becoming a Jehovah's Witness put the proverbial icing on the cake, as it were, and they never reconciled. My mother was able to manage the biting disapproval at intermittent times over the course of her life, but never did they resolve this, and she suffered from brutal migraine headaches, depression, and prescription drug dependency to the end of her days. On a rare good day, Mom was breathtaking, but like the little girl with the curl on her forehead, "when she was bad, she was horrid." Unfortunately for her, she had been christened a Catholic in England and confirmed as an Anglican in Canada, and she couldn't catch a break from anybody. I loved that woman to the marrow of my bones, like no other human being on earth, with a love that was unrequited to the day she died. She would not forgive me either, a heartbreak that lead me to change my first name in my fifties and wreak havoc. The great irony in all of this, of course, is that Grandmummy had four children and two miscarriages in Canada herself. Go figure. This is all in the name of "so the women would have choices". My mother was sneered at by everyone. I would have checked out, too.

Mom and Dad met in primary or secondary school. They lived next door to each other at the foot of the mountain in Hamilton, Ontario, around the corner from the Lifesaver factory, and dated on and off from the age of twelve. Dad once climbed up the roof of the house to her room in the attic and inadvertently knocked the bricks out of the chimney. They never spoke much of those years, only that Grandmummy worked and Mom was in charge of the house. She played basketball, had honours in Chemistry, set fire to a field once, and the boys from school used to like to hang out on the front porch. She had two sisters, after all.

Of course, I was somewhat taken aback to discover in my forties that Grandmummy's father was, in fact, a French Jew from the Paris district. It was quite by accident. You see, Grandmummy and one of my mother's sisters had a love of clothes. Grandmummy used to be taken to the milliners once a year to be measured, and all of her clothes were made for her. It was a trial for her since she had a well-developed set of breasts and felt she would die from mortification when she was being measured. HER father had changed HIS last name after the war, left for England, and married her mother! Oh, for heaven's sake. Grandmummy continued to work outside the home until she was seventy-eight years old and engaged a Czechoslovakian seamstress who continued to make her clothes for her (Grandmummy had a Czech grandmum whom she adored and she used to tell me stories about her in a hushed voice). The same woman would later make adjustments to my wedding dress so it would fit. When a new manager came into the office one day and pointed to her and said, "What is she doing here" it was all over. My grandmother was forced to retire at the age of seventy-eight and do "charity" work into her nineties. Why she chose to tell me about her father at the time she did, I will never know, but she whispered it to me at the front door of a store in Parkdale, Hamilton; owned and run by a woman named Hannah, who filled it with the most beautiful things. Hannah had chosen to confide that she had survived the Holocaust as a little girl and had never had any pretty things, so her sons gave her free rein to put whatever she liked on the shelves. It was a wonderful place, and I loved to go there with my grandmother and aunt and leisurely look at every little piece Hannah had found and put in there. And then we would pick out a monstrous chocolate as a gift. My aunt would make some kind of lovingly mocking remark, and my grandmother would respond by saying, "Tch, well, I have to have something." She used to stuff my grandfather with nuts, and chocolate was the devil because he had acquired a mild form of diabetes in his late eighties...

Meanwhile, Granddaddy was an intellectual. He had won a scholarship to an Ivy League school in Scotland, but he worked at Dofasco and never really fit in because of this. He was Roman Catholic but had been raised in "foster care" in Scotland and hated the nuns for reasons he did not share, which is why Grandmummy christened their Canadian children Anglican. They were a social couple; they danced on Friday night at the Legion, and they were season symphony attendees. She was a member of the Imperial Order of the Daughters of the Empire (IODE) until she was forced to replace her hip. They fought like cats and dogs, which drove my mother crazy growing up, but they were devoted. They loved politics. She practised yoga and walked three miles every morning as the sun came up, a routine she maintained until her hip gave out, which was just as well since she had reportedly lost the volume in her breasts the year before and was quite put out about it because she had purchased a new bathing suit in June to swim at the YWCA over the following winter and by October could no longer fill it out. Granddaddy liked to put on his cap (he was quite dapper) and go for walks. Later in his life, Grandmummy used to fret that he would pitch himself off the side of the front steps since he had managed to catapult himself into the bed of flowers in front of the porch when he first began using his cane. He survived it though, and a couple of hours later, one of the neighbours came to the door bearing a bunch of carrots for her, having gotten them at the store at Granddaddy's request, saying she had asked him to pick some up for dinner. He derived a great deal of amusement from these minor shenanigans. He did not however, find it at all amusing if she was not in his bed in the evening when he got there. Nor was he inclined to allow pyjamas, a little known fact I was treated to the year I got her a nightie for Christmas. I received a phone call from my aunt who somewhat embarrassedly asked if I could give her the gift receipt. Sometimes it's more than you need to know but alas there's always more where that came from.

I digress. When I was three years old, I was spinning around with a glass gallon milk jug and fell on a piece of glass when it hit the radiator. My parents couldn't afford a car so they asked the neighbours downstairs for a ride to the hospital. I remember laying flat in the back seat so the blood wouldn't run all over the floor with my father leaning worriedly over the front passenger seat. When we arrived, a sheet was placed over me, with a hole cut in it over the wound, and they stitched it up. I don't know if it was frozen, I just know it hurt. When it was done, they stood me up on the table and Dad carried me out to the car. Three weeks later a pissed-off family physician ripped out the stitches that the skin had already grown over. Yeah, that hurt too and I still have the scar. Dad pointed it out from time to time and bemoaned, but I didn't really notice. I finally covered it with a tattoo in my fifties, in a fit of rebellion. It said, "A life lived in fear is a life half lived." It was a Spanish saying uttered in an Australian ballroom dancing movie (*Strictly Ballroom*). And since I had friends and family in both places, it rang true.

The neighbours downstairs were Jim and Diane. Sometimes Diane used to tie Jim's shoes for him which puzzled me. I mean, he could drive a car but he couldn't tie his shoes? At our house when we had company, if the women cooked, the men cleaned up. This was great, in my opinion, since my brother and I used to stand on two chairs to do the dishes, one washing and one drying and it would take us over an hour to finish. When Jim and Diane came for dinner though, Jim didn't know how to dry dishes. I resolved that when I was grown, I would only marry a man who knew how to do things. I guessed Diane had married him so she could help him.

We moved to Carlsbad Springs into a little red brick house in the country just outside of Ottawa proper, and my Dad planted a garden behind the house which used to yield an enormous number of green beans which were bagged and dispatched to friends. The Dutch family next door had three boys who were rougher and tougher than my brother and I, and they used to hurl us bodily down the slope between our houses regularly. There was a massive field behind the house and one day when we were out back, I showed them the space between my legs so they would know I was a girl and shouldn't do things like that. My mom used to cut my hair short so I thought they might be mistaken, thinking I was a boy. It was to no avail, however, and the hurlings continued until I started kindergarten. It turned out, I was the oldest of all and I attained a certain cache, being the one standing at the side of the road waiting for the school bus to pick me up. The only catch was that I could no longer stand at the living room window with my brother at eleven o'clock in the morning, waiting for the train to go by. Sometimes there would be more than one caboose and when that exciting and happy event occurred, Mom would put the Everly Brothers on the record player and the three of us would dance jubilantly around the living room until we were out of breath. Ironically, the Canadian Cancer Society was running an anti-smoking ad at the time, featuring a couple of flamenco dancers in black and white, who could not carry out the dance because they possessed smokers coughs that worsened until they were left in a heap on the floor. This had the opposite effect on me, causing me to detest the peanut butter and jelly sandwiches I was consuming at the time, but it was no deterrent to my taking up the habit and keeping it, off and on, the greater portion of my life.

From Carlsbad Springs, we moved into Ottawa proper, just a block from Queen Mary School, where I was to attend grade one and in whose field my Dad would teach me to ride my first bicycle. I crashed into the only obstacle there was, the flagpole, and incurred my second lifelong injury: a dimple on my right thigh, left behind after the intense bruising had faded. We were poor, our bookshelves fashioned from cinderblock and plank board. I got my clothes from garbage bags of leftovers and hand me downs that circulated the Jehovah's Witness congregations and my socks and underwear; surreptitiously sent by my extended family, all wrapped in colourful cellophane at Christmas time. There was a "rule" in the "truth" as it was referred to by its constituents; one was permitted contact with family who were non-believers, but only if it was "necessary" family business. I guess socks and underwear for little kids were necessary "family business".

The snow fell high in Ottawa. My Dad used to dig out the driveway for the regular Tuesday night meetings we hosted at our house and sometimes the snow bank would freeze almost a storey high. In the evenings, when we weren't attending Christian meetings, we would perform plays for Mom and Dad, using the tiger cutouts from the back of the ice cream cone box for masks and old faded baby blankets for capes. There was a marionette that hung on the wall in the dining room. Her name was Esmeralda and sometimes after supper, Daddy would take her down and using a funny voice, would have her converse with us. We were fascinated and more than a little respectful of her. She was a gypsy you see, and should we be deemed impertinent by giggling, she would fly at us in a fit of temper and then Daddy would have to retire her back to her place on the wall. We loved it because we had friends who were Hungarian gypsies, and they looked so different and were so friendly, with their big dark eyes, gold hoop earrings, jet-black hair, and the big pots of goulash they used to feed us with. Oof! Great clothes; they just fired the imagination.

My sister was born here, and my brother and I were entranced. She was all wild silver blonde ringlets and huge robin's egg blue eyes with tiny hands and long fingernails. We bent over backwards, trying to please her, and always let her have the tiger's mask when we put on plays for Mummy and Daddy. She was a pistol, though, as evidenced one night when she let go of a humungous burp at the dinner table. Dad was on her in a trice, looming over her, barking that one did not burp at the dinner table and that when one allowed such a thing to escape, one apologized immediately for the bad manners. My little sister responded by politely and defiantly burping eight more times, excusing herself after each one, forcing out the last two as she shrank back into her chair in the face of Dad's fury. My well trained brother and I were aghast and held our breaths in horrid fascination as to the outcome of this scenario. She got away with it though.

In spite of all my vaccinations, I caught scarlet fever and languished on the couch for three weeks, pale and listless. My class sent home a huge get-well card that everyone signed, which I kept until it fell apart in tatters. My grade one teacher was good like that, always remembering any student who had taken ill at home, sending best wishes and assignments so we wouldn't fall behind.

By the time I started grade two, we had moved to a townhouse on Heatherington Crescent, and I was off to a new school; Dunlop Public School, and taking the bus again. Mrs. Smythe was a nice teacher, young and cheerful, and this school was fashioned as an open concept with gathering space in the centre of a large space for all the students to mingle with and work together. I was bidden to stand outside of class when God Save the Queen and O Canada played in the mornings over the PA system, ostensibly to place myself outside of allegiance to my country and make the statement that I was for God (*Jehovah/Yahweh*) first and foremost. I'm not sure that allegiance and worship is the same thing. Over the years that followed, this effectively separated me from my classmates in more ways than one since I was to be the new girl every three years.

In grade five, I was transferred again when we moved to Bracebridge, Ontario, to live in the back of a red brick house on a hill overlooking a multitude of blackberry bushes. I loved my grade five teacher, Mrs Godet, formerly Mrs Knighte, who garnered the displeasure of her students by making them write and re-write all their compositions until they were grammatically correct and error-free. I was reading at a university level by then, having been taken from class and IQ tested in Ottawa. I'd have skipped grade five altogether but I couldn't remember my multiplication tables, so I was placed in a combination grade five/six class and left to muddle through as best I could. This inability to make sense of mathematics would dog me throughout school until I was twenty-eight years old and finally nailed the quadratic formula via Independent Learning. I was anxious to add mathematics to my secondary school transcript. For some reason, I never had trouble with math again.

One day, walking home for lunch from school, I slipped on the ice and smashed the back of my head outside of Bracebridge Secondary School. I didn't think much of it until my vision started to blur and with an intense headache I hid behind my textbook, gritting my teeth, trying to hold back my discomfort, not to cause trouble with Mr Olds, my grade six teacher, who was an unsympathetic and cranky man. I made it home from school only to throw up the tomato soup Mom gave us for lunch. Dad was promptly dispatched and I was taken to the hospital where it was ascertained that I had sustained a mild concussion. I was poked and prodded the remainder of the night after my release to ensure that I didn't slip into a coma.

This of course, didn't stop my brother and me from taking the toboggan down the hill at the end of our street the following week. It was full of trees, but we had the supreme belief that we would take the reins of the toboggan and gaily steer around them, making it an exhilarating and exciting ride to the street below. That is until we drove straight into the fourth tree at top speed. Nobody moved for a moment. Then my brother shifted and got up. I tried but couldn't stand. I had done something to my tailbone but only knew that it hurt to stand up, so my brother manfully pulled me back up the hill to the end of our street and along the road to the door of our house where we waited in the street until I could muster the strength to stand upright again. We didn't want to incur Mom's wrath; it having occurred to us that perhaps we had miscalculated our abilities and would get into trouble for it. Besides, I was in too much pain for another spanking.

CHAPTER THREE

Corporal punishment was a thing in our household. Spare the rod and spoil the child. Mom and Dad would disappear into their bedroom to conference while we waited on the couch downstairs for the verdict which, more often than not, led to a trip to the basement where we were spanked with Dad's belt. My brother would roll his eyes until the sting overtook him and vanquished, he would retire to the stuffed chair in the living room with a rag on his head, plugging his earlobe into his ear in agitation. He hated being disciplined in front of his older sister.

In actual fact, my brother had an early childhood sleep disorder,, which left him in REM sleep for the entire night. This was unforgivable in our house since the bed would be soaked with his urine, and every morning, the sheets would be ripped off him and the belt administered while my little sister looked on and wept. Every morning, this tableau was re-enacted. Every morning until my brother was twelve years old and the problem was identified, he was sent to school to stand alone and traumatized, by the school door until the bell rang and we were let inside. I left him there to stand alone, partly out of respect for his solace as a male, partly because we had so little time to play, and I didn't want to waste it. I don't think my parents ever got over it. I don't know what is worse, guilt or shame. They had a hard time of it, self-destructing when it was diagnosed, and they threw up and went into shock over what they had inadvertently done to him. Fuck if we don't kill the thing we love the most... Come to think of it, I wonder if corporeal punishment made us resilient. My mother is now deceased, but my father still looks for him, even so, anything to connect with his son so that he knows how much they regretted and how horrified they were. It's futile, but he does it anyway and it's for the right reasons.

I was placed in a combined grade seven/eight class when we moved once again and this time the move was a shock. Somehow, the other students were either more sophisticated or unruly than me and I had a difficult time floating my boat in this arena. When one of my classmates reached out and casually cupped his hand around my vulva during a game of handball, I knew life was going to be different now, and I did the best I could, after I dealt with my outrage, to make the adjustment. Telling my Dad would have no effect except to make him shrink with revulsion at the perceived spectre of his daughter shelling out touchy feelies of her vagina. I knew I had to rely on myself.

In Peterborough, Ontario, I began to go sideways. The pressure from my parents to be baptized as one of Jehovah's Witnesses was immense. Five hours of bible study a week, a minimum of ten hours a month on proselytizing, and doing my part of the housework and school homework was exhausting. My mother began to track my activities so I wouldn't overdo it. The attempt to be involved in other things at school, such as band practice, gymnastics, and being the editor of the school newspaper, was met with a stone wall of resistance. My parents were not averse to writing letters, insisting that I be sent home after school, even though some teachers offered to drive me so I could join the team. I learned to work fast and put as many things into my lunch hour as possible. I could eat when I was dead. This is when I began to sacrifice food for a life that I wanted instead so I would have the time to accommodate it. Besides, compared to my sister, I was a little bit fat anyway, and my mother was apt to be annoyed if I ate too much. We were on a tight budget and an entire can of salmon for a school lunchtime sandwich was considered both selfish and wasteful since the remainder could be used for an entire supper the next day. I used to take a cheese sandwich and an apple everyday except Fridays when I would take a salmon salad sandwich on Challah bread because Mom could get it on sale. Challah is very similar to Jamaican Peg bread, but it contains more egg yolk. Oh, and a wagon wheel, which was good for trading.

I shared my grandmother's love of books and, truth be told, was not in possession of the great beauty my mother and younger sister had. They wielded it as a power unto its own and I was breathtaken at the extreme reaction it elicited from the male population. It irked my father to no end and he compensated for this by on occasion, insinuating that my mother needed him more than she had a right to (even though he was rarely home and sometimes left her alone for weeks to months at a time with their four children to make a living), and that my sister's IQ was not dissimilar to the size of her uterus, in reference to an observation made by her gynecologist that hers was the smallest one he had ever seen. She's a snap at chemistry, so I hope she remembers how superior her ability is to mine because she knows how to blow things up. I pity the Foo, yes Foo, who underestimates her. In fact, in spite of the weeks I spent riding in the Rockies, I believe she is more adept on horseback than I am and can wield a shotgun or pistol just as well as I can. I'd be lost in the woods with her any day. We'd be the shit out there. In fact, my youngest brother can pretty much skin anything, just like I can, so we are pretty self-sufficient in that area.

I was blissfully removed from all the byplay since I was a little bit chunky and not, in my father's opinion, particularly alluring due to the narrowness of my hips. I understood exactly what he meant when he met me for lunch at the City Hall in Toronto. His mouth dropped when a Canadian colleague of Greek origin walked by. My second husband was her son's godfather, and I knew her. Everyone's mouth fell open when she walked by. Oh yeah she had hips for sure. Didn't keep her husband at the time from wandering off whenever he felt like it since they had a son, but I didn't treat him to that particular tidbit of information. One of my parents' friends told me that I looked like a linebacker from behind. This stuck with me all my life and contributed greatly to the painstaking efforts I took with my diet by the time I turned twenty. "Gone are the days when women are chattels" Granmummy used to tell me. "Now you can do anything you like and you don't need to get married at all because you are very clever." That's a relief. I think.

Because of my marks in school (I was one of the top three), I was chosen in grade eight to be part of a team for a televised version of the public school's "Reach For the Top". It was called something else but it was recorded during school hours and televised on Saturday mornings. It was very exciting, and while I was fairly useless at being quick off the mark for all the run-of-the-mill questions, I proved to be useful for the very geeky and very cool questions – the ones that stumped everyone else. We, as a team, were featured in the local newspaper, although as usual, my last name was trifled with and I was listed as Amanda Philp and Amanda Philip in the same article. My last name would always prove to be a problem. I have been recorded as Amanda Phelps, Amanda Philip, Amanda Phillips, Amanda Thilt, and a plethora of other spellings by those who find the name Philp difficult to pronounce or reconcile as a real name. Even some of the immunization records in grade one were written as Amanda Philip and signed off as such by my father, as were a marriage record in Canada in 1998. Of course, after the vows were spoken and I promised to be a lawful wife, I signed my married name on the document, which was of no help at all. I was confused about this most of my life, mostly due to an elopement to Mexico when I was twenty-one, of which records contained my fingerprint but also signed in my married name but never registered with the Government of Canada until I divorced, a divorce decree which also listed me in my married name.

I had my first real crush when I was ten years old, but it was actually a hormonal awakening and somewhat troublesome in my opinion. I spent a considerable amount of time conspiring about how I was to have sex without having to marry someone since I had decided that due to the general malaise in mood displayed by the female gender in my family and the joviality displayed by the men, that I would be sure to get a job and make my own money so 1) I wouldn't have to explain why I needed another pair of shoes, and 2) so I wouldn't get stuck in the house. Getting stuck in the house was a living death to me as I watched what I perceived to be life itself passing me by as I gazed from the window. Even outings with the Jehovah's Witnesses were filtered as though anyone engaged in conversation with me outside of formal proselytization was a threat to my moral obligation, fiber, and love for God. I was tired of being a chosen one. In my life in Canada, I had met lots of chosen ones, but they didn't attended a Kingdom Hall. Most of them appeared to be happier than the Jehovah's Witnesses who, so far, were the most miserable people I knew.

In grade eight, I fell in love with a boy who was Indian and native to Canada. I didn't know if he was a First Nations boy since I had yet to find out anything about our history outside of the World Wars. I was growing up in the era of the Cold War, and since I had played and learned to read and write with black people Jews Muslims and immigrant children whose parents came from all over the world, I had no recollection of racism or whiteness. I was already weird myself and I loved everybody anyway. So what? My friend at school was away for something called Hanukkah and I missed her. When she returned, my parents would write a note stating that I wasn't to be part of any Christmas party and I would be sent to the library anyway. My first best friend was a black boy (*Why do I have to say black? Indians of India-related descent consider themselves to be white but they're mostly brown just like many African descendants. I dunno, it feels weird to say "black" people and I mean, we don't actually refer to native Indians as red people do we? And why are Asians yellow? This makes no sense to me. Next thing you know we'll be calling the Latin peoples olive or green! lol.*) and we agreed that we liked each other the most so it was all good for me in Canada. I just wasn't allowed out of the house much except for school and Jehovah's Witness business. At one point I was entranced with the idea of being a missionary since it was the only way I would be able to leave and have sanctioned adventures, much to my cousins' amusement.

Anyway, we talked on the phone every day for a month over the summer holidays. Somehow he had managed to be my grade eight graduation date and at the last song at the graduation dance – Stairway to Heaven by Led Zeppelin (every high school dance played Stairway to Heaven as the last song in those days), he kissed me on the lips just as the lights were turned on in the gymnasium; a soft meaningful real kiss. My Dad, having been dispatched by my mother to bring me home was standing there right under my nose but his eyes hadn't found me yet and so I was saved from being grounded or pulled up in front of the church elders for a round of scriptural discipline for my wanton and loose behavior. For six weeks I floated before he dumped me which was just as well since I had been zoned for another school and wasn't joining my grad class in the same secondary school. He was Ojibwe and his aunt was Cree.

That summer, before I turned fourteen, I got my first period. Mom had already told me how babies were made, so I wasn't scared.

Secondary school was a whole new world. I had learned by now how to be the new kid. The standard uniform was white running shoes, a black t-shirt, and a pair of Levi's. Wrangler super-wides were okay too, but not as cool as Levi's. My father had permitted my brother and I to cover a paper route for somebody while they were on vacation with their family, so I had purchased a precious pair with my share and wore them relentlessly, wet, dry, dirty, clean, whatever. Gone were the days of being poked in the chest at school and told my clothes were very original. I endured more sarcasm from the Jehovah's Witness kids than anyone else. In desperation, I learned how to sew and my father agreed to purchase materials so I could make my own clothes. This alleviated a lot of pressure. With several public meetings a week and various circuit and district assemblies, fancy clothes were a necessity and everyday clothes, out of respect, were not allowed, especially pants for women, no matter how cold it got outside in Canada in the winter. I'm not knocking them. It was just the rules of engagement. We had to comply to belong. Everyone has rules.

So saying, I wasn't as awkward in high school as some. I had already been exposed to hordes of people and different schools and I was accustomed to being the odd one. I still had to leave my homeroom and stand in the hallway when the national anthem was being played, but I didn't care about being weird anymore.

However, all this unfortunately backfired on my father when that year my mother had gained a largish amount of weight and, refusing to attend the prerequisite parent-teacher interviews at school, had prevailed upon him to attend them in her stead.

"Your daughter is brilliant" my English teacher told him, "just brilliant."

"I don't know how you do it Mandy," he snarled, as he threw me across the kitchen sink. "You always come up smelling like a rose." I was mouthing off again, and Mom was pregnant with my youngest brother and teary, which upset him to no end. Honestly, in retrospect, I don't blame him a bit.

One day my school friend invited me to a party. I had been relegated to the basement at my house since the birth of my youngest brother and had taken to climbing out of my bedroom window at night. Mostly, I just walked along the railroad tracks outside of my subdivision until I met up with my new boyfriend. He was always waiting for me, or else he sent someone to meet me if he was babysitting his younger half-brothers for his mother. My parents had already had him to the house when a member of the congregation discovered a piece of poetry in my Bible that I had written to him, to explain that I could not be his girlfriend, but he wasn't budging. He had red hair and was cocky as only a teenage boy in love could be, and he treated me like gold, always walking me across town back to my house when the sun was coming up, even though his return trip would take him a couple of hours. He wasn't available that night, so I went out and stood on the road until my girlfriend came to pick me up. She was in a car with her current boyfriend, a seventeen-year-old boy who was a boarder at her family's house. I knew him, so I jumped into the back seat and off we went. Before we breached the parameters of the subdivision, I knew something was wrong. There was a strange boy in the back seat and my girlfriend was laughing in the most peculiar way. I was uneasy but I figured it would sort itself out and I wanted to see this party. Parties were a rare and wonderful occurrence in my life and I was excited. Besides, I hadn't been to all these cities and schools for nothing. I knew how to handle myself socially.

They handed me a small bottle, something called a mickey and I drank, then I coughed and sputtered. I was informed that the feeling would pass the more I drank so I waded in and they were right. I thought the whole thing was very exciting and couldn't wait to get to the party to see what it would be like. An adventure! And I was out of the house! Hurrah! It was one week before my fifteenth birthday.

I must have passed out because I awoke screaming in pain. The car was stopped and the streetlight cast a shadow through the back window. I heard my girlfriend laughing in the front seat as I screamed again. The boy's face hovered over me, disembodied and I felt like something had cut me with a knife and set me on fire. The boy was between my legs and I moaned in agony and begged him to stop, trying to get away. I passed out again and when I came to we were parked in a remote area and I was free. I crawled and fell out of the back seat onto the ground at my girlfriend's feet. As I struggled to stand, I vomited. She was furious as it spewed onto her shoes. Bad manners! Bad manners! My brain threw into my awareness. How could you? We never made it to the party.

I was somewhat dimly aware that I had inadvertently lost my virginity. Is that what it was like? What a gross nightmare. And I was annoyed. It wasn't who I wanted to be with at all. And I was in pain and didn't know why. Lots of pain…

A week later I made arrangements to meet my boyfriend downtown and my girlfriend's boarder offered to drop me off since he was going the same direction on his way out of town to run an errand. Unfortunately, my boyfriend, for the first time, wasn't there. Thinking he was late, I accepted the boarder's offer to accompany him on his errand and off we went. On the way back, still in shock from the events of the preceding week, I fell asleep in the front seat next to him. I awoke when the car stopped to find us parked in the brush somewhere in the countryside. As he lunged for me, I knew what was going to happen. This time I was ready. I fought. I fought for my life. He was big, about a hundred seventy pounds to my hundred and ten. And he was tall, at least a foot taller. The most difficult thing was getting his fingers and mouth off me as he attempted to tear my clothes from my body. Blindly, I panicked and fought harder. Finally, bloodied, I fell back against the leather seat as he abated his efforts. "At least you didn't let me do it," he said in admiration and something akin to grudging respect as he drove us back home. I was shaken. Shaken and damaged. How badly I didn't know yet but I would find out. My nipples were in agony.

I closed the door to the bathroom and gingerly removed my shirt and brassiere. Stark, in the mirror, I registered dully with shock the black black skin that had once been my nipples. So black. I heard my mother shifting in the hallway outside and locked the door. My fault, my fault, it's my fault, was the mantra skittering in my mind. It would skitter for years like that whenever I found myself badly hurt...

After that, my attendance at school became sparse. I went, but I couldn't bring myself to the classroom. It was too enclosed. I wanted out of that school. I wanted out. My girlfriend called me at home in a fury, accusing me of leading him on. I tried to explain, but it wasn't what she wanted to hear. When my father overheard us talking, he missed all the parts except for the fact that I had been bailing out of my window at night. He came down to my room, put his head in my lap, and wept. I felt his hot tears hit my skin and knew that as busted as I was, I could never tell him the truth. And so I didn't.

After that, I began to put on weight. Dad was starting another job in Kingston, and my mother demanded that he take me with him, so I entered another new school. I was now a problem child that needed to be monitored.

The new school was another open concept, Bayridge Secondary School. We eventually rented another house across the field, and I attempted to settle in. One afternoon, I left school with a crowd of friendlies to party at one of their houses. All was well until it was discovered that the hostess had incurred alcohol poisoning and so we were herded into the principal's office and promptly expelled from school for two weeks. I had been invited by my Uncle and one of my aunts (one of my godmothers actually) to accompany them with my cousins to Daytona Beach for March break and it was in peril until my parents decided they needed the break from me and let me go.

I had never in all my born days seen a strip like Daytona. I guess every university across Canada and the U.S. had sent their students there. I was mesmerized as I walked with my cousins. We were now fourteen, fifteen and sixteen, respectively, and I fit right in the middle; a brunette, a blonde and a redhead. We walked as car after car cruised the strip. It was organized mayhem. Eventually we hooked up with a group of young gentlemen from the University of Kentucky and for the next few days we partied happily (meaning hung out) with them in their hotel room with all kinds of students wandering in and out. And this is when I discovered a completely different side of sex. On the third night, my gentle American compadre put his mouth between my legs and did the most marvelous things. I was astonished. Who knew people did such things? I was entranced. We never had intercourse and to be honest, nothing actually happened but that American boy from Kentucky State University restored my faith in men, and I admit, I have been a friend of the U.S. ever since. Not the most sophisticated reason I know, but I always felt safe there after that. An American from Kentucky did that for me. He never knew.

My right nipple never recovered. It stayed shy and damaged and buried for the rest of my life. The scar tissue remained. My clitoris had been ripped off of my pubic bone but I wasn't to understand fully for some time. I was too torn and damaged down below. It would be years before it would be cleaned up but I was always uncomfortable and it wasn't over yet…

I took up smoking. I became what my parents would call rebellious. I lost my honors status in school and I hated going there. My Peterborough boyfriend had gotten a job and wanted to come to Kingston to see me even if he stayed in a hotel but my mother made me give him up and so I lost him; the first boy who ever loved me and would have followed me to another city. It turned out that he had been commandeered by his stepfather to help with something and as mobile phones didn't exist yet, there was no way to contact me to tell me in time. It was the only time he wasn't there for me, the one and only time. I never told him what happened. It wasn't his fault. But that boy was the reason I never signed my name until I was fifty-nine years old. Because he was the one. It's not anyone's fault. I was only fourteen, but I was true. It was true.

The Jehovah's Witnesses decided that I needed personal study. I wasn't baptized yet, and as I turned sixteen, the woman who was assigned to provide additional bible study pronounced me "sweet sixteen and never been kissed." I complied and stopped going to school. With no recourse I was moved again and put into another school which lasted a few months until it became apparent that I longer cared. I told my parents I wasn't interested in being baptized; I didn't want and wasn't going to be one of Jehovah's Witnesses and was informed I was too young to make that decision. We moved again, this time to an apartment building in town. I came and went and wandered about the city at night, getting into trouble. Mom and Dad were not inclined to let me come home. My clothes smelled of smoke and they deemed the influence on my brothers and sister to be negative. At one point I successfully convinced Social Services to let me board with a girlfriend's family but the Jehovah's Witnesses stepped in and pronounced I was more than welcome at home if I followed the rules. This was exacerbated by the fact that my father had done a show cause hearing for a boy I had been seeing who ostensibly had shot someone up with a bunch of arrows and dumped him in the river. I knew nothing about this as I wasn't with him at the time but he was apparently ensconced in the local penitentiary awaiting trial. Dad was no longer in the military due to the fact that Mom was too lonely moving from place to place as he was posted, so he had sought and obtained a job in the courts and in spite of his religious conversion at the behest of my mother, he continued to apply for postings in other cities on a regular basis. His position was that, if he settled down, "it" would be all over. My brothers and sister hated this constant moving but a younger me would egg him on with glee. "Where should we go next Dad" I would ask as he perused the job postings listed by the provincial and federal governments of Canada. He was a rock star too. Just a quieter one.

Now there had been suitors in the congregation, oh yes. It would have been helpful if one of them had taken but we never stayed long enough and due to the closed nature of the organization, there was fierce competition for eligible bachelors and always being a little bit fat and on the way to somewhere else, I was edged out. In retrospect, it was probably for the best since I would have been the blight of that poor brother's existence. My mother never forgave me for it.

I was still naïve to many things, not recognizing what I was seeing in the world. I had taken to hanging out at the Plaza in the evenings, a place where there were shoddy strippers who would entertain the military men and the establishment allowed us to smoke pot at the table. The military were sandwiched between offenders from the

Kingston Penitentiary so I was pretty comfortable. I wasn't a pot smoker per se, preferring to keep my wits about me but a very large man with a fierce dark beard would motion me to sit in the chair beside him and he would watch over me as I settled in beside him at the large round table for the evening watching the comings and goings and making the acquaintance of various people who would "pop in" and socialize. One day he disappeared and I was told he'd been arrested. He was a speed dealer, known to be the second largest supplier in the city. I didn't know if this was true. I had only tried speed once, in the form of a pill called a Christmas Tree but it had been laced with strychnine and landed me in the hospital so I wasn't a fan. In fact, I was somewhat adverse to pills after that, albeit vitamins were not a problem for me. My mother was a big fan of them.

Eventually my comings and goings resembled no pattern and I ceased to even try to accommodate my parents efforts to reel me in, ascertain my whereabouts or pay heed to any kind of curfew but one more occurrence led to that and then I was hopelessly lost and unable to get me to see reason, my mom and dad began to cut back on the amount of time I was allowed to be at home. Given that my clothes smelled of smoke and they were trying to raise my brothers and sister to be Jehovah's Witnesses, I was a bad influence that needed to be disciplined according to the creed. I can't say I didn't blame them or that I blame them now..

One day, I was waiting for the bus and a man stopped by in his car. I knew him. He was one of the characters that frequented the Plaza and I had enjoyed many a conversation with him at the round table. He chatted with me for a bit and suggested we go for a beer so I hopped into the car and off we went. Over eight beers I poured my heart out to him and told him everything that had happened to me. He sympathetically took me out for Chinese food for dinner and booked a room for me to sleep in. Exhausted and unburdened, I exhaled and fell fast asleep. I awoke because I couldn't breathe. Someone (he) had me by the neck and had jammed my face into the pillow while he mercilessly and brutally sodomized me. I was broken after that. And I began to understand that I was in no-man's land. When I ran into him later at the Plaza, incredulously I listened to him ask me why I hadn't called him. I told him I had gone back to my ex-boyfriend and in that instant understood that I needed to be attached somehow to a male in order to keep other males away from me or treating me in a disrespectful manner. He backed off and I never had to look over my shoulder. The era of "dowdy" clothes began and I put on more weight. My mother was a little disgusted. She wanted me to bathe and dress nicely but it was too late. No Jehovah's Witness would consider me to be an appropriate wife now and I knew it. Neither could I bring myself to do what my street girlfriends did as I watched them slowly one by one be led away to a man with a warm and safe bed and a meal. This, to my understanding, meant pimp. And so far, no man had been particularly trustworthy. I also instinctively understood that there were some things in life I might not be able to come back from.

One night, after the last girl gave in and was lead away, I stood in the doorway in an alley. A bare light bulb was lit above me in a metal cage and behind me was a locked heavy metal door. The hour was pitch black, the one darkest one just before the light and I knew I could be seen. I dared not go into the alley, into the dark. They would get me there. Here, I would just be unwaveringly observed.

As I gazed up into the starless sky, I prayed I would last until the dawn broke. And I made decisions. I had just watched the last of my street girlfriends being exhaustedly lead away the preceding evening, to a hot meal, a warm bed and a "nice" man. I was the only one left. I decided there were things worth dying for, in order to avoid, since I'd never be able to retrieve my soul anyway. Instinctively I felt this and so came into being my four hard and fast rules. 1) I would not stick a needle in my arm to get high. 2) I would not have a baby with someone who didn't want to be a Daddy – not a father – a Daddy. (I had a great daddy). 3) I would not do anything to earn a criminal record or go to jail. 4) I would not trade sex for anything, ever; I felt I had earned that one already, and I would go down swinging. I would be in my fifties before anyone told meI was the size of a Tinkerbelle, so my swing would hardly pack a punch.

I learned to move through the world quietly, softly, and invisibly. In my opinion, the women in my family were bitterly unhappy and bereft of compassion when they were stuck in the house, whereas the men were not locked up at home, always jolly and always out. I decided the key to life was to not get trapped in the house. I wanted to be free like them, and I got away with it, for the most part, by being useful. The drawback though, was that being locked up was also equated with the classroom. I could never make long-term commitments there, which ultimately led to being certified and designated by any means possible except through university full on. That would trap me. I would not get over this until I was closer to retirement. Turned out, I adored working, just adored it. It was safe.

I was transferred to another school, and this is where I met the "Duck". I was to find a place to stay with him, and I hung in there as long as possible until the place we had rented turned out to be a sublet, and we were booted from the premises by the owner. To avoid wandering the streets at night again, we moved to a boarding house, and I began to cut. This was a one-time occurrence but I was prevented from contacting my parents by a possessive and contrary man who ripped the public phone by its cord from the booth when I tried to call. This cut was to my face, and I landed in the hospital where my brother and mother arrived, to their horror. What were they going to do with me? When I was released, I was as messed up as ever and one night in desperation, I called my uncle in Hamilton and asked if I could come.

CHAPTER FOUR

Now, my uncle was a different and brave sort of kettle of fish and turned out to be someone who I could rely on to tell me the truth and be respectful at the same time without an agenda. He was my cousin's father and the husband of my mother's youngest sister. I hopped on a bus with two young men in tow, and we arrived in the dead of night at their house. The next morning, after having dispatched the men back to their hometown, he let me take in a stack ofpop bottles for the deposit so I could buy cigarettes. I know he did it because I would have something. I usually give food to men on the street, but I give cigarettes and money to women so they can have something. Uncle was almost finished his studies to be an Adolescent Psychiatrist and was preparing for his final exam. I didn't know it then, but he was contracted to work for the facility in Burnaby, British Columbia, and when, after a few weeks, it was apparent I had nowhere to go, he prevailed upon my aunt to take me with them, even though she was six months pregnant with their first child. My aunt didn't want to cause a problem with my mother, but my mother and father were at their wits end so the day came and I was bundled into the back of the red station wagon and we set off for British Columbia accompanied by my other uncle, my mother's youngest brother. Uncle said I was dissociative, which, although I didn't know what that meant, was true, and I barely spoke a word as we made our way along the TransCanada highway, stopping, unloading and camping every night through the provinces. My recollections were strong of that trip. Saskatchewan was unyieldingly flat and there was literally nothing to see but the hugest sky ever. I experienced the only night of my life there when everything was right with me and the world.

We were camping behind a gas station and grilling steaks on a hibachi. The flies were exorbitantly large and we had difficulty eating without ingesting an insect or two along with them. But the sky! We saw the Northern Lights! It was a spectacle I had never witnessed before, and the vision made me and my problems disappear as if they were of no consequence at all. Those lights bestowed upon me inner peace, and I slept so well that night that I snored without compunction to the dismay of my other uncle, who feared we had been beset by a bear! We finally rolled into Kitsilano, a neighborhood in Vancouver, British Columbia, and holed up in an apartment until Uncle could find us a house to rent. That's when I first tried dim sum! Chinese dumplings that were rolled out in little steam carts...har gow, siu mai, binghua jianjiao, Xiao long bao, pot stickers, sew mai, char sui, law bak go...holy crap, that stuff was good. I was in Vancouver for eight years, and for the last four, I went to dim sum every single weekend, come hell or high water. Of course, I was a little bit fat for "Kits". Weird wasn't the thing here. Everyone was fit, and this is when I began to understand that body size was not my friend. I spent the summer locked in my room, scared my Ontario boyfriend was going to come after me, but other than a letter telling me I was an asshole and that I should always be looking over my shoulder, it eventually appeared that I had escaped. I started school this time combining grades twelve and thirteen and spent the first few months trying to walk up the long hill back home without stopping. I had no muscle anymore, just flab, and it was unbearable. Nonetheless, I gamely donned my black t-shirt, white running shoes, and Levi's and went off to school. Standing out in the "smoke hole," as they called it, I was approached by a group of lovely girls dressed in Ashley print dresses who introduced themselves. This was unheard of in my other schools. Standard behavior was that I was acknowledged after I'd toughed it out on my own for three weeks. Of course, I had noted the sports cars the students were pulling into the parking lot with, but it didn't click until the lead girl leaned in fascination and said to me, "So! You must be from the Bronx." I needed to find a new wardrobe and lose some weight.

The gap between me and the rest of the students at Handsworth Secondary School was apparent in my head. I'd already been demolished and lived in the street. I knew I could make it if I could just settle in and be normal but even my brains failed me, and the blessing at Uncle's was that I only had one rule instead of the potential of a hundred infractions as I had been living all my life; I had to be home or call before the sun came up. That was it. I broke it once. They locked the door and I was forced to tumble through the basement window onto my cousin's bed by her good graces. She had arrived in the fall and was going to college. I tried, but I could never quite make it to class. I was a fish out of water. Even my brain failed me right up until just before the very end. I had written a couple of essays that were deemed to be of high caliber and in spite of the fact that I had scored forty-nine point one percent in History, the essays got me over the threshold and twenty minutes before the graduation list came down, on the day of the graduation ceremonies, my name was added. My aunt had insisted I wear some frothy concoction vehemently opposing my desire to wear a white tuxedo with a pink cumberbund and so, I contented myself with a white suit I had made myself for the ceremony and on that evening, hair done to the nines like a B52 beehive, I entered the graduation dance and promptly fell over a chair much to the amusement of my Accounting and Phys-Ed teachers who had witnessed my entire desultory year. I went down in the school yearbook as the only student in history to get lost ON the way to school, and alas, it was true. I had attempted a shortcut through the ravine and taken a wrong turn and had the humiliating experience of having to explain why precisely, I hadn't shown up to Accounting class.

Graduation was fun although I managed to not distinguish myself in any way other than getting my backside pinched by my girlfriend's father during a dance, and we ended up on the shores of Ambleside Beach in West Vancouver watching the sun come up. Somehow, my dad was right. I came up smelling like a rose. However, the bunch of roses he and Mom sent to me listed their first names instead of Mom and Dad, which was disconcerting.

"Another certificate to put on the wall," my mother sniffed in disdain. Granmummy was not like that. Clever, she called me.

Little fishes are a double-edged sword. Little fishes have nothing to lose.

I adored the corporate world and I enjoyed wearing a suit and heels. It made me feel strong and alive and lulled me into believing I had my shit together because I was working.

The thought of going to university was unbearable; four more years in a classroom – another school. It was a moot point anyway, as my most important transcript was in actual fact, an ignominious defeat. I had barely made it. So I applied for Katimavik, and straight from the brochure, now a website, here is what it was:

"Katimavik offers young adults opportunities to gain life skills and work experience while contributing to community development through volunteerism and employment. The word 'Katimavik' originates from the Inuktitut language, meaning 'meeting place'. Since 1977, Katimavik has brought young Canadians together to learn, to exchange culture and language, and to help build stronger communities across Canada. Katimavik aims to help youth become engaged, caring citizens and capable contributors and leaders for a better Canada. We do this through the development of 21st-century skills, experiential learning, employment, and civic engagement."

It was straight up my alley, and given that I had inherited my father's propensity for travelling, I was far more interested in moving on than staying.

Participating in that program was one of the best experiences of my life. I helped to build a gabion wall to stop the advent of erosion in Port Hope, Ontario. Here is where I met Farley Mowat and Valdy; Canadian writer and musician, while taking part in the promotion of the town's Olde Tyme Christmas. I learned how to work, but I also learned the concept of goal setting and working for a purpose. I learned how to ballroom dance and use tools. I learned how to budget and how to cook for large groups. The next place I was sent was to Notre Dame de La Merci, Quebec, where I painted road signs, bottle-fed baby goats after I dug my way out to the barn in the morning, and the Cha-Cha, taught to me by the Québécois (not quite the same as the Edmonton two-step but both dances were taught to me by farmers). I nearly learned how to ski at Mont St. Anne, but I underestimated the time for learning. First off, the rope tow, which I fell off of, I gamely crouched and pushed off, just like I'd seen on television. It was easy, astonishingly so, until I began to pick up speed, and as my skis began to widen in my stance, I passed the base of the rope tow, fairly cartwheeling in an attempt to slow down. The specter of my Quebecois amis with their mouths dropping, yelling "Asti! Elle est mongole!" stayed with me as I picked up speed anyway, taking out skiers from all directions until I finally came to rest, with nary a pole or ski in sight, having decided to continue on without me, merrily down the hill. The French were pretty decent about it, all considering, as they picked themselves up and set off in hot pursuit of my runaway equipment. I tried downhill skiing once more on the West Coast, hoping for a new lease on the sport, but alas, I was instructed rather curtly over the loudspeaker to get the f*** out of the way after I fell off the chair lift, and so I gave it up and tried horseback riding instead. The third and final placement was on Saltspring Island, one of the Gulf Islands off the coast of British Columbia. Hippieville! Oh, I had a grand time hitchhiking from one end of the island to the other. There, I was given my own little tractor to cut grass for Parks and Recreation, and I learned how to record music. Fabulous! Music was my first love, and I used to sing to my brothers and sister to sleep at night. I had always sung, and my mother, who had played piano growing up, took guitar lessons with me when I was fourteen years old. All in all, it was the best decision I could have made. The lessons and, experiences, and exposures to culture were many and contributed to a certain sophistication, I felt, that could not be obtained in a classroom. Most of all, I learned to work and play with people, something I had missed out on growing up. It was a maturation experience. I never felt cowed around a person with degrees after that. They didn't understand how the world worked the same way I did, and the academic rigor they employed was not the same as the hands-on experience. It greatly contributed to my equilibrium, and when I was finished, although I hiccupped a little bit, I knew I had options, and I had a better idea of what was available in the world and how to go after things I wanted to do.

I came home nine months later, having met a sheep farmer on Saltspring Island, and for awhile, I hung out with him and waffled over what I wanted to do next. Ultimately, I chose to cook, mainly because Mom's cooking had been very plain, very English if you will. I was privy to the entire fine dining in the world, and I learned how to cook and clean just about any fish or animal in existence that could be served in Canada. It was spectacular. The world of fine dining commercial kitchens was rife with drama with the heat, the knives, and the temperaments of those who could truly make food into a mouth-watering work of art. I made my way through various venues, and I completed my apprenticeship to become a Journeyman Red Seal. Over the succeeding nine years, I had the opportunity to cook for Liberace, Mikhail Baryshnikov, Michael J. Fox, Phantom Vox, Blue Rodeo, Mitzi Gaynor, even the Shah of Iran, and a host of football and soccer athletes, Lui Passaglia and Roy Dewalt, among them. It was six degrees of separation from the kitchen to the famous, and I loved it. "I don't know what you do to these people," a bartender would say as he was sent back to the kitchen carrying a taste of the recommended wine with a bite-sized portion of the special that a customer had bade him come to me with. As if I didn't know. It was food.

Around this time, I launched out on my own, having determined my aunt and uncle had been of quite enough assistance to me. My aunt deserved her own household. My cousins and I had descended upon them en mass, and she had a full house trying to raise babies, go to school, and keep us all in check. When they vacationed, we would have the most wonderful parties in their absence: toga parties, electric jello parties, and all sorts. On one such occasion, my friend Brent came into the back door downstairs and seated himself with one of my cousins and her newfound college crowd. They were slightly stuck up, and she was anxious to make a good impression, having fallen in love with one of them. She wasn't a big partier per se, preferring to be as respectable as she possibly could with only the odd indulgence in a cocktail or two. My friend pulled out a bag of weed and calmly rolled a joint, chatting easily, totally unaware that she was having a quiet fit of apoplexy. When he lit up and then held his bag to the light, wondering aloud if there was too much shake in the half ounce he had purchased, my other younger uncle took off upstairs asking me to get him out of there. He was in hysterics of laughter. I met Brent on the landing, quite unaffected by the incident, and the party began in earnest. There were many scenarios played out at our parties, blowjobs in bedrooms (Oh grow up for chrissake, it wasn't me. As my grandmother in law used to say, "It's just a blow job; you don't think they had blow jobs when I was a girl?" This, in reference to the Clinton debacle; they do exist you know), breakups, makeups, dancing, heartfelt conversations, friendly get-togethers, guitars, karaoke, plans made, promises kept, friendships fortified, memories, connections, tea and mushrooms in the kitchen, warm fires, standing in the rain on the deck, dragging some guy out from under a bush cause we could all see him lying there from the dining room window, hurling pickles on the front step, finding my good knives being used for hot knifing hash on the stove by one of my good friends who left a year ago and cycled across Canada then spent the winter in the Tibetan mountains, hugs, tons of laughter; shenanigans of all kinds. I resolved to have one great party a year to keep in touch with all my friends. And I did so. Costume parties at Hallowe'en were my favorite because I had always been especially envious of those kids going from door to door, not preaching the good news, but rather gathering candy in pillow sacks. I made up for it with shooters.

    I moved out and shared a bachelor's apartment with a fellow cooking student. On her birthday, she invited two men; her current boyfriend and her ex-boyfriend. And so I met Mr B; tall, wearing Daytons; riding a motorcycle. I was still extricating myself from my university student. I was tired of writing his essays, and he was starting to get a little whiny. Truthfully, he belonged to my college cousin's crowd, and I had snagged him by leaning across the table at a pub night and telling him to kiss me. College boys were easy. It was a little in her face but I had made my point. Mr B was more my style at the time; from Ontario, on his own more or less, and working as a welder, a tradesman like me. We hit it off instantaneously, and after dumping my guy after a David Bowie concert, I came home to find him there and sat on his lap the rest of the night. And so, my first serious relationship was born. Now Mr B was a cokehead, something that was entirely unknown to me. Hard drugs were always difficult for me. It seemed like everyone came down and fell asleep as the sun rose, and I gritted my teeth, rocking back and forth, waiting and waiting for the same thing to happen to me. So, I stayed away for the most part. My last acid trip, after going across the Ontario border to Fat Lenny's at the age of fifteen, was a couple of years before, having ridden the roller coaster at the Pacific National Exhibition while I was peaking. I never did acid again.

Cocaine was okay. It was the eighties, and everyone suddenly owned a bunch of property backed by junk bonds, but I didn't understand that Mr B couldn't stop, for a couple of years. Mr B was my party guy. We worked a lot of double shifts and stayed up most nights. We knew lots of people and we were of the age that we could get away with the houseful of people we lived with. Antigonishe, Vietnam, Ukraine…we had a blast and worked around the clock. I guess I was always a career girl since I didn't like staying at home. My dad didn't approve of career women, but like my welding teacher at 59 said, "Everyone needs a job", so I worked. I worked hard. I loved every second of it unless I got bored, and then I would move on to fill my brain with new things and loved every second of that. I would later reflect and remember how often a drunken CEO at a wrap-up party would tell me that they loved me because they thought I would get eaten alive. And yet, I only got them through because I could translate and mediate. They were on the same page, and they just didn't understand each other. Fear is the only barrier to success. Fear of loss of love, of honor, of ourselves. Crazy, isn't it. Fighting for face time. I've had the honor of working with some of the best people in the world. That's what a generalist is for, which is what I am. Honestly, try not to go off into peals of laughter. Unfortunately, the devil is in the details, but you can't find out if they're there unless you know enough to ask for them so you can put it all together. Line em up and let it run.

Mr B began to go AWOL, and I knew why. Before we eloped to Mexico, he confided that he had been sodomized by a trucker in Alberta when he was hitch hiking to find work. He was about seventeen years old when it happened. I forgave him instantly, but I knew there were some things that you couldn't get back from, and I lived in agony waiting for him to come home as I watched the things I had given him slowly disappear, one by one, to pay for his habit. I stopped sleeping then, and I didn't sleep again until I came home years later to live in British Columbia because all the bodies were buried in Ontario, and I couldn't reconcile the pain except to let them be there without me in it. I was safe and within reach and unless I was willing to go it alone in Manitoba, which I loved from afar, I had to decide in my heart and soul where it was going to be. I do hope my body goes there when I die, for B.C. gave me solace, real solace, and I just felt a deep gratitude; but my mother was sent there, and I would be so honored if they accepted my ashes and threw them into the river since I had the good sense to stay away and not cause them any trouble.

By the time I turned twenty-three years old, Mr B had given me crabs and Epstein Barr, and I knew if I stayed that, I would become HIV positive, so I offered to pay all the bills if he would go into treatment, but he said he wasn't ready and by then he was already involved with a beautiful dancer from Mexico (no irony there) and so, I got a passport and went to Australia.

Australia was very different. I landed and stayed in a hostel with my girlfriend and two random "Kiwis" from New Zealand who were running from the law. Oddly, I never feel threatened by "criminals" because I recognize "private industry," and in the end, criminals are usually too busy to bother with the likes of me. Only very important people like to kick me around, mostly for not having threesomes or giving blowjobs in hallways, and frankly, it astounds me that someone would think I would behave in such a manner. It has always led me to believe that too much formal education makes you into a useless, entitled twit. As my mother would say, "Oh, for heavens' sake, just get on with it," and my other favorite, "Oh, for heavens' sake, Amanda, you've seen one. You've seen them all". Penises she meant. Penises. This is not strictly true because I haven't seen them all but I've seen more than one.

When was that? It was December 16th. Mr B had killed himself on the 13th; blown his heart out in the bathtub with a shotgun we kept behind the bedroom door. I was long gone by then. Uncle says I bailed, but at least I didn't have to wipe away the blood and tissue exploded onto the tiles. I would never have known if Linda hadn't felt it necessary to track me down. Why? Why would she do that, I wondered. She always flirted with Mr B and had photos taken of them together at parties….so why?

The answer was on the table. Mr B had loved me. No one would touch the table until I arrived. It was my job, apparently. The table was full of all the trinkets we had collected when we were together, and he had them arranged separately. But it was the spice rack that killed me. He had purchased it for me and since we had no money and I was apprenticing as a cook, I had pasted my own little handwritten labels on them and filled them with spices. Mr B had always taken it everywhere with him, even though he travelled light, and put it over the stove. He had loved me. Why is "I love you" the great panacea for all the shitty things I'm about to do to you?

CHAPTER FIVE

Immediately, I went to the Sydney Opera House to see a chamber singer and was in heaven. And then I went river rafting in Tully. My girlfriend went skydiving but I didn't have the stones since that had been Mr B's gig in Abbotsford, so I went rafting. Military precision was required and they made us into a squad that could drop and roll on command. They drilled us and drilled us and drilled us and then like true Australian men they took us down level four, five and six rapids. I was almost dragged under once and someone grabbed me by the toe, literally my toe and I flipped back into the boat like a fish and tucked my toes under the strap like I was supposed to for the rest of the ride. As we came over the rise, I felt wonder and then fear. This was it! This was level six and there were people lined up along the rocks and guide wires strung overhead. Our guide shouted out commands, and we "dropped and rolled" just like we were taught to. Didn't we have the ride of our lives and sail out the other side? I loved it so much I later dragged my boyfriend to Tout le Monde in Quebec to river raft there but that is another story. Australia, although someone did in fact pick me up and throw me bodily across the street because I wouldn't partake in a threesome, was the only place I've ever been in the whole world where I could just go by myself and sit in a pub at the bar, watch a game, drink a beer and eat lunch without anyone bothering me or looking at me sideways. I was just a normal person and I could breathe without censure. I guess that's why I value the freedom of movement in my home country so desperately. At the end of the day, you get to see "what's out there". Life! Wonderful, wonderful life. And I never begrudged that man who threw my body away. Good for me. I know who I am. My mother's and father's daughter. Uncomfortable for them as it might be.

I traveled by bus to Brisbane since I met a new girlfriend who lived there with roommates. We sat in the open market, drinking champagne surrounded by large baskets and listening to the quartet. I will always remember the soft, warm breeze that wafted through the place, and, in the end; it was my favorite moment of all. Much later, when I married my second husband, I hired a harpist to play in honor of that memory. Weeks later, I flew out of Cairns, but the airline employees were on strike, so we only had enough gas to get to Hawaii because the airstrip wasn't long enough to accommodate lift-off with a full tank. This same thing occurred years later in North Bay, Ontario, but only because everything was frozen and the plane was smaller. I never got to pilot my own plane, but I did get to fly in a four-seater yellow Sandpiper, and it was a total illusion because I could have blown that propeller myself if I'd had the lungs of a bagpiper.

My aunt picked me up from the airport, and since I still couldn't stay in Vancouver because I was afraid I would run into Mr B and weaken and inadvertently contract AIDs, I went back to Ontario because my friend had tried to commit suicide twice and my parents wanted me to see if I could do something. I had made friends in Port Hope, Ontario, during Katimavik, so we hooked up, and I was able to complete my cooking apprenticeship and get my Red Seal.

I was working at the University of Toronto and catering at night. I had learned how to do this at The Lazy Gourmet in Vancouver, working off a freezer top and producing an alarming array of fancy food for society weddings and those kinds of events. Actually, it was the first place I put in a twenty-two-hour day, so I knew how to prioritize. And then in walked Mr L. What is the problem? I couldn't even look at him. I was just a twenty-five-year-old goofball, and I never felt as unsophisticated as that in my whole life. I never wanted to have kids until I was forty-six years old, and then only for six long seconds, and I was so relieved when the feeling was over because I couldn't breathe. It was horrible. And Mr L is when I became a fancy girl. Lucky for me, I could muster up enough French and Spanish (thank you, Canada) to come up with three languages, but he spoke a Dutch dialect as well and, so for most of the next six years, I lived anywhere but home when I was at home because no one ever spoke English. It was exhausting, and his ex lived in town and was far too thin, beautiful, and apparently accomplished because she went to university and I didn't. I became fancier and fancier until I got a great job with Bell Canada through my aunt and finally stopped coming home. In the meantime, however, he wanted me to go to visit his family's farm in Spain so I got a British passport through my father because I couldn't get it through my mother so unforgivably again I put my uncle as my other relative instead of my mother because I thought it wouldn't count if my relatives were female. I think I might have inadvertently created myself as a legitimate member of the Philp family since I'll never know where the hell that grandfather actually came from. Everyone in our family is a sea captain after two generations ago.

Now you have to appreciate that I am no more interested in someone's family farm than the next guy and since it was going to his brother I accepted that he had it worse than me. I was straddling provinces but he was straddling countries! We flew into Heathrow and missed the flight from Gatwick because they were moving a plane from one storage area to another. Usually, it's sheep or goats or cattle but this was an actual airplane, and it took forever. I was so annoyed that I gave them what for since I had already narrowly missed my foot being run over by a bus and was still trying to fix my hockey bag because it got caught under the wheels. Mr L waved me off and applied his never-ending diplomatic linguistic skills. We stayed with an Indian family at their bed and breakfast, and boy, were we ever grateful. It didn't cost us a mint, and we were welcomed, made cozy, and fed. In the morning, a fellow guest asked Mr L if he knew his cousin who had a gas station in Calgary and I tried not to laugh. Mr L was European and the gentleman posing the question was from the United States and so Mr L just looked confused and I realized that to Americans we only have five thousand people in the whole country so we must know each other personally. And so we boarded a ferry from the White Cliffs of Dover to Boulogne. It reminded me of Ireland immediately, even though I have never been there. We took off and walked those cliffs and I thought that I had the best life in the whole world even if I had to share my companion with his first love. In fact, I had my period and accused him of not being very nice to me and he just looked at me sideways as I burst into laughter because I was wrong. We stayed in a boutique hotel and in the morning as I haltingly spoke my Canadian French, they were the most understanding people in the world and just told me to take my time, and they weren't offended at all. It wasn't until later that I recognized that Quebecois are offended by my francais because we learn Europian French not Canadian French, in school (even though Canadian French is our official second language). I understood immediately when we boarded a train in Luxembourg and Mr L was not easily understood because the Letzeboiesch, his mother tongue, had evolved past his baby years and they were having difficulty understanding everything he was saying. That was funny, too

Belgium. Ah me! Belgium! I'm so not cool enough to be Belgique, but I was told I look like that in Europe. I ran straight to the underground subway and bought a chocolate bar from the vending machine just to see if Belgium chocolate was really all that because I used Callebout in Canada. It was. Although I have to say that Italian chocolate is better, much to my surprise, but not as conducive for baking. After settling into the farm; it was an actual hand built farm, I was taken to meet the relatives. I like relatives but it's always tricky because there is always someone who came before you who bailed because they hated them and then they miss them after they are gone and now they get to hate you. They were pretty good though and six weeks later I could converse somewhat intelligently for a whole afternoon. The food was heavier and I got heat stroke every time I went outside between noon hour and four pm but that didn't stop me from accompanying my best friend and his brother on ten kilometer runs through the hills. I always lagged behind but seeing the look on his brother's face as I came over the rise was priceless. The headaches were worth it. The first time I ever went topless on a beach was probably as a dumpling at Wreck Beach but by the time I got to Cuba and Spain, I looked much better in my opinion, so as I lay on the beach towel I gingerly removed my bikini top and lit a cigarette. Within five seconds a young Spanish girl asked me for a light, and I had to get up anyway. I liked Mr L. We travelled together alot. He was offended by me alot too but he got used to me eventually. He was not afraid to travel and I admired him for that even though he was far too good looking for me and alas, he would not let me have a baby because he was still enamored of his ex, so on Fridays when he put on a silk shirt and cologne to see her for coffee, I fumed and fumed and eventually ended up in the hospital again (endometriosis). We travelled to Cuba around the same time period and it was singularly the most pristine water I ever swam in. There were armed guards there; I had seen them before in Mexico; and we were restricted from riding our bicycles past Castro's billboard. People lived on food stamps and lurked quietly, hoping to give us their money so we could buy them shoes. Any shoes. They would stuff Kleenex into them so they would fit. We had chicken and chocolate at Christmas, and then the food disappeared from the shelves, and they had to line up, even in Havana, for water. The sad thing about it is that the Cubans were very well educated and well-spoken, and I wondered if it had to do with Guantanamo Bay. I danced like I never danced before on New Year's Eve. It was the best New Year's ever. I was twenty-eight years old and I was going to be okay. We found a spare empty beach and laid on it until a man on a donkey rode by. We talked and he shared a dram of rum with Mr L and handed me a can of grapefruit juice. Kind. And just as well because I had to get it open so Mr L wouldn't fall over from the booze in the heat.

What is a lawful spouse? I am confused about this. If I take my husband's name, isn't he supposed to take mine? And if he's working all the time and has money but doesn't get to see the kids, and I'm not allowed to work but have no money then what the fuck exactly? You can't imagine what it's like to wake up in the morning and have your children ask what there is to eat because there isn't anything. In the end, we end up in bed with someone else because we are lonely. Don't kid yourself. Men drink so they don't have to feel the pain of sleeping with a woman who's not their wife. And women left alone too long are preyed upon by other men. So what gives? Truly. Just in case you thought I shit on men. I like men. I just can't take them seriously because, for some reason, they don't have the power either. And I guess if you are going to struggle to have any kind of quality of life, you are going to become a dangerous person because then, as all good books say, we seek to dominate each other. Which, I guess is the reason that we don't share our resources since apparently only a few are entitled to live. We grab onto our children and choke them to death because if we can't work or don't want to, or are considered whores if we do, then they are the money, and in the end, they will never do what you want them to. When do you have to beg for a job and get fined for working or looked down upon because you don't have the money to pay for credentials that, in the end, protect you from litigation? That is a lawyer isn't it? And I would ask Jose to step out of the back bench and thank her for her balls. Because when you threaten the safety of a woman's child she will kill you. A man will stand back because he gets to ejaculate with impunity and since he is excused from not being able to control himself, it is the women who will fight to save you from yourselves in the end. Don't kid yourself. Or hide them away and be ashamed of everything you do.

I loved Luxembourg because that was my name, and in Luxembourg, you get to be your name. It'll cost you, but that is the reason. A little blonde girl followed me around. sang American rock songs and gave me her school picture. I will remember her face until the day I die.

["I'm sorry" he said, almost reverently, when she told him she had no children. Surprised, she hastened to assure him that she had never wanted any (in spite of the fact that she had raised four). Too late, she realized her response was purely cultural and that she had only confused him, not reassured him at all.]

Furiously, her mother had hurled at her "Satan will make sure that you are never happy," when she discovered that she'd had an abortion. She had been pathetically grateful to Dr Morgentaler and told him so. A week later, the place where she had lain was bombed; only a large hole in the brick and mortar remained.

The doctor retired shortly thereafter and Mr L, free to carry on with Ms E, had already convinced me to move in with him alone, although the activity of moving furniture the next day caused me to bleed, and I forgot myself and lost it (objected politely) outside of the restaurant they were intent on dining in. Bad manners! Mr L was disgusted. I went home instead because I had to work the next day.

They were so disappointed with me on the west coast when Mr L and I broke up for good. Engaged to be married twice, I could never bring myself to go through with it, having ended up in the hospital three times to clear out the endometriosis, a byproduct of his extracurricular activities with his (ex) wife. My extended family appreciated his good looks and his Luxembourg bloodline and would have preferred I flew back and forth with him to the palace for tea in the Grand Duchy. Her uncle would later tell me that I had never been okay because I refused to compromise. How hard can love be, I wondered. What did I need a palace for?

They wanted to kiss my engagement ring at work. All those diamonds made the wearers of the massive solitaires jealous. I just wanted Mr L to come home. I gave it back to him, and he sold it in the end. It was a relief, although, this time, it was his mother who was disappointed.

When I finally left Mr L I felt badly but I had competed for so long, I just couldn't bring myself to be the consolation prize because I could forgive him but I couldn't stay. Because I am my mother's and father's daughter, and I know who I am.

My job was at a standstill. I always wander off when my brain doesn't have enough to do, and while I learn slower than the average person, once I get it, I can do it better than anyone, so off I went to my next challenge.

CHAPTER SIX

My father spent my entire childhood telling me that whatever I did, not to get married and have children, so I never signed my name because I only gave it to the Government of Canada so I would always be able to work and not get caught out like my mother. Ultimately, as I neared my thirties, he began to chafe at the bit and ask why none of us kids did the normal thing; got married and had a family. I was truly astonished. Really? So, I married my next guy because he was divorced and had two children, and I thought, "great! Now everybody has an heir and a spare, and I can go back to work." My mid-thirties to my mid-forties were the shit. I mean it. I worked around the clock, shopped for groceries at 2:30am, went to the gym at 4:30am, showed up in the office before 8am and I made sure those kids had the best childhood I could give them so their mother would know that I would keep them safe. Unfortunately, she was also way more attractive than I was, so hoo-ha; I was batting a thousand in that department. I did some of my best work in those years. I was fast, smart, knew how to handle myself, and I was contributing in a meaningful way to my country of birth, which was the best way I could think of to thank them for giving me such a great life. I never felt so badly sitting next to her at the kids' baseball games, so I bailed out of respect and went on to record my second CD. I didn't know it then but I was to learn how to stand in front of a crowd and share. Not stand my ground but share. Share every thought and feeling and nuance without regard for myself and as I grew, I knew I was finally at play in the fields of the Lord, and I gave myself over to it. Not before I threw up, but hey, faith and Noah and all that jazz.

He didn't make me angry…he hurt me.

On My Impression of Men:

Please understand that I accept full responsibility for my part in all of it.

You hunt us, you seek us out, you put us in cages and wonder why we rattle the bars and become vicious; when you thought we would tend the hearth, make apple pie, and rub your feet when you return from sticking your cock into another and are repulsed when instead we waiting with our legs spread. You know why I would never lay shamrocks from the front door up the stairs and lay waiting under a rainbow surrounded by gold, only wearing a green hat? Because you would be four hours later than you said you would, and when you arrived you would give me that look, that beleaguered long suffering look to convey, that, oh god, now you have to rise to this occasion and how selfish could I be knowing how tired you are from working yourself to the bone providing. Never mind that I might be pregnant with your child, sacrificing my body, that I might have acquired stretch marks because of it; or scars, or that the pussy you waxed so poetic about shaving bald now has ingrown hairs that hurt. These things you will use to defend yourself against me, telling me with words or with the look in your eyes how repulsive you find me. And if I seek to eradicate these flaws surgically or via other means, then I am a whore, and you will fuck me or ask me to suck your cock dry and then satiated, but repulsed, you will wonder where your dinner is and go sleep on the couch.

I take a bus, and the man behind me tells me he wants me to come home with him. I sit in my car in traffic, and you drive by and tell me how beautiful I am. You pull up beside me on the highway and pause in the fast lane, plastering your phone number against the window and making motions with your hand for me to call you. You have me get up in a boardroom and ask me to write on the whiteboard so you can watch my pants ride up the crack of my backside. You ask for unnecessary explanations so you can bathe in the sound of my voice and then claim you don't understand. When you discover that I am on to you, you call me a disrupter and then another steps in, offering to fight for me but we both know what the price of that will be. And then you have the gall to ask, who do I think I am?

Do you expect me to take you seriously? Heaven forbid, no, you don't.

You love my mind, sharp and penetrating – it's so hot, you say. You love to engage in longconversations, thinking you have found a woman who respects you and that if I spend my time with you in this pursuit, then you, too, must be brilliant. And if you want to fuck me, sudden, brutal; and wonder why it hurts my flesh because you believe it's so obvious that I need it. And then you call me a bitch because I asked what the fuck are you trying to do? Get off me.

Who do I think I am? Not yet. When I sing to you, you close your eyes and immerse yourself. You bathe in the sound of my voice. Then you take my picture; tell me that now all I need is a bustier to wear. You blow the picture up into poster size, laminate it, find out where I work, and show up unannounced, to present it to me. You pick me up bodily and throw me into the fountain; across the street, off the bed onto the floor when I object to a ménage et trios, refusing to share our bodies with another. The one time I give in to you, the one time, and it doesn't matter what it is, you never forgive me for it and use my capitulation to wound us endlessly until one of us dies. And then you ask, what is wrong with me?

You want me to stay forever because you are afraid of being abandoned but you don't make it possible, insisting that I prove my unconditional love by accepting whatever you choose to disperse and then not respecting me for it. You tell others our secrets, holding me out for disdain, judgement, and marginalization. When I tell you my association with us is at an end, you ignore me and then call me three weeks later to go for dinner, and when you discover that I told you the truth because I took you seriously, you show up at work with flowers, calling my name causing a scene, in an attempt to make me look cold-hearted. When you realize that I did love you, you stand in the street sobbing hot tears down the side of my neck into my shirt while I compassionately hold you.

Where is the lover I will be true to? The one who will be true to me.
I will not allow you to speak for me in public because you are my man, but I will kill to protect you, and that is no joke. Not like they tell you in books; we do not own each other. We do not have to stay. We choose truth and loyalty, and we create together. We have found ourselves in the other and are the eye in the storm. True loyalty is rare, but it must be in order for the creation to survive. Survive it shall because there are no boundaries except what he and I agree to. I will remain until creation is betrayed.
Who am I? Am I ridiculous? This simple little woman...
I am a reflector, a purifier. I am Eve, and I am Lilith. I am an angel, a chaos wreaker, an avalanche that buries, a steaming kettle, a gentle brook, a warm bath, a song writer, a singer of sounds, an echo, a clap of thunder, the morning dew, the pouring wetness of cunts and vaginas, the blood of women, tears, rivers, oceans, ponds, lakes. I make you feel so you remember what it is to be alive. I show you who you are if you have the courage to look at me; a teller of stories, an object of love and hate, a rabbit in a costume, a tree standing alone in a desolate desert, a dancer, a lover of cock but I just need one, a cat's tongue, a swan; always a swan, an ugly duckling. I love in spite of you and me and all the others; a protector of children. If you take me for granted, you will rue the moment you did, and, helpless to do anything to prevent the karmic re-balancing, I will be forced to watch and weep for your agony.

Raising those boys on behalf of that woman was the worst and best thing I ever did, and I will never get over what I did to her trying to help him. It wasn't his fault necessarily, but looking back, I bet he thought he was made in the shade the first time, and in the end, he lost me. He lost me because I just couldn't do it to the mother of his children anymore.
She could feel the blood draining from her face as the sixth needle went into her body. And so it begins, she reflected. It would go quickly now. Her hands went numb, and she was suddenly icy cold. As the seventh needle was inserted into the base of her vagina, a moan

escaped her. The nurse peered curiously at her as the eighth needle pierced the entryway of her canal, and tears began to pour quietly down the side of her cheeks. Suddenly, the bed was released. She could hear the cranking of the metal, and suddenly, she was upside down. The nausea subsided as the freezing took. Slowly, the bed was lowered until she was nearly flat. The surgeon began to work.

"Will I ever be able to orgasm again?" she had inquired of him.

"I should think you would be more concerned about whether you will live," he replied.

Did the flesh he cut and cauterized with the laser smell? That smell... no matter. Her clitoris was re-attached to her pubic bone, and the scar tissue was removed. He did a superb job. No stitches. No scars. Only time would tell. He could do nothing about her nipple. One had healed, but the other was too badly damaged. She got herself a nipple cup after her physician insisted on yearly mammograms. The cup worked; kept the scar tissue stretched and supple although she couldn't help but wistfully wish she had a man who would do it for her with his mouth instead. She would never flatten her beautiful breasts into a mammogram machine again as long as she lived. Just so they wouldn't mistakenly diagnose her with breast cancer again.

Mr J paid for it with his own money. I know why. He felt for me. He really did.

I had completed my last post as a Director of Project Management for a small company. It's work at an intermediate level. Basics like job descriptions, financial numbers, dealing with the executive team (who kept acting like they forgot there was only one of me. What did I care? These guys talked more about nothing than any woman I ever met. It was awesome to get all that information because eight months later, I knew I had to leave because I finally found the gap that put us under water. I traded my job so that my brilliant, gracious smart as whip guy from Bangladesh and my Filipino Sr PM who walked on water because she had the common sense of an entire country could keep their jobs. Someone offered to fight for me but I am not a head nurse for anyone so I thanked everyone politely, fired my brand new arrogant little shit of a PM; replaced him with someone who actually worked hard and left). Besides, they made me take golf lessons with the girls so I could "be a leader". Shoot, thanks to North and South Carolina, I could golf like a rock star already, meaning sometimes I had to pull back not to embarrass anybody but if you ever heard a man berate himself for his stupidity from the depths of the ravine where he'd dropped his ball, popped it up and out, to bounce off his golf bag right back to where he started, you would understand completely.

I had seriously begun to wonder if I existed. The notion of the phrase "my people" began to intrigue me. I had spent my life push-pulling against the endless responsibilities to the group, ironically becoming the caretaker of many and never being close to anyone. I had attempted it, it was true, but most of those had ended in power struggles or abandonment. I could never keep enough secrets or be sufficiently open. Where was the happy medium? And in the end, at least for the moment, I faced Mr G's same question – who would miss me? Did it matter? Had my dreams ever changed? How many lives could one have? As many as we liked, I suppose.(*The Second Best Exotic Marigold Hotel, Judi Dench*)

Golfing was a great passion of mine, thanks to my second husband. I chipped my way up every fairway in front of hordes of self-satisfied jeering,what business did I have, being on a golf course men, for three years, until I could knock it out of the park, so to speak, no matter if there were crocodiles. And in the Carolinas, there were crocodiles. Mr J and I went down every year in the fall and played eighteen to thirty-six holes a day. It was a perfect way to make yourself stop working and just play hard. We played with a couple of men from Kentucky after meeting a group of Quebecois males who just couldn't get over the fact that we were actually married to each other. In fact, they invited us to eat in the clubhouse with them later. It was such a novelty. I love the Quebecois. They just take a licking and keep on ticking. Great food, great music, great clothes, great art, great everything. Anyway, we played three holes, and our partners never so much as uttered a word to us. I started chafing about it until Mr J said, and I'll never ever forget this. He said, "Relax, let them take their time. They are not used to it. This is the south and their land." We were on a cotton plantation, for god's sake, and that man, that beautiful black man with ancestors from Ghana, gave THEM time to accustom themselves. I would give my life to the kind of person who sat there after all that brutality and just waited for them to be okay. It was like Jesus or Nelson Mandela. Turns out, they told us they had a great time playing with us and you could see in their faces the surprise they felt that that had happened. The last hole was fraught with crocs, so I drove it up the far side of the fairway to find myself in front of the clubhouse full of rather large hopped-up men who were all on the porch finishing their last beer. Ah! the worst. I took a breath, prayed for grace just this one time and I popped it over the water and onto the hill without rolling it down the other side and it just sat. Mr J, who was carded for five or six sports, had already done the impossible and I brought up the rear. A little white chic and a black man. It was a real moment. By the time we cleared the clubhouse, it was empty. They had gotten up and left. But they saw it and we did it. Together.

I ran out of work. I realize now it was probably because I wasn't popping out offspring and since by then I had stopped menstruating and was pretty relieved that I was no longer the usual twenty thousand dollars in debt, I found myself on an allowance. I thought, sing or die, baby, sing or die. I just realized I was going to die like my mother at sixty-four, but probably of cancer and I remember thinking "it didn't go very well did it". So I mustered the strength and joined a choir. It was either that or university and since we didn't have any money because we had raised kids, I had to do something to ensure I wasn't stashed in someone's back bedroom like a granny. I'd drop dead too or get high. Why not? Millions of grannies all around the world have their stash, so they don't poke your eye out AT BEING RELEGATED TO A ROCKING CHAIR. Besides, wouldn't you rather be high as a kite from your own drugs so when they dump that shit into you to make you die sooner, at least you won't remember that they killed you knowingly, with their fabulous authority given by hundreds of thousands of dollars in credentials? Too scared to live. Too frightened to die. It's why I'm always being asked to leave the doctor's office because in spite of my minor smoking habit, I blow respiratorily like a teenager because, again, in spite of my running habit, I am told that both are bad for my health and I must stop immediately. I mean, that's your multi-million dollar professional opinion? Thank god you didn't deliver my baby.

BRIMMING WITH COCKTAILS
Amanda May Philp

What's the use
Of telling the truth
When you don't want to know what
I think or feel
You want me to make you feel good
So you can be real
And so I'm brimming with cocktails
Cause I should be lying
Instead of trying
Your patience
Cocktails of timing and rhyming
I'm brimming with cocktails

CHAPTER SEVEN

The first time I walked into choir practice for a lesson in singing Italian, he saw me. I didn't know it yet, but it was going to be the greatest heartbreak of my life. Because Mr G had cancer and either knew it or was in remission and didn't want to die. Or he didn't have cancer until he met me. I'll never know.

The year before I belonged to a massive choir and learned to sing in Celtic Scottish. Now, there is an ethereal tongue bender. I could only just manage it because I was a mezzo-soprano. I could hit two notes above a high C comfortably. I just couldn't live up there.

In fact, I was to witness the beginning of unforgiveness to the nth degree. In the end, that is what killed him, because he wanted to retire and work and keep living and everyone objected with vitriole. I guess people miss their parents and their kids and in the end, everyone thinks we are a piece of shit because they can't find us when they need us, and we can't pay for their lives or sacrifice ourselves for their precious bloodlines. I don't know why we get cancer because we are alive. Our legal names are granted to us the moment we leave the hospital, or our birth parents wouldn't be permitted to be our mummies and daddies. Apparently you might get a name on your birth chart of some kind and don't people use that to grab what they need from you to complete themselves? What a crock. Everyone in the whole world has a talent, an aspiration, and a work of merit, and those of us who are not adept at living the adventure of life get bitter because we imagine someone has more than we do. I hate the thought of older, healthy people dying alone because someone objects to their choices, their freedom to have another go at it, and the spectre of loneliness looming because their children want their stuff. And so, they die of hopelessness because once their assets are redistributed, there is no interest by the families who grabbed them, to pay for their care or to actually come often and keep them as part of the family. How does it feel to pay for childcare now? Shortsighted. My father drives very, very well at eighty years old. In fact, his only accidents are when someone else makes a mistake; because he's been doing it for so long, it is second nature, like a farmer driving his tractor.

I did a lot of singing in "old folks" homes, and can you believe the only time I got a standing ovation was for an Italian opera solo *in Italian*? And I'm Canadian; with British and French and Swedish blood. And so I cried for Mr J, who wanted to play professional soccer longer than he did because he got cut and was still on top of his game, even now, at the age of sixty-five. Sometimes I wish that children after the age of twenty-one, never saw the people that gave birth to them again so they could have a shot.

So, you throw soup at great works because you disagree with how they came to be. Too bad Mozart died a pauper and Picasso cut off his own ear. But you just can't let them have it, can you? Because you object. All those Germans who lost their lives in the Holocaust along with the Jews, the Bible Students, the Gays. And we never ever forgive each other because we weren't there, and we have no idea the behavior that lead up to that great disgusting event in our history that the Germans will be held to account for generations. I know, I have eyewitness accounts from many people, some who were abandoned in cattle cars, some who lost their identification because their father went to the bathroom and didn't return in time. And since I am also a Bible student with Jewish blood, you can fuck right off because I have to feel it all just like you. We are not paying our parent's debts or our children's. We are paying for our objections, just resentful that someone might actually be successful or beautiful or happy, no matter if they worked a hundred times harder than you will ever want to. So go ahead. Object. Object all the way to your grave while the rest of us get on with the business of living our wonderful, wonderful lives. My mother's mother lived to one hundred and four; she was willing to wheel herself around on her own if only she could get out and have a life. She would escape my aunt's house in her wheelchair at ninety-six and go for coffee. When it rained, they came after her and found her sitting in her chair under a bus shelter. She refused to board the van and informed them she was just fine and would be along when the rain stopped. Everyone spoke to her. Everyone. She just loved and mourned and lived and laughed until I wasn't allowed to take her back to my place because everyone was objecting to me being there in the first place, so she died frightened while her daughters held her head as she faded away. Her *married* daughters, by the way…

Do you know that I saw a woman like that with her groceries hanging on the back of her wheelchair, powered wirelessly? Her food was hanging too low, and she was stuck at the crosswalk while a couple across the street were just sitting there watching her. They just sat there. What the fuck is the matter with you? I pulled over and lifted the groceries so we could get the signal back, and off she went. Same with the old Polish woman who waved me down in my thirties. She was so cold her feet wouldn't lift off the pavement and she was helpless. I'm sure the taxi I flagged for her didn't appreciate my request to help her up the stairs when she got home, but for all you know, she might have been making a bank deposit for her daughter who had four children and was the breadwinner. I hope you are satisfied because every time you object, you are the one who has to pay exorbitant taxes to the government because they were doing fine until you decided it was "inappropriate," and now they have to pick up the tab. This is why I always ask why a man isn't at home with his wife when he wants to know what I'm doing working outside of the house. It's hardly his responsibility to put clothes on my back. It's mine. So stay behind your computer and data mine everyone else's money. Be an isolated freak. Because at the end of the day, you will be as bitter and alone as everyone else you decided you were better than.

My Mr. G. Well, I finally thought I was going to be allowed to have something, and I almost died. In the end, we fought every day, all day, even to the point of helping Mr. J so he could stay in business, but you know, my irish didn't like Greek, and my Greek didn't like English, and my English didn't like my jamaican because of my sicilian, who tied all of our families together through Africa and the US. So the breeding mares and their progeny objected to the tune of two million dollars, which he needed to survive the rest of his life so he could keep going. And for the first time in my life, I made them pay. I had to go down to the place I had married my first official love and drag him back home because none of them would do it. And then every private school known to man fought for his puny two million dollars that he gutted out for so he wouldn't be a burden. It is the only time I hated the medical establishment and our collective families. Because he earned it, all older people have earned it, just so they can pay for themselves and babysit for you, looking a gift horse in the mouth. I lost my first and last official love to death. Permanent death. And my second lost me because he was a landed immigrant, and we were fodder for babies, so he could just procreate and procreate at will. Not to say people (women) didn't get smarmy and snide calling him a Provider, which, if you are not born in this country, is a disrespectful and dishonorable thing to say because then you never ever get to come home and not be castigated for it. Listen, chic peas. No one sleeps when they have kids. No one. My second husband had balls. And compassion. Held my forehead when I puked where I just shit. Got his kids to their mother, their grandmothers, and great grandmothers, worked around the clock, played sports, accommodated our other varied interests, and he paid, and he paid, and he paid and he paid and he paid. I forgive him EVERYTHING. So just let him have it. Because we were the shit. We were. IN spite of YOU. In spite of everything. In the end, I just don't get it. You'd be better off running with the wolves. No one is ever going to love you enough. Get it? So get your ass up off the couch and get a job because apparently, I have to pay the government of Canada nine thousand dollars a year to work, when I have the credentials, and yet I'm supposed to pay for you sitting in front of a computer, not paying your share like a weakling. You have your own bloody names. Stop being a coward. Women pay more taxes than men do. They pay to carry any man's name who is the father of their children or they are accused of being whores, whether they are married or not. No wonder they sue you for abandoning them. They have to pay for you to begin with. Aren't you a peach. They're kids. They're your kids. And they are leaving. Not with your names, with THEIR names you idiots. If you're lucky, you will become great friends with history. Or they will go their own way because they have it in them to aspire. Or they have it in them because they are just like you.

When you live long enough, you can see a lot more than you anticipated. If you're strong enough to endure when you are very young and stick with your first choice, eventually you are forgiven. You will die young for your bloodline and be in some goddamn registry, or you will forgive and live a wonderful, beautiful life. While EVERYONE objects to you being there. I get it. I meet people who started on an island far away and they have married and had children and married and had children over and over again all across the globe. It is a hell of a ride, but how do you expect your children to honor your country of birth over their own or over the one you dragged them to and expect to fulfill all your cultural proclivities? I don't know. They sure as hell don't either. People will only come for you if they need you and for no other reason. Or live your life in the house that is falling down around you because it is "home". Is there any reason that you are too special to clean up your house and your life, and take some responsibility for yourself? Many, many people have come for me and loved me and cried until they thought they would die from the pain of losing me. Make no mistake. That was my second husband, the one you sneered at and never forgave me for, and I will love him until the day I die. But I have to work for my mother, which is what my last love did and why I lost him too. At the end of the day, I can only grieve forever. No wonder I didn't have children. You think I don't like them. I do. But there are too many rules, and I'm not willing to be shamed for having them since apparently, it's a crime. So I do the only thing I can. Help you pay for yours because they are somehow related to my family.

You see the problem?You never cleaned my house or raised my children or paid for me. I did. I worked and worked and worked and worked around the clock. I painted, groomed the yard, went to work at six thirty am until six thirty pm, and ran like hell for the subway so the kids could get to hockey practice. In the end, if I had born children to my second husband, he would have died so I paid and I paid and I paid and I paid and I hope one day, he forgives me for some of it, because we never do forgive you for resenting us. We excuse you for your ignorance and for all the insults you jeeringly spoke to our faces and we live with the loss because we already know it happened to you too. We just pull ourselves up by the bootstraps and do our duty so we can maybe see each other again someday and still be friends. Landed immigrants, citizens…..what do you do when your birth mother is widowed in a strange country only it happens to be the one you were born in? That's what I did for my second husband; gave him back his mother because his father's name is safe in Canada. Pffft. And like me, he mourns. This is what kills us. The potential and the resentment that we might actually get to have something. What the fuck is wrong with you? You are Italian and you fucked an Armenian. You are English and you fucked a Saudi. We love it. But heaven forbid your mother believes she is not fancy because she is a landed immigrant who married once and that you are a whore for bearing her son's children. So now you are pimping us out? YOU pimp us out. YOU. I don't care if you are seventy-five years old and widowed in a "strange" country. My grandmother worked until she was seventy-eight; did her three miles in the dark before the dawn with her walker so she wouldn't upset anyone and everyone LOVED her because she loved her life and didn't give up. So kill each other. Go ahead. I will forgive you. Why? Because the kids need things don't they? And if you have enough children in one country, they will pay for everything for you and live in quiet desperation. I love my life. I miss my mother. I miss my loves. But they didn't have a choice either. And I cry for the pain because if I don't protect myself, you will object to me being here and loving your people even though my people love you to bits and in the end it's the women that have to ruin their bodies and hope they don't have to beg the government for food stamps. It's not your fault. It's not theirs. I gave in for my last living birth parent. Who lost BOTH his parents before he was twenty-one years old so he's old and even though he has his own ideas about what his daughter should do, I have to honor the people I lost and so do we all. Healthcare is never about sickness, it's about you objecting to their honest love. And I eat cake. I eat cake. Well meet me at the bakery baby, because you eat cake too. I've seen it with my own eyes, without a degree even…

Mr G and I went to New York City to sing. His cancer had abated but suddenly began rocketing through his body even though he came home in remission. We floated through the Christmas holidays because we thought we were actually going to make it. We had a Jewish music teacher who had worked very hard to get his breathing corrected so the oxygen could flow back into his body and I could hear the difference in his voice. Everybody could. His diabetes was gone even though the medical establishment had given up on him and refused to stop his medication even though it was making him lose his balance. I know all about it since I was prescribed Metformin after my second concussion, obtained after ice fishing and being thrown from the quad I was riding because someone had cleared a bunch of snow on the lake and I couldn't see it in the dusk. Someone at work had leaned me up against a wall and asked what I was on because my eyes were "funny". I knew because they wouldn't take me off it and I was losing my balance and was going to lose my job so I just sensibly stopped so I could function. And eventually your doctor tells you he won't see you anymore because what? You're non-compliant? But they can practice on you with impunity. I might really trust you but in the end, I have to tell you to go fuck yourself because you haven't the power to adhere to your oath because what? Oh don't tell me you have to meet a quota so you can write prescriptions for the drug companies. In Europe, physicians used to get bonuses for keeping their patients healthy and herbalists weren't the devil.

We struggled that last three months. We went down there and we sang and when it was over, we stood in the foyer and I saw the look in his eyes. He was dazed and exhilarated. I knew he felt it. That connection. That real, free flowing connection. With our hearts and all the people's hearts that were there. "It's good isn't it." I said to him and he met my eyes and spoke a breathy "YES". And we did that. We felt that. Together. It happens once in a lifetime.
She hunched down in the alleyway, rocking back and forth as she listened to Ruby speaking to her from so far away. An armed security guard had stationed himself in the street a few yards away from her. He had settled his stance there after pacing restlessly back and forth, fussing as she smoked cigarette after cigarette in the dark.
It was dire. Mr G was blind in one eye and had developed thrombosis. His weight was so low; one hundred and twenty-four pounds on a six foot four inch frame. They were pumping him full of big fat bags of nutrients. The airline would never let him fly. He could no longer walk anyway, but if he died, she didn't know what to do. He had become snarky and stubborn the day after she arrived and there were no instructions, just the words of his sister, sobbing, as she booked her flight "don't let my brother die in a foreign country."

His face turned grey and as he slumped over, I could feel death and I stood in first class for an hour holding his hands and saying "I'm here. I'm right here." I was to drag him home as he fought for his life to his last breath because everyone was PISSED OFF that he might make it, that he might get to be happy, that he might GET AWAY FROM THEM and they killed him rather than let him have it and then every lawyer known to man ran over me like a truck. I no longer had the ability to distinguish the difference between family and friends apparently. Except that Mr G's mother was from Germany and served in the military in Greece and my secret lover had been greek so he could stay in Canada with his mother and when that came out, even my italian godfather's people couldn't abide me because my best girlfriend's mother was also from Slovenia like my soulmate's companion from the old neighborhood. In the end, they would have killed me or I would have to level up or down or something because somebody pulled my hair and asked me if I was a whore. For what? For working? For loving one of my own or your own? For not staying in the house? For not being a useless eater? Get the fuck away from me. You are a part of my family now just like everybody else. And by the way? He had irish relatives. And jewish ones. Mr G and the dragon. Suck it up. Everyone has been a slave. Everyone. And I watched the dragon sob with despair; sheer agony because no one would let him have it and now I apparently "slept with anybody". This deemed by my aunt's Irish friend and his Italian wife on their second or third round so you tell me. My "money" indeed. What kind of pair of shrinking testicles has to get permission from his daughter or his mother to live his life? My parents never asked me for permission for anything they did. They did what they did because they knew I didn't mind and I would come if they needed me to. Even my mother who never forgave me until my father took that monstrous burden off my back; **she wouldn't get a job because she was afraid of breaking a law.**

I stayed with him until he took his last breath. He was devastated because it was me and not his daughter, although he had a son. He fought until the end, standing with a crushed disc because no one gave a shit whether he lived or died and the only thing I could do was insist they all come to say good-bye. I believe, in the end, it was more expensive to kill him than it was to save his life. I might have paid that bill too. Shame on you. Because now I want to know exactly what I am paying for and I want you to ask my permission to execute your "treatment plan" and tell me precisely what you are intending to accomplish or else I need to bring a lawyer to the hospital with me. Because you, physicians, lie to my face. And I can prove it. That man literally dried up and stayed with me as his face paralyzed and he became a husk. That's how badly he wanted to stay.

And then I had to forgive. Because they never forgave him for loving; or me for anything. But my second husband did. And he was saved even though he will never recover fully.

I found the pictures of the other women. My soulmate had a proclivity for a different kind of sex life. There were rolls and rolls and rolls of film. My second husband was holding his breath, waiting for me to come back. He wasn't sure what happened but since he had an "obligation" to continue to have sex with his other wives, he panicked. He wasn't working and we would have to pay the mortgage all over again. In the end, I just couldn't do that to those women. I tossed the whole lot in the garbage. And wondered how I would survive because now I had nowhere to live and a shitload of estate lawyers calling for atonement due to a bunch of church record filings. Do you have any idea what that did to Stewart, Conrade and George? They wept to the marrow of their bones, the same as the women they chose or were loving. I forgive them EVERYTHING. Everything but the scorn. Religious scorn. Cultural scorn. Academic scorn. Putrid. And those men died for it. I recognize prostate cancer in the early stages when I see it. They were sacrificed as well as the women. For a bloodline. Get the fuck away from me for knowingly killing your children. Even my father couldn't stomach it. Fifty-four years with one woman, the only woman. I'd rather die than be "special" in my bloodline because I could never live with the blood on my hands. Not ever.

I don't know if Mr G ever paid for his children or if his wife at the time had to do it. All I know is that he died and I had to go to Mexico to get the second man who died when I brought him home, because the first man I married down there took his own life by the time he was thirty, too late to have a legitimate child. I'd have killed myself too if I had realized why .

CHAPTER EIGHT

On regrets:
Only regret I ever had is that I had a tough time getting laid. I never met anyone who was really hot for me. And I suppose I will remain wistful about that until the day I die. In the end, I shall be reduced to simply making money like I always do. Sex and love, the final frontier, not to be explored in this lifetime…I missed the train. Will I succeed in being close to someone before I die? I am extremely disillusioned with Ruby. And she is wrong. I will sell what I have and leave. Where is my home and the lover I will be true to? Because where I am isn't good enough for me.

The butterfly was fitful. Dad had sent a text to her and she was flummoxed. Why now? Nate sent word that he received the package so she guessed the game was on…she didn't see the problem; if there were two names, there shouldn't be an issue with her claim on one of them. Wouldn't it be a kicker if they named her Philip after all.

ANOTHER NAME
Amanda May Philp

Call me by another name
So I can be yours
And yours alone
Call me by the only name
You have for me
So to the others I can atone
Call me by my name
Because your name for me
Is my only name
The name that makes me free
Call me by another name
That makes me feel at home
Broken when I found you
I was broken
But still working
Working until the day
My name
Brings me home to you

Oh my god, what a great day! So much accomplished so easy creative flow. Fear is a strange thing to some living men and women, but fear also wakes others of these, up. So much read and written this morning and then I played in the kitchen and inadvertently accomplished more. Tending to the plants and restoring the table was fun.

I'm happy when I come here. Is that okay? Think I'll clean up the brass on the piano and finish sanding the strip.

Tonight my aunt told me that no matter what, she always had and always would love me. The cascade from grandmother to mother to daughter had landed on me but it had nothing to do with me. She's seventy-two and she thinks eighty-three is young. Her husband is much younger; twelve years as a matter of fact. Good for her. My grandmother couldn't figure out what was "wrong with men these days". My grandfather had been "good to go" until he was admitted to hospital for stomach cancer. He was ninety-three and I held his feet because Mr B and I came for him and he was so upset they put him in diapers when he was perfectly capable of relieving himself on his own. Chained to the bed with no dignity.

Whose kisses are the best in the world? Haven't the vaguest idea…does it matter? Yes, it fucking matters. The first ones on George's couch were in a class of their own but they never turned into anything

So

Still, they were enough to get me to come back. Just misty for you, I guess. Would I forget about him if it were over?

Probably

I don't like pain.

Mr L was a dick; why did I spend six years there? Because he was fucking his first wife so I didn't have to be faithful, meaning, I could work on my career and travel. Kind of backfired didn't it? Caught in his own belief that his mother would die, trapped on the farm they had to leave his brother….poor guy. I hope she took him back and they went home to Spain….

Mr J was a semi-criminal like me but I had to protect the boys – the boys who didn't belong to anyone and forgot about you anyway because they weren't allowed to see you…that poor man and all his family. He worked as hard as the dragon….

Why did Mr G matter? Because he made you <u>believe</u> and didn't you nearly die from that bit of subterfuge…

The butterfly paused. Did she want to stay or go? She understood. Her child was the earth and she wanted to fight for it. She would wait to see if the dragon was telling the truth. They rarely did, although sometimes they saw the writing on the wall in time. Would he be able to do it? Would he want to? Would he try? Actually, they never saw the writing on the wall in time, but he asked and she agreed, so until…
Meanwhile she wrote. She had been lucky, extraordinarily lucky. Why Jill and Hightower (*Runaway: Diary of a Street Kid, Evelyn Lau*) had ever put her in the car, she would never know but they had saved her life while fighting for theirs. Ann had done the same, getting work for her. Did she want to spend all her time with them? Not really. Did she still owe them? Did she want to spend her life with anyone?

Yes, she really was too wise and naive for this sort of thing. She didn't want a husband, not ever. But it was time to face the fact that she needed a spouse. She'd had enough partners to last into the next lifetime. She was a girlfriend now, she believed. How novel. It wasn't so bad after all; so many things she still didn't know about. The dragon was really good. In her soul, she recognized that she loved him. It was her healing heart that needed to catch up. Who knew what would happen? His heart was damaged, too. She could feel it. Adjustments… And the dragon wept

Huffle Me Muffle Me
Amanda May Philp

When did I say yes to you?
You weren't asking the question that I answered
As you slid down the length of my heart
I asked myself
How long will it take to get there?
To get to the place
Where you get to face
The end of the race
And never have to chase
The length of that heart again
Can you say when?
On how long it will take to get there
The place where
You won't turn a hair
To bare your soul
And be whole again
And now you're chasing me down
Like a hound
And I can't keep you at bay
So hey, take a number, k?
Cause I paid my way
And part of yours too
When we were two
And yes, sometimes
I miss you too

TIL DEATH DO US PART

Amanda May Philp

(for Gillian)

How brave am I to love you anyway
Even if I don't forgive you, sometimes
But you think everything is a choice
Don't you
Have you met my family
Who can't stay put
And believe they know who they are
I'm not brave at all
Some things aren't a choice
They are simply part of me
For reasons you don't understand
And so I can't forgive you sometimes
But I can't stop loving you
Because you're always going to be
A part of me that I can't forget
Or let be
Or forgive for
Because I'm brave enough to love you anyway
Til death do us part
And then you'll live in my heart

CHAPTERNINE

How much do I love you right now? Endlessly, honestly, deeply, truthfully. Tomorrow is another day.

The best thing I ever heard: "Fuck me like you make more money than me."

Pain is just the result of a misread, misstep, or waiting for time to catch up with you. Pain is out of step with what you desire.

Where do all the horses' men go?

I don't know what love is and yet everything I do is for it or because of it. Love is the only thing that matters. I know it when I feel it and when I don't. It sucks when love costs you. And it always does, big time.

Wait! What do you want? And why are you wet all the time?

Can I love you without being in love? It's the safest thing. Can I be in love with you and not lose anything?

What is it? What? If a man has a bird in his hand, does he cherish the bird or look for two more/ in the bush? I know because this is my younger proclivity. If I had a bird in my hand now, I would cherish it. No way of knowing unless you stand still.

And it was my task to fly through the funnel; having spent a lifetime on practicalities…learning to fly from the house of soul was my purpose in this life.

Sometimes, I think you freak out internally too much, but then I realize you are processing and integrating little by little. It's actually a lack of resistance.

What Mr G did was give me a chance.

Girls wanted to spend time with him, so he called his wife and told her he wanted to take a break.

No more running

Always running to be one step ahead

Always running until the day I am dead

No more running now; I don't sprint anymore

The long run is over

The finish lines are gone

Wait, where am I?

My eyes reflect what I see without prejudice. Can you look into the mirror at yourself? You will see who you are.

Always remember that I loved the promise of you all my life until I finally found you. (*The Firm- paraphrase*) And then I loved you beyond the edges of my soul and will to the end of my life; maybe beyond, it remains to be seen.

How many times do you make love with heat? Every time? I don't think so – moods are different.

What one fears can strengthen, can heal…

How do you know when the timing is right? You wait for the universe to tell you.

And so today, the butterfly went from "I'll love you forever" to (just) another woman; handy because she was willing and able to drive the distance. Did the dragon realize he had just cut her or whatever…

The butterfly would flutter back to the city earlier than the dragon had requested. The proposed alternatives had been communicated after she arrived. She was askew (off-kilter), but she would survive it. She had songs to write still, and a book to finish after all. Perhaps the butterfly had secretly known all along…..fuck. Oh well, the dragon didn't have a strong physical desire for her anyway; mostly it was a brain and companionship thing.

Why was it so difficult for the butterfly to get laid? She would be too old to be attractive enough soon. Maybe she was lying to herself and that time had come and gone already.

A life without a connection that way. Would she be able to heal her soul herself, or would she always remain incomplete?

And so at last the butterfly Mr G had tried so desperately to pin down was in love, torn wings and all. She could still flutter and her wings were mending. Mr G couldn't stick around after all, but he made certain she stayed behind in his cage, and he called their home. He didn't know that for the butterfly, home was where her heart was, but he did the best he could. And now the butterfly would stick; the tears of a woman she had finally wept. And so now she had more than wanting. She loved the dragon truly, and it was okay because she would never get over what she and Mr G had failed to do. Stay.

Okay, so I'm weird. What of it? I'm the same as I was yesterday – different but still weird. You have to own a good set of balls to love a weird woman. So what of it? What? I'm still free.

Marriage – on the Subject of:

Some people say marriage is for having kids. Not me. For me, marriage is for true love. You marry to protect it, so the world cannot insert itself with the claim that you have no right to it. Anyone can have children. Look around you at all the abandoned wee ones…One union ends when the obligation to bear fruit has been met, the other does not. And by the way, it is my opinion that anyone who believes that sex isn't all that has never had an orgasm with someone they care about, nor have they ever had the occasion to foam at the mouth with sheer lust. Poor souls. Who needs a cheeseburger or box of chocolates when you can have that?

---PS---

What was to be undertaken would require a fair amount of inner strength. Her natural inclination was to bury herself in something else, anything else, until it all went away. It was a hard lesson but if nothing (else), she had learned finally to just wait for times to change. No matter what name Mr G had given her, and in spite of Ruby's haranguing about knowing who she was, she did in fact, know herself on an unconscious level. She was Amanda May Philp – very funny Mom and Dad – Am a Philp; am a Philip – Amanda may be this, Amanda may be that, just like Nathallia Brown; liar, no liar. Together, they made a happy woman and a freemason's wife, and it was going to stop then. Amanda the happy madman so be it. She hoped she would be able to stay with the dragon. She hoped the dragon realized who he was. At this point, finally, it didn't matter anymore. She was going to do what she was going to do and everyone else would do what they were going to do. Too bad, so sad, "Bite the weenie Riz".

(*Grease*)

Drunken sex in grades eight and nine; classic coming-of-age years. Wonder if the guy who did me was the same way…likely doesn't remember me. Wow, men are different. And we walk around under some hazy glow of enchantment. And they are enchanted but we are not singly memorable are we – only collectively so. Is it a mythic fairy tale? A lie? Or just a carrot; a remote possibility until he has a little girl of his own? And yet friends mean more then…but how often does a respected friend get thrown over for a helpless fragile twit? Often enough, I daresay. Friends might escape judgement but they are in a different category and men just love a rescue don't they? Guess there's no throwdown for a woman like me if I just go into shock and yet don't you want some man to do just that and not let you up until you come hard and deep and long, just so you know it was him and that only he can make you do that. Of course, you will attach in spite of yourself, and he does not you to ever do that. If it doesn't fly with the dragon, perhaps the future will be peppered with random hot hate sex until someone doesn't let you walk away. The dragon's chick – what a thing – so who wants love, Dragon, on anything after that. No wonder it's difficult to call him that. Expropriation. How odd that the more risky it gets, the braver and more self-contained I become. Back to masturbating two or three times a day…thought my drive would wan with age but it doesn't so sucks to be me with a tongue in my cheek. Did he want me to give him a blowjob when he was hung over last weekend? Would have thrown up all over him…and in the end I am different and hot and beautiful but nothing special. Not even to my mother or Mr G, so my G-clef is safe and belongs to me.

The impossible dream will always be the one thing I failed at. And yet, it is the only thing worth living for.

Do you know why you will go back to your very first lawful wife? Because your kids will force you to so you aren't pronounced compromised by early signs of dementia. Ironically, they won't get anything for it except your death, and their children will remember how to do it to them. No wonder you have to leave the country. I will never ever do that to anyone. And I look down upon those of you that do. And in the end the dragon was horrified to discover the truth and so were his children. Well fuck you too. That was my godfather before he was yours. Show some respect. I showed it to you in spades.

And still I wept…

MY BITCH
Amanda May Philp
(*for Jane, because she would appreciate it*)

Didn't I say you'd be my bitch
Mostly cause you don't know which
Way you goin' now
Do ya
It would have gone without a hitch
But you wanna keep your niche
And now you don't know which
Way you gonna go now
Do ya
Ho now, hey now
Which way you goin' now
Cause now ain't life a bitch
Don't it make you twitch
And you really do
Think I'm a witch
That you'd like to ditch
Mostly cause you don't know which
Way you goin' now
Do ya
Ho now, hey now
Which way you goin' now
Cause now ain't life a bitch

After that, I was pronounced bi-polar and charged nine thousand dollars every time I filed my taxes. Then, I was accused of not being able to manage my money since I didn't have children. I was not allowed to work or be with anyone, and the only reason I made it back home was because my father, my judgemental, prone to female submission and headship father….called the hospital and said I will take her. My eighty-year-old father has very little except the love and goodwill of his second wife and family and the Jehovah's Witnesses, and was on the hook because I was a disfellowshipped Jehovah's

Witness and his wife had to share their money with her sister because her husband had committed suicide. That's my dad, people. He forgave me EVERYTHING. And so I paid the money so he could see home again before he went home. Ontario to Newfoundland that is. He has nothing so try not to be jealous. Pension money is puny. Go ahead. Begrudge it. Do you think old people are spoiled and worthless? You wait. What you do to them is what will be done to you. He would have sat in the streets with his arm around me and we would have been separated and perhaps MAIDED out. So please, continue to object to others instead of paying attention to your own life. Let your parents die of loneliness. Begrudge everything so your life also is cut short just when you think you're actually going to be able to have something. Drop dead at sixty-four like my mother. Do it. Seriously. But that is your decision and there will come a time when it will happen to you and you will be bitter too. My only grace is that I was there. I came every time someone asked me to and I was there. I will still do this. Be happy if you know me because I would come for you too.

COMMITTED

Amanda May Philp
(for my father)

And so you forgave me
Everything
But that wasn't the point
Because you wanted me anyway
And as it turned out
I was the easiest of all to love
And you wondered
Why you hadn't done it before
Because committed
Made you the happiest of all

My father remembered my history too late and the cancer ripped through his body so I ran. Back to my uncle who would have done the same for me until I realized I had to stop making men (other people) responsible for my decisions. Of course I'm sure someone else's son is making objections but my understanding is that he is now embroiled in the same dance. When you are twenty, you are either forbidden from doing what you want or you cannot hear yourself anymore. I know it. My friend UV never took anyone of his daughter's suitors seriously and she will never take him seriously either which is why I run the gauntlet and laugh. And help any one of yours because we all get kicked until we're dead. Unless you get over yourself, under the guise of "we just want you to be happy". If my dad's beloved died and he could go again, I would be right there supporting his choices even if he had to endure the demise of three or four more women. I would support his choices, his ability to love, his right to life all the way. He'd still be working if he was permitted. He loved working. My whole family does. Too bad, maybe there'd be more housing at reasonable prices if you got your ass up off the couch and worked two or three jobs like your parents did. And maybe you do. So you get it too. And I salute you. I really do.

RUNNING FOR NOTHING
Amanda May Philp

I guess I'm a bad girl
A bad bad girl
Who comes running for nothing
With apple pie and beer
For fear
That you might leave me
If I don't take care of you

I'm sure I'm a bad girl
A bad bad girl
Who comes running for something
With guts clenched in fear
In case
You will be leaving me
If I don't give you what you want

I know I'm a bad girl
A sad, bad girl
Who always comes running
For nothing
Because you'll leave me
No matter what I do, for you.

Ok, so this is me giving in. I wish I could have what I really wanted, but I know if I want something badly, I will never have it. Doesn't that suck... maybe I want something no one believes in but me.
In the end, I couldn't have children, you see, because I had been "raped" too young and my body was unable to form an able-bodied child. It wasn't anyone's fault. It just happened that way. And so I worked...

TEARS OF A WOMAN
Amanda May Philp

If pennies fell into the ocean
Every time I cried for you
I don't apologise
For loving you
Even if you don't love me
Enough
It's the only freedom I have
And pennies fall into the ocean
Every time I cry for you
Don't deride me
Or abide me
It's a privilege to love you
And I do
Even if you don't love me
Enough
The tears of this woman will fall
And you don't have to fight for me
Cause these tears are free
And will fall
While pennies fill the ocean

CHAPTER TEN

I wanted to be a rock star; not a heavy-duty one (is there any other kind?) You know, singing with a hairbrush in front of a mirror to Ann and Nancy Wilson, Helen Reddy, Marianne Faithfull, and Lee Aaron. I thought Teenage Head from Hamilton and RUSH were the shit; same with Max Webster, Kim Mitchell, Gordon Lightfoot, and a host of others that I remembered crooning in the backseat of the car with my siblings on family road trips to the beach or grandparents house. There, my brothers and sister and I would sing to the Beach Boys, Nana Miskouri, David Soul, Roger Whittaker, the Kingston Trio, and Chicago; anything my parents had the eight-track recordings for. We were older then, and my mother's brother thought we were fancy because we had a tape deck rigged up under the glove compartment in the car. I know my dad put it in there so he could get from point A to point B without having to stop for a bathroom break every half hour. But the first Drive-In movie I ever saw was Funny Girl when I was seven years old, and since she was singing on roller skates, I watched Barbra's first television special, and she knocked my socks off stomping all over that Canadian mink on the floor at Bergdorf-Goodman singing I Got Plenty of Nothin. I howled with laughter. Right there, was what I wanted to be.

I have often wondered why one child is worth more than another. I mean, on a basic level, I really don't give a fuck where you come from, who your parents are, or what order you are with your siblings. The meanest, most entitled people in the world believe they are legitimate or some kind of distant royalty. How one comes up with a name from the past when two parents don't have enough money for a name is beyond me. I think I'm supposed to be English for some reason. What for? There are all kinds of people in the world who have no idea they were brought up with a household name that isn't the one on their birth certificates because their parents have it. Of course, who gives a fuck if they can pay for their own kids. People with no name last forever; people who pimp out their children believing the ones they make babies with are whores. How lovely to be smug your whole life. I guess someone decided you weren't enough at some point in your life so you thought you would prove them wrong. Too bad nobody loves you. By the way, you know that, under the law, people are capable of loving more than one person, right?

It's rare to be able to keep something you worked hard for, which is surprising because I would be so embarrassed of myself and on behalf of my mother and father if I behaved that way; begrudging someone's accomplishments. My mother always said my father was a pessimist because then, if something good happened, he could be pleasantly surprised. He and I worked for our governments, and I know that he hated that I followed in his footsteps, but at the end of the day, it was me, mom, and him who loved the adventure. We just blew in together from nowhere. It was just that she got left in the house for weeks on end and that didn't change. I know she resented my freedom. But I would die for it. I would die for someone else's too, if I thought they would be sacrificed, but only if I could do it anonymously. Who wants to be known as a martyr? So many are murdered on behalf of martyrs. It's a backwards claim to fame that is more than likely a misunderstanding.

Why are we so nasty? Why do we let our bodies go to shit? Why do we allow ourselves to be pumped full of prescription medication when it is no longer required?

Where did all the self-hatred come from?

And even the people younger and older than me are just as fancy as I am. Do try to remember that.

Mr Trudeau was the only Prime Minister of Canada that I ever voted for. And frankly, I don't give a shit whether you approve of him or not. He had a job to do and lost his family. And yet you begrudge his ability to continue by hook or by crook to parent his children. How would you like it if you were in his position and had to actually orchestrate all that COVID bullshit? I'm pretty sure you wouldn't have done any better. So, I support the Prime Ministers of Canada, no matter who they are, because I worked for them and I would do it again in a second. I think my government is the shit, even if they had to move me on. They gave me a great life, and whether you approve or not, they seek to give everyone in Canada a great life. The fact of the matter is that we follow Common and Civil Law in the same country and have a massive unprotected border with the United States. It takes remarkable skill to administer that. You have absolutely no clue what kind of effort that takes. And you want to know why your fancy potatoes cost so much.

I know many of you hate Trump. But I get a great big kick out of American politics. The perpetuation of the sins of our "Fathers" just greases the wheels of Hollywood which is still run by the Jews. I think it's marvellous. Please don't jump all over me because I'm not an "expert," and I don't possess enough DEGREES to know what I'm talking about. Sorry, but the Emperor isn't wearing any clothes, and I don't need to be in school to see with my own eyes. Get a sense of humour. I'm no patriot. I'm a living, breathing person. And I will protect you no matter where you come from if you need my help because so many people have protected me when I needed their help. You see, in this country we are constitutionally protected by our whacko jurisdiction. Everyone who resides here is permitted to go from one end of the country to the other, whether they have to travel through your community or not, and are protected from bodily harm. How can you beat that? It's not Korea, it's Canada. And yes! You do have to work like a dog. That's the whole point of having your personal freedom. What, you thought you were going to come here and be taken care of? Hate to break it to you, but everyone here has to do the same thing as you, so quit knocking the Government of Canada for flying in water to feed your babies. We do actually have to build pipelines and roads so get your ass off the couch and do your thing. Ever heard of a rain barrel? We used them in the city of Toronto because the water is so chlorinated it burns my stomach. CPP is for people who stand up and make a contribution. Nobody owes you anything. Scary, isn't it? That your life does actually belong to you? What are you playing the victim for? I can't have children but I work and I don't care if you hate me for it. I'll work even after I am retired. What do you think a useless eater is? Someone who expects their parents to pay their bills. Get it? Awesome. I'm going to go do a few sets of weights so my boobs don't hit the bed when I lay down. I used to do push-ups before I could afford weights or go to the gym, just so you know. I borrowed $450 from my father once on Friday, and he had it back by Monday. And that's the only time I asked for money to pay my bills. The only reason he loaned it to me was because I had never asked for anything in my life except my freedom. And guess what? He's safe. Know why? Because you objected.

I would love to work again to pay for all my misdeeds and pay for the children who aren't working or not having kids because I'm nobody special. Except that, apparently, you need my help. And I so don't mind. I like to work. In my next life, I will bear as many, if not more, children than you can shake a stick at, just to confuse you. So I can laugh some more. And get everything. Because I will do the same thing I did before. Work around the clock, teach them some manners and a work ethic, and most especially, not to sneer back at people who sneer at them because they think they're more special. If I was from another country, I would do the same thing as my fellow Venezuelan compadre. Slovenia and Venezuela in a pissing match with Italy. Right under our noses in Canada. Astonishing! And almost the most fun I ever had. My poor dragon. Another rock star! All of us Canadian-born people just want to be Canadian but you won't let us, because we're just a bunch of shitty shitty people who took the native land away. Well, I don't know, where exactly are we supposed to live? Because a bunch of us are now native as well, so your boys can't keep their dicks in their pants either. I guess they like cake too.

So I was picked up off the street by a Northern Ireland bloodline. Mine is from southern Ireland; Galway, I believe. I was never a hooker, but there might be a police report saying so because there was no other way to "code" it. It makes me a dark horse like Aritrea. And I'm pretty sure that most of you are also coded in a criminal fashion because there was no other way to provide anecdotal evidence to explain how you came to be in the position you're in. I'm really, really sorry for this because we have to pay for this false incarceration, and the cost is exorbitant. At the end of the day, you're not allowed to physically damage someone because your joint beliefs don't coincide. That's divine law. There isn't a true religion on the face of the earth that doesn't have this principle at its core, which is why I am not afraid. Did you cut off someone's nose because you didn't like something? It's actually not your right. And I'm not afraid of you. Because you just trumpeted to the world that you are afraid of a woman. Which means you have no penis. Why am I even talking about this? Enough said. But I have orange crystals that signify my connection to all women, and I know what has been done to them by some men who are afraid. Wear your physical scars as a testament to the fact that a man was afraid of you. That is the ONLY reason you got cut. Because you made them feel threatened. One little woman.

I have this courage because I come from courage. It's in my blood and in my DNA, and it is a gift from which I will never back down. When I am terrified, I know I have to stop, turn around, and face my fear. So that it doesn't scare me again. You can come with me if you want. I don't mind. I will take care of you.

So, what is a legitimate child to do? Be glad you aren't one of them for you will have a much better life than they will since they have to pay for their children and if they don't have any, well, then they are kind of useless. And they can't have sex so they are naive. Weird, yes? Where did all my money go? Oh right, I'm running a company now so I have no soul. How special can one little woman be? I swear I glow in the dark.

I'm pretty sure President Trump doesn't really mean for Canada to become the U.S. of A's fifty-first state. That would make us the most powerful state in the country and nobody wants that. I can never fully comprehend why a gesture of accommodation or respect or even tomfoolery is taken and used to offend endlessly because somebody doesn't like it that a person waved at us. Get a grip. Queen Elizabeth waved her way around a good portion of the world, and there is still a magazine dedicated to the goings-on of her internal family. King Charles is so lucky because now he's supposed to reconcile his late mother's position in the world, which frankly, didn't have anything to do with him. Let the good times roll. So, how well do you play with the other kids?

And if you are illegitimate, lucky for you that you have soooo much money. You get to work and have babies and do whatever you like as long as you produce. Too bad, you'll be sneered at and kicked around by everybody since apparently everyone is legitimate somewhere. Didn't know that, did you? You are legitimate in a family line related to your birth or blood family. So riddle me this. Who's the whore for loving? Who's the whore for procreating? Exactly who is the whore in this scenario? Lots of people will give you their only bloodline freely, but if it's not the right one, you're just a piece of shit for muddying the waters. Oh my god. If you were so pure to begin with, then I guess you are the whore who likes cake. Thank god I'm a mutt. My immune system can kill stuff you would be scared to go near. Because guess what? Black doesn't run. It's solid black. Every black family in the world wants to know how white or black their baby is going to be. Too bad Mrs Markle's baby wasn't black enough. He would have been the toast of British Democracy, adored by millions, the same way Mr Obama was. And you're right. There is no private enterprise. Public service will always prevail. And how nice it is that you are financially compensated for your inconvenience when this occurs. You object because you built it yourself – "treading on the rights of the little guy" you scream. Oh wait, didn't you just disown your child for marrying someone they loved? No? Oh their "person" is just a "friend" who is a "whore" and doesn't know who they are. Spectacular! Now you can fight over the kids or leave them severely alone. And piss on the government at the same time. I had a good friend who wrote screenplays in college and yet she refused to work on one with me because she didn't have a degree for it. I married a Laird for my mother who was a Davidson in Canada but wow, his birth record was rooted in the Ukraine and he didn't graduate in the same province as I did so you know, he got scorned. So I married a Brown and tried again but wow, his birth record was rooted in the United States, no! Wait! It was Jamaica. What? No? It's Ghanese? Really? Fuck, I can't do anything right. She wanted a King and so did my dad but if you think I'd marry English after I lost my ability to bear children, think again. And I don't even blame them. I don't blame anybody because if you think I'm going to cower at "home", give your head a shake. It's never ever going to happen. Not ever. Not for you. Not for anyone. That, and my ability to love, is all I have left. My heart, my soul, my brain and my freedom of movement. Lucky for me my cousin's Canadian born (A)merican daughter married a Massai, so I can never be accepted or forgiven. Wait until we get to the Italian branch of our family. Oh yes, one of my grandmother's brothers married an Italian after the war and we haven't seen him since. This is why my Anglican godfather is Sicilian. I just love that shit. Just love it. Canada is not for the faint of heart. Don't come here to be safe. Come because you have the guts. Then you can be snotty, too. But at least you'll learn to be polite about it because that's how we roll people. That's how we roll....

And by the way? If you are "triggered" because you aren't identified "appropriately", no one is "dissing" you. You are supposed to wear a nametag so "we" can be "kind" and not "label" you. It's not any easier for anybody else, so just do it or shut up about it. And I will still love you. Truly. No matter what you decide.

Sometimes mundane is still mundane. Don't assume you're brilliant just in case what you are producing is mundane. Don't assume that mundane is supposed to be reclassified as brilliant because you come from a damaged minority. Then you're just handicapped. Don't assume that marginalized work isn't brilliant. That's arrogance. Socialization is the only innate leveller in existence.

The pandemic fallout was never about disease. It was about prejudice and loneliness. That's it.

Oh, and there's another thing you should know. Your family's retirement home is a nightclub. They get laid left, right, and centre. Just for your information. In case you begrudged them a girlfriend or boyfriend on the outside. And they get to drink alcohol like rock stars. I can't wait until I get into one. I get to be fifteen all over again, and no one will blink twice! The food is atrocious, though. No wonder they drink. It kills the mould....but if they fall down and hurt themselves, no one is allowed to help them up. Don't worry. The place is just as filled with prejudice and inflexibility as anywhere else. They will feel right at home dying on the floor as they would have in their own home. Staff? What staff? You mean the people who work there? They're lovely, but as usual, they're not allowed to "help" if your family sues them. What a great opportunity! Here's why:

They don't staff enough people because they are run from a different country and applied for corporate "welfare" in Canada and were turned down since they are supposed to be hiring residents of Canada. The "medical" staff is private and they work bankers hours only because, well, you know, they should be able to because they have student loans to pay off. There are rules about the hours they are permitted to administer "medical" care. They are only open for business five hours a day so they don't have to pay union dues. Or they're retired" from public service and work for private services and don't have a license to touch you. How's that for bait and switch? Brilliant eh?

Are you really working or are you faking it?

So how much free stuff do you get for your child? Such a great gravy train. No wonder you're pissed when they're grown. I made very sure my stepchildren were involved in anything they expressed an interest in. I wanted them to understand some of the possibilities out there. And I hoped they never abandoned their private hopes and dreams since I continued to follow mine right in front of them. I did it because I never wanted to blame my life path or lack of "choices" on them. I still have my aspirations. It's what keeps me alive. I can't grovel in the dirt or mud wrestle anyone over a child. How graceless. My mother, my grandmothers and my aunts would never lower themselves to such a depraved level. They didn't walk on water. They used their own two feet their entire lives. It's the same with the fancy ladies in my life who came "fresh off the boat"; in sandals and high heels no less. Can you do better? My second husband taught me something very important. He said he only went places where he was welcome and since I'd seen him in more than one establishment with his back against the wall, I understood why. He also worked for the government, but since he was "black," he could be shit-kicked by a bunch of northern Ontario hillbillies even though he was the one hiring them. Never underestimate what the person standing in front of you is capable of or how hard they are working on your behalf, unbeknownst to you. And if "your woman" catcalls my husband, I will forgive her and let him have it. But if you need to object, I'm pretty sure the objection isn't the presence of my husband. Touch him, though, and I would do the same as he did for me – break your ribs. Just "Cause uptown bump don't give it to ya" isn't his fault. (*Mark Ronson/Bruno Mars*)

THINGS I REGRET
Amanda May Philp

Do I love you
Can't you tell
Do I love you
Go to hell
I'm not beautiful
Anymore
But I can tell
You want me to love you
Anyhow
You're not beautiful
Anymore
But you want me to love you
That's for sure
Do I?
Do I love you
Can't you tell
Then go to hell
I'll love you
Anyhow
Any way
I can get you

The most outrageous comedian I've ever heard was Ali Wong. It used to be Eddie Murphy (actually, they're tied), but the shock of a woman letting it fly like that made me choke and spew coffee through my nose, and I was proud and more than a little scandalized. Oh, it was thrilling. I wanted my grandmother to know because between me and her? We had a love of adventure, and while I was subject to strict English scrutiny, she and I thought it was so exciting when we were alone together. We got away with all kinds of stuff. In her later years, she had a pole installed by her bed so she could pull herself up in the night and onto her wheelchair so she could go to the bathroom by

herself. I teased her that she had a stripper pole installed, and clearly, I was going to have to keep an eye on her since "this sort of thing goes on with you people all the time" (her favourite "go-to"). I just really like old people because they've seen and done things that would curdle your short and curlies, if you still have any, and are secretly more rebellious than a teenager. They're your best friends in the whole world – literally shock proof. When they're old, like, older than eighty, they are strong enough to last if they got that far, and the only thing that costs you money is if you don't take them seriously because they'll get on a bus and go to the airport to get away from you!
Or the casino.

UP A TREE
Amanda May Philp

Why must you run
So far away from me
You don't know who you are
The only chance you've got
Is to finally be free
Free to be you and me
Remember?
Remember you?
Remember me?
Or be in exile
Up in a tree
So far away
From you and me
Because you run
Up a tree
Where you think you can see
But you see so far away from me
Nothing
But yourself
Up in a tree
So far away
From you and me

SOMEDAY
Amanda May Philp

(for the dragon)

You're so unrepentant
Because I don't love you
Like I loved him
But you had all your children
With other women
Loving you that way
Would leave me high and dry
And would be a lie
We're perfect for each other
And you know it
Hear my laughter
And wonder why
You still make me happy
Because you're the guy
But I'm not ready
For you to carry me away
Not yet anyway
Not yet anyway
But someday
Maybe someday

Am I a Karen? Nope, I am as frustrated as every generation before me and every generation after me. It's why we turn to religion. For solace. The way it is set up now, it looks like to me that every house is a whore house with children. Or you don't get to live in a house. Yuck. Come to think of it, I think I'm kind of offended by that. Check your privilege if you can find it. Mine is long gone. Forgiveness is immaterial.

GARDEN OF RATIONS
Amanda May Philp

They never let me have anything
And wonder how I survive on nothing
I live in the garden of rations

Frogs wail, snails hail.
Rain rocks onto your path
Don't tell me your lies
They're just fireflies
In the garden of rations

If you were to imagine
The whole world in a passion
What do you think it would be?
Too much glee for you and me

If you were to imagine
The whole world in fashion
What do you think it would be
To much pree for you and me

Cause we live in the garden of rations

Have you ever noticed that people associated with great wealth usually look like they're starving? I wonder why. I don't envy them. They are clearly on rations of some sort. Doesn't look like a privilege to me, that's for sure. Doesn't look like privilege either, when a public servant stays up all night working and goes to work in the morning. Doesn't look like a privilege when you're up all night with the kids and have to chair a meeting at seven thirty am either. Come to think of it, religious robes don't look like a privilege, but they sure do confer privilege, don't they? And why is a wife, not family? What on earth would a woman entertain marriage for if she's not going to be family? You mean I only signed up to be a sanctioned whore? A breeder? Well, there you go, that's privilege right there, isn't it? No wonder you don't get your kids. Whoa! Why would I have your baby then if I'm not family? Do you need money? Why don't you get a job? That's what I usually do...

So why is your family entitled to your money if you aren't family? Sounds like fraud to me, but hey, what do I know since I'm a little light on university degrees.... There was a guy in Spain at the airport who was a little rattled, and his friend said, "eiy, tranquillo...don't get desperate". Isn't that the next best thing you ever heard? I tell myself that every time I see someone else rattle for dimes or whenever I am terrified. Tranquillo! Don't get desperate. Have some common sense. Please. Grace works too. Works like a charm.

Mr G was the only person I was ever jealous of, that I didn't meet him sooner. I was jealous of his history because I wasn't in it. I don't know why. He was the first man who could keep up with me. When we were in New York City, we talked to everybody we met. It was such a relief not to be shushed for once and he confided that his girlfriends gave him a hard time when he spoke to other women because they complained that it "opened a door". I do have to say that sometimes I wanted to pipe up and say, "You know I'm standing right here" because women just loved him but how could I begrudge him that? He was hot as hell. No lie. It used to happen all the time with my second husband because he was hot, too; he carded for five sports and was; a semi-pro soccer player. Girls would actually slip their panties in his pocket with their phone numbers on them. The high point came the night we both had phone numbers tucked into our pockets, surreptitiously, by others. Qu'elle, surprise, I finally caught up. Seriously though, doesn't it creep you out when a man other than your husband touches you a certain way? I don't mean hugs for chrissake. That's just decency sometimes. Or handshakes. However, men are weirded out when I extend my hand. Don't know why. Don't men shake hands anymore or has that gone by the COVID wayside? I hate that he died. I've been around births all my life, and that was my second death close up. To fall in love with my first and last and have them die in the same country (Canada/Mexico). It's a real pisser. And to lose my second, who grew up here, just before he retired. Super sucks. But, as my other dark horse used to say "Get up. Clean up your room and take some responsibility for the person you are going to become." (*Dr Jordan (Bernt) Peterson*). Just like my grandmother would.

It's a drag, but somebody has to do it.

I'm not sure why I have so many names. You have to be married to understand and I've ventured twice into that debacle and I have to say, if my assorted family members objected to me being single, which they did, they sure did make me into a whore for attempting to be a wife. Apparently (great word for all the aha moments I experienced), I don't have enough names for children because I'm supposed to provide them or something. Laughable, since I suppose I would have had one in spite of everything, but frankly, didn't care if I did or not. There's so many kids out there being sneered at because they're not the right bloodline, name, color, branch of the family, profession, trade; to name a few. Well if you're not going to care for or forgive your own blood, then I can't help you. I can only help them. You wonder why you're old and there is no one to give a shit. Unfortunately, they're not allowed to come near you because you married them to somebody you saw them hanging out with, even though there is no actual record. It's a real bummer, isn't it? More bitterness. And I have a secret for you. It will come as a huge surprise. They aren't going to do what you want anyway. Half the people I am supposedly married to, there is no record for, since I'm supposed to be there. The other half needed my help even though my puny little one name isn't enough. It's why I don't apologize. If you love me but you are going to kill me, duh, I need to leave. If you are going to go and off yourself because it turns out I actually did have a shit ton of names under my puny little company, well, it's not my fault. I thought we were in love, not doing business. That's a hooker, isn't it? But yes, I will pay my forty years and three hundred thousand dollars because

I know why you got that way, and I forgive you. Completely. Because I do what I want to when I realize you were looking for me to bail you out of a situation, not make a life with me as your beloved companion. I really don't need to be anything to anybody since I suddenly realized you all live in little bubbles. Well no wonder you came looking for me. (Pretty Woman, Julia Roberts) Just don't try to marry me because a horde of bills will appear because somebody objected. I am sixty years old and fuck am I hot! And what a relief. I've only ever been abused when I have been married because someone is frustrated at the sudden demands thrust upon them that they cannot meet. And they are always emotional ones wrapped up in a big wad of cash; oddly precipitated from the outside by the very same who attended the wedding in the first place. Is there some kind of glee attached to the taking of bets on how long the "pussy-whipped" man goes before he dips his wick into another "whore" who will give away her name for the "privilege"? How grand to become a long-suffering Mrs since you obviously trapped him in the first place. Soooooo, he gets you, children, a mistress, a career, and his family of origin and you get bupkis; less than bupkis because the house is in his name. How lucky can a woman get? Some trade it for protection. Helpful, especially when you discover you have an STD when you take your child to the doctor. How's that working for you? Of course, since you have soooo many children, you have to find work off the planet, er, continent, so how selfish can a woman be to demand sexual fidelity when she's the one who gets to "stay at home" with aaaaalllll those children. The very thing you want to escape from. Pfft. Now, everyone gets to hate everybody. A prescription and a Big Mac is just the ticket for the pain. I see why men downgrade women, but I don't understand why they take a good one and turn her into a Mrs. I think all woman should be Ms. It's not your business why I'm working, shopping, socializing, raising kids, going to pub night, recording a CD, pitching a song, writing a book, have an opinion, telling the truth, having dinner in public with someone who isn't my husband or brother. It just isn't. Can't fathom why you think it is. If I'm in real trouble and a lawyer can't help me, then there isn't any trouble. It's just an illusion. If you like to go home and watch the game, but I like to work out, I fail to appreciate why you have anything to say about it. Don't think I've ever been afraid and didn't still do what I had to do. Remember Solomon? The wisest king? Know why? He understood that since "there is nothing new under the sun", if you have a question, then the answer exists. (*Ecclesiastes 1:9*) If it didn't, you would never have formulated the question. You wouldn't be able to come up with it. And that my friends, is the reason life is soooo exciting. You can always find the answer if you look for it. Or you can be precious and snotty about "what's out there," but you will certainly be the last to be pulled onto the boat since operating "out there" is pretty much what life is. Can I laugh now?

Do I make "Daddy a sandwich?" You bet I do. "Daddy" fixes stuff that I don't have time to and he buys tickets so we can go out together to cultural events of different sorts, and he gets my car washed, pays the mortgage (I pay the other stuff – all of it – it amounts to about the same) and sometimes he even cuts the grass if he can figure out how the lawn mower works. Why wouldn't I? I take extremely good care of my "Daddy". Why? Because I chose him and he agreed or vice versa, and I'd like him to stick around, you moron, and principally, because I'm the only one sleeping with him and I'd like it to stay that way. Duh! He can open jars and lift heavy stuff too. Don't get me wrong, I can do that as well, but it's faster if "Daddy" does it. And yes, ladies, I prefer a head of hair and a flat stomach too, so don't get huffy about that forty pounds you think is your privilege to feed and then get harpy about the fact that boys don't like you. Honestly, if that's your jam settle yourself inwardly and go find your kind. No biggie. Really. I have to work at it, too. Trust me. Both of my husbands had exes who were way hotter than me and didn't everyone take great pains to let me know it. So suck it up. The great beauties of this world don't have it any easier than you do and at the end of the day, men look used up too when too many hands have been all over their bodies; their penises shrivel as well. Nobody gets away, so stop thinking everyone's got it better than you.

So! Aha! I've got you! If you really loved me, then you would wear black after my demise and you would never work or love or play again because if you really meant it, you should have died when I did. Hot off the Press! News release! I'm still alive. And perish the thought. I can still do it! When I think of it, I think my parents are still alive, too. They're pissed that I got married in the first place to a non-believer instead of taking care of them like a freeborn legitimate firstborn should. Well which is it? My father remarried after fifty-four years of marriage, three months after my mother died. I just about had a nervous breakdown because it would have been nice if he could have waited over the winter but if you have ever cared for an invalid you would have jumped at the chance to have another go at it too. And as soon as possible. That's guts. And sheer determination to live wonderful, wonderful life. He did very well too. She was a peach and thank goodness her family was nice to him. But I didn't cut him off. Why would I? He's my dad. Are you mentally incompetent or something? And in spite of my disgraced position in life (how droll), I'm still alive and kicking and having a great time! And yes, I do weep. I weep in my sleep. I weep in front of the television. I weep when I'm driving (yes! I can do two things at once – you see and breathe at the same time, don't you?). I weep on the treadmill I was forced to purchase since it's suddenly considered bizarre behaviour to go outside. I weep for the love I lost and for the objections and misunderstandings. It's horrible. But do kindly refrain from doping me up so you have to take care of me. I'm heartbroken; emotionally traumatized, not mentally ill. I'm perfectly capable of living. And I can do it all by myself. Ever notice that no one wants to hear the answers to the questions that are being asked? Don't insult me with formalities. Nurses have no issue at all with shit-kicking you at night because they "hate their lives," too. Healing and immunity are your personal concerns, not anyone's corporate business. Be glad if your son or brother or father or friend, cousin, uncle, etc, loves me. Because I have stamina and loyalty and I am a capable person who will care enough to do what has to be done. And I'll do it because I mean it so I won't be snobby about it. And if he needs me to, I will step in and care for you as if you were my own. Anyone who will touch my feet when I'm ninety years old will have only my heartfelt appreciation. And frankly, I'd prefer it if you were female and of color. You're alot nicer about that stuff than my people are, and I'd be grateful. Mr G's mother's best friend was of Indian origin. And I like the way women of colour speak. They lilt; they don't crisp. No, people of Indian origin think of themselves as white, not brown.

Can I talk about this? My fellow sisters? My best girlfriend from Germany (she is deceased, so no need to soap her windows) once told me that Harvard had to allow a certain number of black people in because they could never pass the entrance exam. I hope you are on the floor laughing with tears coming down your face since, according to history, they can do math in their head well enough to put a rocket ship into outer space. And they don't look like a dust bunny the cat dragged out from under the bed while they're doing it. They don't wear tights to work with their hair wet, generally speaking, from what I've seen. We've established that I don't stay at home, right? And in spite of the fact that I have been given a hard time at work by some men of African, Asian, and Iranian descent, I can't say that once we've established that no one is throwing anyone under a bus, I recall any one of them doing that to me. All in all, they usually know what they're doing and because I don't get offended (because we are working), we end up working quite well together and accomplish great things. I don't really understand why you're offended, as women. Stop talking about nothing endlessly, so much. Even I get exhausted trying to figure out what exactly it is you want. Get on with it! Food does touch other food when it's on the same plate. Jeez. And as for "compliments", well, if someone thought I had a great ass, then good for me! Maybe I do! Doesn't mean someone is going to touch it. What are you ... twelve years old?? The workplace is not the arena for these agendas. There's no time for that sort of nonsense. Take your high horse to the farm and ride it yourself. And yes, it's a fact of life. Twenty-five year olds are gorgeous. They're everywhere. Are you jealous? They have their own brutal kettle of fish. Don't worry about it. You'd think being happy was a low down criminal offense but it isn't. It's free!

And this whole men and women thing. Why is it even a thing? I've had men turn me down because they're in love. Men generally aren't as ridiculous as you'd like to purport. I've had men cover me with their bodies so I don't get hit with flying glass (*Canadian Russian*); they've fished me out of the water when I've been sucked into an undertow (*Quebecois*). My second husband broke a guy's ribs because he ran his hands up my skirt in a tavern and when I turned and said "that better not have been you" he responded with "yeah, what are you going to do about it". So I slapped him. It turned into a slap because I unclenched my fist at the last moment because I didn't want to get arrested. He fell backwards and my husband said "what did you do to her", because I don't go around whacking people. Do you know this guy had crawled his fingers into the cracks of four other women's behinds and they complained to the bouncers and nothing happened? What did you think was going to happen? It's their job to break up fights, not to keep strangers from touching you. That's your job. He dragged him down some stairs and left him outside, cracked one of his ribs in the process. He didn't hit him. He removed him from the premises (*Jamaican Canadian*). My uncle rescued me off the street to allow me to abscond with him and my aunt so I could finish secondary school. It saved my life (*Irish Canadian*). My daddy was an awesome daddy; swimming, horseback riding, tobogganing, riding bicycles, running together, let me make my own clothes, got me my first nail polish (tasteful color lol), my first necklace, hayrides, movies (*WelshCanadian*). They've shown up with tents when I'm running in team marathons for charities; so I have somewhere to shift sleep (*Canadian Italian*). And I've never had a shitty male boss. Tough, moody, biased, antagonistic, but never shitty. I've never encountered sexual blackmail at work. Ever. Nor have I ever not been paid for my work in full. I haven't made top dollar but I haven't eeked out my existence either. And when I've done the work myself, men at work have ALWAYS given me the credit when it's due; not just lip service, hard cash; financial compensation in the form of a bonus, raise or promotion. It is why I enjoy working with them. It's an exercise in character. It's always about the work. The rest is just banter. It works if you enjoy competition because that is how you are propelled to excel. Seriously, put your boobs away. They're only kidding. And this is no slag on my female bosses; I'm just not referring to them at the moment.

You can sew, can't you? Where is your hatpin, stick pin, or darning needle? I used it all the time when I got swarmed on the subway, riding back and forth to work. They are amazingly effective. It all just stops and goes away without a sound. Stop expecting men to protect you. It's not their job. It's yours. You are as grown and competent as the next person. Take care of yourself! You don't need to "swing a dick" to be "safe".

And as for this whole "do you feel safe" latest bizarro-ness, why are you even on this page? Are you precious? No one ever asked me such a question until I was fifty-nine years old. I've been to Australia and back by myself. I've been to Mexico and back by myself. I've been back and forth across Canada many times, all by myself. I've changed my flat tire on the highway at night in winter, with semis flying past me, by myself. I've wandered around Manhattan at midnight by myself. I've skied, surfed, skated, rode my bike, skidooed, ridden a horse, driven my cars, a tractor, a quad, a backhoe, a hay baler, and a catamaran as well as a plethora of other semi "dangerous" things by myself. What gives? And why do you feel the need to ask me that question. Are you okay? Might I help you with something since you seem to be confused; it's the same world as it was twenty-five years ago. There are just some different people in it. Safe is a big bad word these days. You should be so unfortunate to be "safe". It's a trap. And a waste of the life your parents and god gave you. It seems to be a big buzzword these days because this generation has been deprived of ordinary and necessary socialization because of the pandemic. Suddenly, everyone is afraid to "leave the cage" of isolation that they protested about in the first place. And if you're living your life according to some weirdo estate law because you lawyered up, since you are very important, then bully for you. You are a bully.

Congratulations! That should trigger an awful lot of people. No wonder you have to stay at "home".

So here comes the whole "high risk" behaviour question. Since we are socializing healthcare, then shouldn't we have the right to determine if we think you are worth it? Don't we get to judge you first? Who decides that? If a golf ball smashes into my hip in a freak accident, am I or the other person engaging in high-risk behaviour because we didn't don a suit of armour first to make sure we are safe?

Are we safe, or are we just ridiculous?

Are we safe, or are we just too scared to live? Well, I'm not. Just saying.

You make us pay double and triple for our houses if there's only us living in them but criticize us for being alone. Then you fine us for finding someone to live with because we might be touching each other. Are you mentally competent? Or are you just being corporately insolent? Because all those objections land you in a facility where you can't go to the bathroom and have to wait until someone deigns to change your diapers. Ain't that a bitch. And mangle your kids in the process...

Thank god you're safe. Nobody loves you. Nobody likes you. But you're "safe". Pfft.

Too bad you are objecting to the nationality, marital status, and perceived sexual orientation (which is none of your business anyway) of the person who is holding your hand while you pee. Thank you, my Canadian Acadian French-speaking friend, for that bit of enlightenment.

CHAPTER ELEVEN

I wandered past a group of men at the Rattray Marsh in Mississauga, Ontario, on the trail. They were listening raptly to a Mullah. I recognized him by his height and his "uniform". I was uneasy because I wear shorts but I forced myself to pass them and disappeared on the other side over the rocks so I could walk in the water. I always do this kind of thing when I am in a part of the country where women wear coverings that don't even show their faces. I don't have a problem with it because a bunch of us spent a lovely half hour skipping rocks together so I don't get freakish about "who knows what's under there". But I do have to consciously force myself to walk without forgetting that I am safe to wear shorts since my female flesh doesn't drive men berserk. Anyway, I came back up onto the path later and looked back. There he was, the Mullah, with his pants rolled up walking in the same water. It made me happy to know we could share the same water, the same simple pleasure, and that he enjoyed it as much as I did. Years ago, a taxi driver wanted me to explain to him why Canada didn't do something about the Mullahs coming in and running their neighbourhoods, but hey, since I had a somewhat "jewish" granmum, a "black-ish" husband, and a Jehovah's Witness-ish father, I didn't know what challenge to address first and told him so. Then he wanted me to get upset about marijuana, but in my experience, it's usually booze that causes more trouble so I couldn't help him there either. I don't think Canada or any other country is responsible for policing religion except if it's killing people. And that's policing criminals, not religion, so I don't like to discuss anyone's approach to their version of the divine. If it's divine, it's not your providence, and if you worship, it's your personal choice. It has nothing to do with me or the country you reside in. The Holocaust sure wasn't about religion. That was politics and money. Religion is a great mirage to get the people on board, though. People will kill you for religion more easily than for hate because the former is associated with god and the latter with the devil. And citizenship names do feel pain. As do passport names and married names and dare I say it? Legal names.

My mother begged me when she got sick. She panicked, and she pleaded mutely for me to do something. And all I said was, "the answer is no" because she was trying to escape to go outside in the dark in the middle of winter to finish recycling. When your mother dies, you cry at inappropriate times, suddenly, out of nowhere. I'll never get over it. I don't know why. I would have done anything she wanted so she could live, even fake my way through baptism and pregnancy. I would have traded places with her. If I could take it back. If I could take it all back...and do it again properly so I wouldn't fuck it up and she would still be alive. If I knew that I could die from producing a child, or kill my own mother or father, I would never ever have a child. And what kind of fucked up world kills your mother because you were born in the wrong place. Is that why Keanu Reeves rides around by himself? I get it. I so totally get it. Why would a man or woman ever have a child if it's the kiss of death? Why didn't I leave my country and go be a stranger in a strange land? Why did everybody insist I get married if I couldn't be married? She died believing she did a terrible thing. And it was because of me wasn't it. It was because of me. And all that fucked up religious estate law bullshit.

They say six kids completes your bloodline. Whose exactly? Every couple with kids that I know, fights over them. Why? They fucking adore you both to the ground and they always will, even when they know you can't stand them. Some people are meant to parent, some definitely aren't. I can't fathom why folks get their knickers in a knot spewing that you're some kind of whore when you are a female provider. Sorry, did you want to take on my responsibilities for me? Why on earth would you do something like that? Don't you have your own? And why precisely, am I a whore because I'm not asking society to pay my way? Isn't that the big complaint men in general have? That we are after their money? I never met a man who had any. And I certainly have had the occasion to be chased by two men in my life who I suspected were well heeled since one of them used to send a limousine and the other had a spare bathroom redone in pink for me, but seriously, would I trade money for love? Nope. Don't even have to think about that. I can make enough money on my own. I'd go for love every time. Every single time. Love walks on water.

So how does the new commonwealth work? It's a commonwealth of nations but the "English" colonies are part of it as the former English colonies. Well, if the King is in England then does that mean that the Commonwealth of Nations is subject to Common Law? What happened to Civil and Admiral Law? Because no matter how you slice it, Canada is now a republic like China was (are they still?); except we're not sure now if we are allowed to walk across the land. So what is the state of our constitution after 1982? What filibusters have been put through at midnight? Because it's happening the world over and each country, depending on its current political state will be behind or in front of us, which means we are being organized into voting blocs. Now, I love the dirt of this land. I do. My "family" winces because they think I'm a patriot or patriotic but it doesn't have anything to do with that. I just love the land. I breathe it through the pores of my skin and I guess I would die for my freedom to move across it or anywhere in it. I'm not arrogant. I don't think I'm more entitled than someone who wasn't born here although I am tired of being looked down upon by those who come from other places and think they are better than me. I get that alot. It doesn't affect what I intend to do. Nothing does. It's just that I can escape to the hills anywhere here and feel safe. Doesn't matter to me if it's a "country" or a "company". Doesn't matter to me if you are a "woman", a "man", or an "other". I just think people are shitty when they think they have a claim on something you did yourself. That's shitty little jealousy. If you want what I have created, go get the same thing for yourself. You're just as capable as I am. That goes for men too. I laugh when a man feels I am not entitled to what I built because I am a woman. One little woman, with all those men lining up for my stuff. I am the shit. I guess like with Diane and Jim, they need the help.

Might I rant about our so called medical care? Everyone raves about our medical care in Canada. I've had physicians fire me because I am "non-compliant" and yet there is evidential proof that my prescription drugs are no longer necessary and are doing harm. I've witnessed the same callous treatment metered out to my loved ones. I have to question your sanity. You already know that diabetes, hormones, mental illness, weight loss; to name a few, drugs exacerbate the very symptoms you are trying to eradicate. They tell you to your face on television and follow up by giving you a pamphlet repeating the same thing. And you just roll up like a moron and swallow anything they give you so you swell up like a balloon until you are on seventeen or eighteen prescriptions. How intelligent are you? Can you not read and reason for yourself? My teachers told me in school I was fifteen pounds overweight and needed to relieve my five foot four inch frame from one hundred and twenty pounds to one hundred and five pounds. Over the years that followed, every time I jumped to one hundred and twenty-eight, my physician would tell me I was too pretty to be fat and to lose ten pounds. By the time I hit menopause in my mid forties, I jumped from one hundred and twenty-three pounds to oh god! One hundred and thirty pounds!!! I was massive. And my physician proceeded to anxiously <u>inform</u> me not to lose any more weight. This! while my family nattered on about me being anorexic and/or bulimic, my whole life. But what was I thinking, running on the streets at night, to get some exercise, because I worked all day long. How can I take any of them seriously? Ever? Or you for judging me?

Have you noticed the disciplinary tone a medication ad takes on because you are not aware of the latest Research and Development drug? Swim little fish, swim as fast as you can, to be the next contestant on The Price is Right. Or, Let's Make a Deal to see what part of your body and sanity you are willing to trade for what's behind Door Number 3. I've had the privilege to be treated by a few excellent physicians in my life. The rest are too busy, too important, too beleaguered, too judgemental, too arrogant or too incompetent to know better. They are just people who know how to study and pass tests – doesn't mean they are adept at practising medicine or that they chose their profession because the health of humanity is their core reason for living. Don't try to check you're naivety if you're not the one checking your privilege. It will enable you to get along with everyone for the twenty-eight years you will be permitted before you never wake up again. Oh, you want to know who they were? How's this? A young Asian woman, a much older private practice gentleman in Yorkville who probably saved my life, and a guy my uncle knew who closed me up, and wouldn't touch me. They're Canadian. And Dr Morgentaler of course; my knight in shining armour. If you're not paying for my severely crippled child with no discernible brain activity yourself, then please fuck off and die before you get your gun. There are a multitude of caring competent health care workers. And when I broke down, they were there for me one hundred percent. Sometimes I cried because of their gentleness because I really really needed it. Please assist your physicians by monitoring your body and don't expect them to fix your life for you. They are caught in a twenty-two just like everybody else.And you don't get to be stupid because you are sick.

I have encountered in the last five years, a number of women who claim they would like a baby but are stymied as to how to get one with only a biological contribution from a male since they already know they have to pay for the child themselves anyway. I have only two points to consider in this scenario: be careful what you name them and why do you feel it necessary to tell them they are the father? Did you need the help? Then why don't you anonymously invitro? Oh yeah right, I forgot. Men are cheaper than invitro. That's irony right there. Go for it. Then you and whoever, can torture that kid too. I suggest you hand them over immediately so you can leave and get a job and get on with your life. Don't change your name though. In case they need you after all. Apparently women who are providers are whores and men who are providers are hard workers and meet their responsibilities. This is why they make more money than you. Because sperm is worth more than a uterus. The egg? No, you're confused. The egg is the little microbe that becomes a body. It just doesn't know what sex to grow until the sperm gets there, because the man decides if it's a boy or a girl. All your kids are unisex if you follow the science. Are you mentally ill yet? Are your physicians tested regularly for sanity before they work on you the same way some people have to pee in a cup before they go on duty? NO? Are you able to distinguish friends from family? Why are you even talking to these company workers? Why would they give a shit about you? Smell the coffee yet?

I want to understand why fat people go to food banks and scorn us out for "body shaming". My body has been shamed all its life for being alive. I want to understand why physicians are unable to prevent death because they need the hospital bed, so administer "comfort care" in the form of morphine to shut down your lungs. You think the sixties hippie culture was drug addled? You make us look like innocents. I want to understand why the members of the boards of hospitals get such outlandish bonuses for keeping costs down, not keeping deaths to a minimum. You're stinking rich already since that single father who has been waiting all night for you to see his daughter with a 104 degree temperature, will likely lose his job, and you'll have the pleasure of charging him hundreds of dollars and associated administration costs before you even deign to look at her. Oh, the effort it takes to put that box out to collect money from the peasants. People are so inconvenient. Cadavers were way more interesting. Besides, that little girl? Pfft, she's just a breeder. There's lots more where that came from. I hope you triple check your math before you launch that rocket....

Of course, now men are so confused, they are prone to pretending that any woman they are seen with, are their wives, mothers, sisters or co-workers. What a grind because now they "as a man", have to be everything to everybody. I'm never quite sure whose flesh is the more pristine.

I don't really understand why we fight over names. My granmum used to call it "money" but I think it is a setup. I was "married" to the first man" I "brought home" even though I never engaged in intercourse with him. We were friends and he had three kids already but his "wife" had absconded to Australia. Truthfully, I came of age the same way my mother did – at the birth of somebody. For her, it was me. For me, it was my cousin. Funny, we were next to each other all the way from Ontario to British Columbia before he emerged from my aunt's body.

The things that kill me inside? That my first husband was so alone, so alone that he killed himself – couldn't find me, couldn't find anyone just to grab him and hold onto him and say "its okay, it's okay". You're not alone. You're not bad. You didn't do anything wrong. I didn't abandon you. I just had to protect myself from you but I am still here". That my little boy who needed a mommy through no fault of his own, can never see the woman who loved him and taught him as a child. What if he kills himself because he can't find me so I could grab him and say "its okay, its okay. It's not your fault. You do have a real mommy. It's not her fault. Neither of us will abandon you. Even if I'm a piece of shit, I promise. I promise if you need me I will be there." That the psyche wards are full of people who just need to be forgiven because they paid their debts in full. That you cut us off from each other because you hate that we love. You hate what we love. And you will make sure if it's the last thing you do that we pay for loving it. What does that make you? It's what you wanted in the first place. Take me to church. I'll worship like a dog at the shrine of your lies. I'll tell you my sins and you can sharpen your knife. (*Hozier (Andrew John Hozier-Bryne)*).

So I grew up as my mother's best friend and my father telling me "well, YOU, can do whatever you want, but I'll give you a bus ticket". When my mom died, I heard over and over from the Jehovah's Witnesess, that she "needed him so much". Huh? Explain to me why I was supposed to "do as I was told" by my second spouse who ostensibly, had jurisdiction over me! He had babies already, with other women, for chrissake. Apparently he and his wif(v)e(s) needed the help. All these important people who need the assistance of teeny tiny li'l ole me. After we split (sixteen years), people from other countries kept asking me if I needed help. I'm so sick and tired of people questioning my right to live in the country I was born in. It's laughable. And apparently YOU need MY help, not the other way around. My siblings dance this way as well, even though we are third generation Canadians, depending on who objects. I will never bow to a man or woman born in another country unless I'm being honourable, or someone who has a shitload of kids that I am working to pay for. I think it's funny when you get a bunch of education and have a mess of children so you can elevate yourself above me. Go ahead. It's actually your life, not mine. I was "given" in "marriage" to some guy I was only friends with, so I could sleep with my lover. That's so great because that makes every other woman in his life, including the mother of his children, a whore. I wonder who pulls her hair in Australia.

I write these things to those of you who have been deemed "mentally ill", since I've discovered that a mere soupcon of humanity is deemed to be sane if they have the credentials. You and I get to scrabble in the dirt like the rest of "the great unwashed masses" (*Edmund Burke/EdwardBulwer-Lytton*). You're not sick. You're right to life has been heisted for legal or religious or malicious reasons or, because someone needs to prove they are better than you because they needed your help. You're being used like a ditchpig because you are probably on the verge of having something. People are so jealous when you are not unhappy. Look at every artist who's gone down in cultural history and died penniless. Someone realized they could make money off of what someone else has or can do. Be happy if you've been taken to a psyche ward. Someone begrudges you. If they kill you with drugs in there, guess what? Your legacy is made in the shade. You will take it all and there is nothing they can do about it. See? Martyrdom does pay.

Every family's probate is taken out of their hands when one member is sacrificed for another. It's the law. Jesus, move over.

Legitimate people are companies, and therefore, useless eaters; avatars to be supported and worshipped. Fun eh? They are your bank. They don't last long because they are not allowed to go outside. The irony is, that they are levelled up at birth; TRUE COMPANIES. Not people. Be kind to them. They have no idea who they are. Feel better now?

Things I Object To With My White Privilege:

Your torture of others for your own personal need for reconciliation. Wow. I can't fix the slave history of any nation for anybody – not for the blacks, the Jews, the natives, the gays, the women, the Ukranians, the gypsies, the Russians, the Americans, the Mexicans, the Irish; the list goes on and on; please apply a smidgeon of graciousness to the aforementioned since I am certain there exist those not stated who did, indeed, have it worse than any of them. Because love and money aren't enough to heal you – no matter how much you get or have. And I eat cake because one little white Canadian woman loves you to bits. Fine, don't ask me for anything then. Then you can still blame me for being the racist bitch with sooooooo much privilege. Get over yourself. I try and pass it to you every chance I get, but since I'm not good enough, you spit on it. Well it's your privilege now so you do something with it. I can't wait to be a second class citizen. Oh wait! I'm a woman so I already am one.

And you need my help. What an epiphany! YOU need MY puny little help, so you can pull my hair while I'm fixing it for you.

Just so we're clear? I'm not from an immigrant family line. I'm actually Canadian; always will be. That ten generation or whatever number you put on it before you get to be a real Canadian? How lovely that you get to live here and pretend you are better than me.

Everyone is better than me. It's a crying shame. After I spent my life being spit on, I get to spend the rest of my life being spit on. No wonder my immune system is in such great shape. Please! Spit away!

ALWAYS AND FOREVER
Amanda May Philp

Did you go sideways on me
I didn't notice for a minute
Was it something I said
You doubted me for a moment
And went inside your head
That's okay
People do things when they're afraid
They're going to die
Sometimes when you love
You have to let things fly
And if you fly forever
Because there's no leash here
Then you were just a kite in flight
Who got lost because
You thought I let go of you

AND THAT'S WHY THEY HATE US
Amanda May Philp

I can come with or without you
You don't own me
Did you think I wouldn't notice
That you needed me more
Than I needed you
For your babies galore

BOVINE SEX CLUB
Amanda May Philp
(*for my "Canadian" boyfriend lol*)

He asked her to kiss him
In the backyard by the BBQ
He didn't want her to be a bitch
Just a witch by candlelight

He asked if he could show her pink
So she could drink his head
She didn't want him to take her to bed
Just to clinch her in a fight

He asked her to remove her panties
So he could feel what Canadian pussy
Felt like
I guess he liked his cake white

That Canadian boy
Who didn't know who he was

CHORUS
Whoo hoo oh ya
I'm coming for you
Whoo hoo oh ya
And I got more than a few
Good things for you

RIFF-RAFF
Amanda May Philp

I'd rather be riff-raff
Than a grand old lady
I'd rather be a whore
Than the woman whose sons
She bore

Its riff-raff comin' for a laugh

I'd rather be the mistress
Of myself
So no one can put me on the shelf
And I'd rather be myself
Than anybody else

Its riff-raff comin' for a laugh

I'd rather drive my car
Than be a star
Because then I wouldn't get very far
In my very own jar

Bubble up.

GARDEN OF RATIONS
Amanda May Philp

They never let me have anything
And wonder how I survive on nothing
I live in the garden of rations

Frogs wail, snails hail
Rain rocks onto your path
Don't tell me your lies
They're just fireflies
In the garden of rations

If you were to imagine
The whole world in a passion
What do you think it would be?
Too much glee for you and me

If you were to imagine
The whole world in fashion
What do you think it would be
To much pree for you and me

Cause we live in the garden of rations

CHAPTER TWELVE

I had to get myself "disfellowshipped" and my "married" name turned into a legal one, so I asked and received, and then paid another nine thousand, so my second husband could get his pensions out. I couldn't leave him high and dry. I think his parents left him the house. It was the least they could do since they'd pimped him out mercilessly. It's always easier for a man to get work than a woman. His credentials are generally recognized through his transition so he can continue to provide. A woman has to explain why she dumped a "good man" and then she never gets her credentials back. Or the house for that matter. Since the woman has to take full responsibility for the state of the relationship. I know they have their own ways of getting their own back for being trapped or abandoned or poor. Some have children impregnated by other men so they can be smug too. Some get pregnant every time he pisses her off. It's a crapshoot. I've been friends with both kinds. It takes my breath away. That kind of warfare I personally don't have the stomach for but I can't honestly say that if I was trapped by a whoring man with kids and little cash, I might be tempted to do the same thing. I'd rather take my chances corporately. It's easier to swim with sharks than dance with wolves, in my opinion. At least I get paid for it and I get to go outside without putrefaction. Kids are the best thing in the world but there's nothing like being able to get up and go to work in the morning. Every morning. It's the breath of life for me. I can do both. It's worth it.

I've been reviled by both of my mother–in-laws. I don't know why. If I pay the bills and raise the kids, what exactly is your problem unless in your mind I am the next breeding mare. I've been openly asked if my husband is the type of man I like to sleep with because if I was just going to be a whore and not bear more children we can't pay for, then I could have just slept with his father and gotten it out of my system. Repulsive don't you think, and certainly not rooted in any moral obligation, if that's your ulterior motive. I thought you wanted your children to be "happy". And they're not, so it must be my fault, not yours. I didn't realize I was supposed to fix it for you since I thought that was what the last woman he had was doing before you made him bail. In the end, if you're going to be that way then I'd rather he visit you without me because no one is going to pay for the next round except me, and I'd rather not sacrifice your children, my family name, my reputation and my body for the privilege of bearing your son's fruit so he can abandon me and you can love me while I'm pregnant and tell me I am a whore after I bear you a grandchild. He never comes home anyway and if I don't go to work, I'll have men sniffing all over me because my "man" is not ever here. Either way, I'm a piece of shit because I'm raising somebody else's children and paying your bills. Wait until the kids turn on me because I never ask about their birth mother. Right? I can't ask about her because she hates me too. Like I said, in my next life, I'll get pregnant every chance I get and claim I don't know who the father is, so I can have six kids in my name and get the government to pay for them while I go to school and get the government to pay for that too, as well as daycare. A fully fostered real live Canadian family! Then I too can get laid with impunity! But it won't be because I like sex. Oh no! That would be nasty. It will be because I have an overwhelming natural urge to be a mother at all costs! And you'll just love me my whole life because I have six kids and a career and wonder who the piece of shit was that abandoned me. Then I will be honoured. It's a great Moneyball and Green Book play. And my kids? Because mommy worked so hard, she did finally pay 1.8 million dollars for her children and now they will get whatever loan they apply for so the possibilities are endless. It's a way better road to house ownership than the one my fellow sister was advised to follow by her mother and her aunt; she was a nurse but they were pissed off that she didn't "sell" her body by dancing, so she could afford her own house. I guess there was a "dancer" in the family and she made a killing showing strangers her booty to music, so they deemed my fellow sister mentally incompetent. Pussy, apparently, is in much higher demand than cock. Pays more too. For some reason men love strange pussy more than anything else. Why they pretend they want a family in the first place is beyond me. Why don't you just tell the truth? You want a son and you want me to pay for him. Will you pay for my daughter if I want one too? Then why don't you just pay a surrogate via invtiro? You make more money than I do anyways. You can afford it. Then you can have both; your very own boy and as much strange pussy to ejaculate into as you can afford to pay for. Why be coy? You're a big strong man. You like to "run the world". Why don't you just tell the truth so you can be happy? I won't object. It's your life, not mine. I won't judge you either because you're not hurting anybody. Don't know who's going to raise your son but he's your very own so I'm sure you'll bend over backwards to work something out. We all do it anyway when we have children we are responsible for in our lives. It will give the endless hours you work meaning.....

One of the things I've always loved about working is the expectation that I am going to do far more than what is on my job description. It has got to be the finest most generous opportunity a company could extend to me; learning for free, while I'm getting paid, on the job. This is corporate caring in the most finite way. I get to do more so I can be promoted to the opportunity to be paid more to do more learning on the job. I don't begrudge any of the hours I dragged myself to work on Sunday after I was up all night orchestrating a test or a "go live". I know how to do so many things because of my employers. It makes me feel good. It makes me feel generous. It makes me feel like there is some decency in the world. I don't mistrust institutions. I worked in them most of my life and they gave me everything I ever got to keep. They ensured that I became competent and able to live my life without relying on someone else to "take care of me" and I will never ever back up on that stance. I'm pretty sure they'd love to have me back if you weren't objecting. But yeah, I don't fling poo at the government or its institutions even if the medical establishment irks me. The Ministry of Health doesn't police drug companies. They assume you still have a half a brain to be able to do that yourself. But hey, if you want to be agreeable about it, buy drugs instead of clothes; charge them back to the government along with your living expenses, and prove you are a real person so you can sit outside on the curb hacking sputum onto my clean shoes when I walk by you on my way to work. Sneering is so much more fun that way; while you're drooling from being high as a kite on sanctioned pharmaceuticals. Dear me, let us be elegant or die. (*Louisa May Alcott – LittleWomen*) That's dope. Since music is my jam and nobody thinks it's worth anything, I lucked out. I used to resent it until I realized that the only reason I got to have it was because it was "worthless". I love all kinds of music. Certain songs that accompanied me as I grew up in Canada are more treasured than others but that is a private matter. I'm not a huge country aficionado, much to my aunt's chagrin, but I did have the honour of seeing Willie Nelson perform and I take it all back. He was deadly. Just deadly. Not as deadly as KD Lang of course, but deadly enough. Various artists that I had the privilege of witnessing doing their thing gave me the internal impetus to keep writing my own stuff. Legendary performances that I saw with my own eyes were; Lenny Kravitz's drummer from Santana; Cindy Blackman Santana, who sucked the wind out of me and then let me have it. I was knocked out. Neil Peart of Rush was a monster drummer, world class; but Cindy laid me out and wouldn't let me up until she was done. Melissa Etheridge was sick as a dog and her girls in the audience wouldn't give an inch, so she damaged herself laying down a performance that made me humble. Pink Floyd mesmerized me. Kid Rock disappointed me because of all the truly inspiring things he can do, he denigrated to pole dancers. Anybody can do that. But Jackson, Mississippi? I forgave that hot and sexy talented man instantly. He just loves black women I hear. Is that true? Good for him. My father likes them too. Admires them actually. They come on to him all the time. It makes him blush. My grandmother in law was quite open about it. She was a darling barracuda, always dolling up with lipstick and a sandwich when a repairman came to the house. I was secretly pleased "she still had it" as she simpered down the hallway. Oh my god, black women got him into so much trouble. I'm surprised he's not bitter. He's a man of god though, so I've never seen him bitter, not even when my mother died so young. I guess they like cake too, so I always let them have it. Besides, my English grandmother told my second husband that she would be his granma, when his died. She relished kissing him on the lips when we took her out for dinner. No change ladies, I still had to finally say "you do know I'm sitting right here". The final blow came when she was ninety-five; we were out for dinner and he ordered a second bottle of Barolo. The tannic acid level was a tad too high and she sneezed seven times in a row and was on the verge of dozing off at the table. I paid the bill whilst Mr J swept her off her feet and into his arms, and, as the maitre d'hôtel held open the door and thanked us for coming, she threw her arm over his shoulder and said "I know it's awful, but I had a great time!" What a pair of rock stars. I followed them out the door carrying the coats. She was dressed and ready for church at six am the next morning. And you need a mental health day. I believe she was already two world wars and countless children in...

Now you probably already know that Britain doesn't get along up close; that the Scottish don't necessarily like the Irish and the English don't particularly trust the Welsh so when I see African immigrants all pissed off that their sister is "dating" someone from another tribe, I totally get it. Same when the Sunis are annoyed by other Indian "factions" and "Asian" gangs don't mix "China" with "China" or the Jews and Palestinians trade bombs. The list is endless. You can't help it. You are fighting for your privilege which apparently, I have. Would you like it? I will give it to you freely if only you would stop fighting about it. But alas, nobody wants to take it from me, earn it off of me or even want it in the first place, because then you can write me off while you continue to slaughter each other in my country of birth right in front of me and blame me for your behaviour AND for not taking sides. Don't you think what's "out there" is more fascinating all the time? I do. I don't have to travel, you bring it all right to my doorstep and I get to see it in living color. Most of the time you do not notice me at all, you're so busy trying to impress other immigrants with your superiority, and my countrymen; with the fact that you and your country already had it all figured out before you got here. Soooooo, have you come to enlighten us? That is so generous of you. Is that the reason you're leaving your country or is it because you want to make sure your Canadian born children adhere to your homeland jurisdiction without having to actually live in it. Makes you a little nuts doesn't it? Doesn't enlightenment prevent harm to all life? No? Would you enlighten me then please? Cause my little sister might be having your baby and I want to be sure she is safe and that no one is offended by that; especially you.

Does a white woman have privilege or is it only white men that fit into that "special" yet demonized category?If so, what on earth are you joining the Commonwealth of Nations for? The king was a white guy the last time I checked.

I can't tell you the number of times, I have been deprived of my favourite haunt in Canada because it was bombed, shot up with machine guns or burnt to the ground. I've dodged bullets, glass, jagged metal, knives, drunken females, staple guns, enraged males, fists, bears, foxes, rattlesnakes, wolves, piano wire, chicken wire, axes, golf balls, arrows, spooked horses, spiked heels, chainsaws and Rufis... You believe that you are the only ones that come from violence or a "war torn" country. You are sadly mistaken. We have been war torn just like the rest of you so that pound of flesh you think you're entitled to receive from us? I'm afraid someone else already got it. Live a little. Go outside. If you're so much better, then please, you should have no trouble at all navigating our, now yours too, land. Just be polite and try not antagonizing your fellowman unnecessarily. You could face a dead shot from a woman. The United States of America is similar. We hunt too; trap and skin. It's no biggie. And if your woman is to be taken care of and sheltered from society, then please go home to her, do your job, and stop hanging around me. It only breeds confusion and resentment. On your part, not mine.

Do the men in my family support me? Yes! They don't give me money or a home; they know I can do it myself. And, as much as they hate it, they do step in when another family wants me to pay more than half. It's only fair. The other half of my money goes to my family of origin so you don't have to pay them for me to be your breeder or the second or third Mrs nobody at all. People do get lonely; especially when they are deprived of seeing someone they care about. (*Away From Her (Gorden Pinsent, Julie Christie)*)

In my country, the one who dies from the final blow is the "winner", because the other guy is automatically tagged with the murder no matter the source of the instigation. It's an easy rule to live by because there is no real danger anywhere except random sudden exceptions which means "time and unforeseen occurrences befall us all" (*Ecclesiastes 9:11*). People are generally kind as a nation, here, and I do not believe we are misunderstood by the rest of the world. I believe the perception is that Canadians are peacekeepers because we can hold the line in small numbers; stubborn motherfuckers; ride your horse to the border types, but soft spoken and kind of naive looking; the kind that ask for directions when the bullets are flying and say thanks (*reference BillMaher show clip of the Parliament buildings under fire*). We're not known for diplomacy and personally, I loved that clip of the new Mr Prime Minister Trudeau elbowing his way around the melee on the floor trying to get them back into their seats. (Yes, he's hot too. So sue us). And when our (then) defence minister Paul Helyer crossed the floor. I love Mr Poilievre's stamina and we'll love him because he's from Alberta and Ms Danielle Smith is batting a thousand right now. Also, he has a hot wife, just like Justin and Jagmeet and Brian Mulroney; the guy we only left one lonely seat because we were pissed off about the trade agreement he cut on our behalf with the U.S. Guess we're levelling up or down to that again. Doesn't really matter; ironically, Mr President Trump is facilitating the Canadian's provinces solidarity with each other, meaning suddenly we're playing nice with the other kids again. Thank you sir! Truthfully, Chretien was my favourite but we have a love affair with the Trudeau family and I got to dance with John Turner (*Canadian premier*) on Saltspring Island once. Kim Campbell was our female prime minister. I'm not saying we're smart, I'm saying we love what we love for a reason. It's just history and it's our history and since you weren't here when it was all going down, please try not to criticize us when you live in a glass house yourself. Don't bring your political, religious and cultural history issues from your country of origin to ours. We don't care; we have our own so get on board and educate yourself or go home already. It's not polite what you do when you expect us to manage your expectations. It's not our purview, it's yours. That is how respectful we are of you. Yes, we do have some random stuff;cthe Green Party, the Reform Party, the new Blue, something purple called the Peoples Party, but we basically just stay Liberal and Conservative and Socialist in the middle. Every once in awhile, the Bloc Quebecois kicks our ass. You just never see it coming. Fact: Quebec has our utmost respect. It is the only province in which the natives bore arms. They weren't shot to death so move over Hamas. That's class. I'm not even going wax poetic regarding our role in the "abolition" of slavery through the province of Nova Scotia. Some of us gave our lives for you to show our solidarity for you as human beings even though we had to maintain our relationship with the country to the south of us so the entire continent didn't go to war. And you want compensation. I suggest you seek it from the country from which you were permitted to be taken. Africa is much bigger and more powerful than Portugal. Kindly get a grip. And stop marrying us if you hate us so much. What in the actual fuck is wrong with all of you?

We have tons of resources under the Precambrian Shield which no one can afford to get at so it just percolates and feeds the land to the south of it. We have people north of that but they live in houses, on islands. You can't tell because everything is frozen the majority of the time so it's indistinguishable. Up there, the sounds the northern lights make in the sky keep them awake; all that crunching. Kind of reminds me of why we can't "see" villages in the desert. They are indistinguishable too, to the untrained eye. We are Highland Fling and the Jig in the east and Ahs and Ohms in the west, and the middle is flat and hardy and rocky hilled and Two Step. Hunting is better once the farmland runs out and like nearly everyone, we have fish. We love to golf but we tend to mountain climb instead and we don't tend to drink as much in the west as we do in the east I've noticed, although I have no clue why. We pound on the floor for football and spend a lot of money on hockey. Our downhill skiing is epic. It's not very English but when I was in primary school, God Save the Queen was still sung next to Oh Canada. We don't do that anymore. Most of our "colony" people were so thrilled that they were allowed to come and start fresh after the war, that they had no problem with England because they allowed them to do it, along with the U.S., if you came by ship. Our mosaic hasn't changed that much. We have always pushed immigration. We are very large and we don't have enough people. It's a leave you be, in harmony place, that will come to the rescue just in time if you take a super dive. But the rest of the time, no one really notices or cares what you're on about. They are pretty self-directed and focused on something else. I like that, then everybody can come here. But it's definitely wild and even if you have people, you are generally on your own.

That's my sixty year general impression. Ha! It's the only place a security guard at the airport wearing a turban will say to me "Welcome home". I don't think this is a fancy place. And by the state of most of your dwellings, I am vindicated by that statement. We don't do well in small spaces. We think ninety minutes to the nearest something, is normal. I understand why people from other countries find it to be too vast. You can travel by train from one country to another via Euro Pass in less than an hour. Now this of course, is not my academic opinion by any stretch of the imagination but it's a "boots on the ground" feel for the place.

I think our socialist system is burdensome because I have to become a sloppy breeding mare in order to have my medical paid for (I'm sorry, I know its wrong and I don't know where I get it but its how I really feel); I can't work as a provider like a man can, because my credentials are in various names; and no matter how hard I work, someone is always "upstairs" deeming me to be not legitimate enough or, they work a few hours a week, then choke the life out of me or someone else, so they can "get it back". I am flummoxed by all of this. I could work two or three jobs still, but am prevented from doing so to give the younger ones a chance, except that most of them want more money than I do and since I am still expected to support them, I haven't the vaguest idea why people sneer because one way or another, I'm going to have to find a way to meet the expectations without so much as a facilitation. Who knew I'd have to explain:

1) why I didn't bear children
2) why I divorced a drug addict
3) why I chose to raise two children and not ask to be paid for it
4) why I'm not working because nobody will hire me but am still filing my taxes
5) why I am not a whore, but rather a provider
6) why I would go to another country to bring home someone I loved
7) why I loved a man who wasn't "white"
8) why I loved a man with a "greek" mother
9) why I loved a man who wasn't of my "faith" (if you can nail that one down, you're smarter than I am cause according to various people, unbeknownst to me, I am of more than one faith, kind of like Billy Ray Cyrus back in the day; one man, two haircuts)
10) why I had the temerity to love anyone at all but you. (Please, if YOU would kindly stand up so I know who you are; so I can spit the 'cake' out of my mouth and be acceptable again).

I'm more than happy to work to help provide for you and yours or mine (if anyone could figure out who my "people" really are). I don't begrudge anyone who benefits from me working since I'm not allowed to support myself. I'm only permitted food, drink and shelter if I'm supporting someone else. Now YOU can fight about where my money goes. You do it anyway. If I were you? I'd work around the clock for anyone who would hire me and I wouldn't quote "the rules" when someone asked me to do something you might consider "extra". Strange how some women believe the children are "theirs" but don't consider the man they made them with, family. Is that a Madonna? You want me to believe that because you were married in a "church" or some other religious "facility" that your children were immaculately conceived? Now that's NEWS!(*Moonstruck, Olympia Dukakis*) Are you ruined? No? I thought you "needed" your husband so much. Don't only "whores" work outside the "home"? You mean he bought and paid for a home all by himself and then asked you to marry him so he would have one ready to provide? For whom? The kids or you? Well whose kids are they? Good question since they're only your "best friends", that is, until you dislike their choices. Then they are or aren't "yours" and are a problem. Mark my words, marital breakups are usually precipitated by one or both parties engaging in extracurricular sexual conduct. You can scream "possessive" all you want but if you're not going to pull your weight, then be a lightweight instead and don't expect anyone to take you seriously. Just be sure you don't get "the house" because you will be taxed exorbitantly every time you leave it. All this in a country with so much space we can drive for hours without seeing any signs of civilization. Yeah, "we the people" in Canada are rock stars! (*preamble to the United States constitution*). Now you see us, now you don't!

I watched a young woman's post on YouTube. She was very shaken because a man had spit on her when she was buying groceries and told her to get out of the way or he would rape her. We had a bus incident where a man slit a young man's throat on a bus without provocation. I've been assaulted too, on our subways and streets. But here's the thing. You can live your life in fear or you can develop some resilience. There's no way I would stand down and watch one of my fellowman be slaughtered right in front of me. Or raped. All it takes is to put yourself in harm's way, in front of that person, for it to stop. Why you have no sense of personal power when you encounter "evil" is mystifying. That kind of stuff is always committed by someone who doesn't know who they are. Your ability to object to "harmful" behaviour is based in the same golden rule we all adhere to no matter if you believe in the divine or not. In the end, it's what you will or won't do. Nobody else. Do I believe in the inherent goodness in people? No. No, I don't. But I do trust in the idiom "it ain't over til it's over".(*Yogi Berra*). There's always a reason. People don't become "a certain way" for no reason. Lots of times, I just get out of the way in time. Or else figure out what it is they really want and then the rest is easy. And rarely, is it something you were "hired" to do. The principles (I use that word purposefully), of dignity and honour mean the same thing to everyone; the manner in which they are achieved, differ. You can be ruled by fear or choose to learn by experience. Living and growing or stagnating and dying. This is my philosophy. Curiosity.

I claim my family as so many nationalities because my family of origin has these in them or are related to them by child, marriage or are relatives of relatives. Most everyone gets sniffy if you get too close. Most of us are friends by now, which you have to do when you get older. We all made choices that changed the trajectories of our lives but, once we became accustomed to it, we acknowledged that when things changed, they grew. Which is the whole point anyways. I have twenty-eight designations and/or certifications but, as a woman, I can't use them unless I am working for the "family" name the credentials were obtained in. If I were a man, I would be permitted to use them under my given name, in order to support my organization. All men have more power than I do; black, yellow, red, white, brown. Just not the respect…all that work for nothing. How ironic if I am still paying for my education that I can no longer use to work. Are you biased against me because I have no children? I know many men who have no children. I know many men who have children but do not pay for them or acknowledge them; some are paid for by the mothers of the children because they bore them instead of aborting them, because the man did not want them. I know many men who grudgingly give a pittance to feed their children and want to know why the mother is ordering pizza instead of cooking full on meals. They can't afford to, that's why. I think you're gross. And I am to be in some kind of fairyland where a man "protects" me? From what? From who? You? Who is a woman protected from, when a man protects her? I'm not being a bitch, I really want to know. Are you intimating that a man has to protect me from other men? Why did you leave then? Fuck somebody else? Have children with other "unprotected" women? Even Africa knows that female industry is what keeps them going. Read the Bible to find out who is sitting at the gates debating the intricacies of "God's" law while the women are running the city (*Proverbs 31*). I think you're just lazy. And proud. It's a blessed thing that we, the women, are so agreeable. I'm sure Dr Peterson would concur. Even he doesn't know why we do it.

Why is there something wrong with me if I would rather work at something other than becoming a mother? Why are LGBTQ++ individuals deemed to be competent but, as a woman, if I don't produce offspring from my womb, am deemed to have some sort of disorder? There are plenty of men who have no desire to reproduce. Is there something wrong with them? So how come they get to work without being scorned for their lack of progeny? Not everyone is suited to everything that "society" "decides" they should be doing. Your degree does not trump the truth, no matter what you paid for it. Neither does it mean you can take a random bunch of "symptoms" and use them to fit a particular diagnosis because you are running a drug trial. I believe that sort of behaviour is considered antisocial, which makes you a bit of a menace. And you wonder why I hesitate to trust you fully as a professional. It's not paranoia, its common sense, something, you are apparently not taught in medical school, along with basic nutrition. I guess medicine is the new "mommy's little helper" (*Rolling Stones*) and not to be taken seriously as a concerted effort to maintain the physical health of a living human being. It's just another choice of which seesaw you'd like to ride (*Moody Blues*). My mother died this way. And not that it matters a whole lot, but she didn't like staying at home raising children either. She had too many brains for that. The sheer fact that she was looked down upon because she had five children is why I shied away from following the same unfortunate path. I like my self esteem right where it is, thank you very much. Women with children are needy and that is the least desirable place to be in society. It's not viewed with respect or accorded any honour. In fact, my observation has yielded the unfortunate conclusion that child bearing is the most effective way to destroy your marriage. Any hope of marital fidelity fades and becomes statistically impossible when you use your womb to pump out offspring. Prove me wrong. I dare you. Precisely how many children and degrees do I need, to be permitted shelter that is not threatened by the notion that I am "spoiled" because I live in a structure that I have managed to pay for by working *like a whore* - because my children and my job are clear indications that:

1) I have spread my legs and
2) I eat food.

I mean duh, how much more useless can I be?

CHAPTER THIRTEEN

I enjoy academic rigour. It is applied simply. I don't enjoy writing tests but once I decide I need the paper, I do it. The reason I don't enjoy doing it is because academic rigour doesn't work in the living world. I have to study to learn the answers that are required in order to pass. I can't tell the truth. I can only achieve expertise in a vacuum. I loved it when a multi-university degree'd person came to "head" the department. It meant they would never be there because they didn't have a clue how it was really done, nor did they care. They were put there so we could continue to operate without a question as to whether someone in charge was qualified. They just sat in their offices to all hours or, we just never saw them at all. I've no idea what they did other than perish from sheer boredom but they did it. And made a bunch of money doing it. Singularly thin people skills. Tough to mingle from a great height. I preferred running from one meeting to another with a lineup of people at my desk, getting things done; knowing what was really out there without conjecture. Not to say that if I had the time in this life, that I wouldn't love to get a PhD in mathematics but that would be impractical at this juncture since everyone uses a calculator now instead of their brains. Am I writing this bit to be contrary? Yes, a little. The time and money it takes to achieve the formal education which may or may not get me to where I want to go, will rob me of the freedom of movement to just do it myself. And put me in a box. What happens when you've used it all up? Besides, education doesn't make you accountable for your decisions. And that's the bottom line. It seems to give you a "buy" on any of the unfortunate outcomes you've orchestrated. Besides, university students are a) snotty and b) imagine they are special. I've done the courses. They're so upset when life deals them the same shit as the "working class".

The same conversation is taking place now as it was when I was a teenager. We are ruining our earth! We are not fair to people of colour! We are not fair to women! We have too many people on the earth! We should have only one child, not to be selfish! We should have many children, not to be selfish! White men are bad! We don't like Russia! We're not fair to the Jewish people! We do like the gays! We abhor the smarmy attempt to be inclusive of everybody! We are on too many drugs! We are too thin! We are too fat! We don't like the gays! For religious reasons! Now gay people are religious too! Oh god, what are we going to do, since our ancestors fucked it up for everybody! Stop littering! Stop oil and gas! Take down the wall of Berlin! We stole the land from the native people! We are racist, sexist, misogynistic, homophobic, polluters! We need to put women back in the home where they belong! We need to burn our bras and stop shaving our legs! We need to stop war! We need to fight against the man!

I believe a bunch of us "hippies" went to India for enlightenment.

Good lord, next thing you know we'll be calling for the destruction of the Great Wall of China for some unbeknownst hitherto reason that befell us when we were insisting on "Truth! And Reconciliation!"

Honestly, I don't give a fuck who you are in bed with unless it's a minor. I think you should pay half for your child. I think get married, just don't take his name. You have your own name, what do you want his for? Are you weak? You have to poach off of his? I did this. Both times. Stupidest thing I ever did but again, apparently, I am a whore if I don't. If I get married in church, I only get a first and middle name, not a surname. There aren't enough to go around in heaven. If I'm the only child, can I keep my last name then? Or do I need a degree and to become a professional whore so no one throws my cake out the second story window onto the garden below where I grow green beans and potatoes?

I lost my second husband while I was working and raising children because I didn't have my own children with him. Would have been nice if I could have paid for one but I was already a widow so there was no chance I was going to be allowed that, even if I could have pulled it off. Kids are wildly expensive. I ate very little when I had them; there just wasn't enough time or money. Have to say that I miss them though. Other than the football, baseball and hockey parents who inevitably tried to engage us in extramarital affairs and swinging parties, it was a great time. A really great time. I'd do it again. Kids are the best. And I'm pleased that I feel that way because I don't yearn for one of my own. You know those beleaguered parents who desperately need a sitter and can't find one? They should hire me after I retire. I'm sorry we lost the house. There were lots of kids that came to stay when there was a tournament. They came to our house because we were respectable and we were both working. Even university kids need a safe place to stay when they are playing...

Now please forgive me for only speaking of which I know. I try not to say too much about things I know very little and/or cannot verify for myself. Sometimes people are offended or annoyed when I don't know enough historical detail about a particular place, subject, event or discipline, but then I doubt they are reciprocal in this respect, since such ones are usually experts about very little so the life experience is "stinted". Most times, this is where the offence springs from. It springs from within and more often than naught, it is coupled with a lack of understanding due to the lack of breadth and depth of their living experiences since expertise is a finite and not a broad based application. Exposure to life is a precursor to wisdom. And if you want to regulate entitlement to that exposure, then we have a dominance problem not a propaganda problem. Be sure to establish your "regulations" in the correct continuum won't you? Application of a little academic rigour to religion would be most helpful. And no, I do not mean academic posturing in order to prove one faith is more real than the next. You are working for yourself not God, if you have denigrated to that platform. Anything not open to scrutiny is afraid of what will be found out, not found...Eileen Wuoros was a victim of this type of abomination. We can never agree on what a true crime against a human is. Kill or be killed is nurture, not nature. And your manuscripts, even the vaulted Vatican ones, are recent documentation. The earth and its peoples are older than the current native cultures who've laid their claim to the homeland. Not even the bible can say it is the final word on what is divine. No one can say for sure, what God's name is or conclude with any real finality, what God wants. I don't believe God wants anything. If you think you are that important that you must dedicate your miniscule life to what God might or might not want, then you are lost. You have no more of the holy spirit than anybody else and to pretend that you do is what makes that whole ball of wax go round instead of greasing your way through life. And you do know that ten virgins only remain virgins if you don't have sex with them right? So what is the point of the sacrifice? I think if your honour compromises another, then you do not fully understand the concept. Murder erases honour instantly and transforms it into cowardice. That's science. Most murderers are cowards. I could never understand why potential victims won't fight for their lives, not compensation, their lives. Your life is all you get. Ever. Nobody cares after you're gone. Sorry, but it's true. A fact of life. And since young people cannot grasp that it takes a lifetime to have something, they will endeavour to take what you have earned because the ones that do inherently believe themselves incapable of accomplishing at the same level, tell themselves that you had it easier than they do. Unless they eclipse you, of course. Climbers and gold diggers are everybody. What exactly are you made of? Even the aristocracy cannot survive without the people since they climbed and dug gold to get there, or else their ancestors did. It is an interesting dichotomy because meritocracy is not the answer or else we would be fighting over the opportunities to establish our merit and lying about who or how we did our work. Remember Alexander Graham Bell? And I love that phone company. Myself, and a few of my immediate family worked for them for years. It's how we were able to afford sheets for our beds because the mortgage was killing us. Charles Darwin and natural selection and all that...

You all lost your minds over Covid. And yes, there was some questionable but necessary oversight that was exercised and it was a very creepy time since everyone just freaked out from the isolation. But that is all it was. I worked with Public Health. They are low tech. They have to be because they track potential trajectories in a very particular way. They will be the last to adopt genetic engineering.

Public Health actually does give a shit about you. And yes, some people experienced adverse reactions that ended their lives. It was a new vaccine with the usual MNR parameters which is why it was openly stated on the airwaves that it was a pilot project. I almost died on the road from the scraping that went through theventricles of my heart and then it stopped at the last second and I came to. I didn't react well to the scarlet fever vaccine either. But the vaccine was a mandate, not a law; and both the private and public sectors changed to accommodate both parties; the vaccinated and the unvaccinated, everyone kicking and screaming all the way one way or the other. I vaccinated when it was almost over, mostly because I had relatives who were questioning my sanity, and because I tracked the adverse reaction statistics over a three and a half year period that were openly provided and was comfortable with my odds. There was a virus. Nobody can pinpoint the exact location or origin of its inception but it is there and we elect governments to "protect" us by making decisions for the greater social good by providing a public service to the best of their ability. Why, you attribute godlike, dictatorship powers to ordinary men and women who are managing the country to the best of their ability by your own consensus; is beyond me. The longer it went on, the weirder you were to be around and I have to say, it really freaked me out. Kiss of death for Trudeau or anyone in power and there was no way anyone else was going to fight for that spot until it was over so lucky Justin. You're beginning to calm down now and I'm relieved. Thought I was going to have to level up without you lol. Hopefully, you'll start wearing your nice clothes again and we can socialize without having to bring cake. It's bad for my complexion, my digestion and my teeth, and frankly, you should know better. It was so awful, I nearly gave up alcohol altogether. Soon, I feel, I will be able to savour a glass of red wine again without being the devil. I like red wine and big salads. Or dance without be assessed as to why I am in public. Yeah, you all really freaked me out with your baggage. Hopefully you're close to getting it all sorted out now; emotionally. Once your emotions even out, your brain will kick in and it will go back to normal. WhichI believe, is what we all wanted in the first place. You are all still real people. You haven't lost your chance to be happy. There's still time aha. But do pull yourself together. There are still women to be plundered and money to be made, as it were...it ain't over 'til it's over after all. For the life of me, I cannot fathom any other reason mankind strives to be alive. Sad, funny but true. And kind of boring...if you could manage to accustom yourselves to moderation, a lot of the studies we waste our own (taxpayers) money on, trying to figure out how to rein in your voracious appetites so you don't hurt yourselves, would be quite unnecessary. Fodder for the "Karens" and the delusional souls who advance themselves on "peer reviewed" material, is what you make of yourselves. Do try and play a little hard to get(*Overboard*). If you could refrain from having your second wife disrobe in public, that would be helpful too. At least put her next to Gaga on the red carpet so you can be taken seriously. No wonder you're always in a bad mood. Everyone knows what you have at home.

CHAPTER FOURTEEN

Why do women compete for men? Why do women compete and then when they have won, do they lower the bar? The competition ain't over honey. If your man idles at too high a level for you, then you need to become more familiar with who you are, because you are taking time up in another person's life. Men do this too, but I am not a man so I cannot speak as a member of that sex in order to poke at the perceptions because I cannot, in all honesty, identify the commonalities for the male species in a way only they could and achieve some sort of consensus. For me to attempt that would be conjecture and grandstanding since I have no idea what I'm talking about (like Dylan Mulvaney; even men thought he was way off the mark trolling a type of woman that doesn't actually exist; men generally don't really think that little of us). That being identified, I do find it curious that men and women aren't better friends. I find it VERY curious that such a small percentage of women achieve vaginal orgasm; a natural freely god given bodily function. It means that men are generally impregnating a less than optimally healthy female; not a good idea. Men are no slouches in bed so is it you or is it them? In my case, it was me because I did not function in a normal healthy way sexually until I was fifty-nine years old. There doesn't seem to be a spate of crimes committed against men where they are tied up, sexually assaulted, tortured and killed like there are against women. Even the Emanuel Jaques and William Gracey murders that were sexual predator crimes victimizing men were committed by men. The Lorena Bobbit type of criminal act is a rarity and that involved dismemberment not murder. Thank goodness Mr Bobbit had medical insurance or it could have turned out much worse for him than it did. Why do women compete for men and when they lower the bar on them, do they stay, even when their offspring and their person is abused?

We need to get it straight, the difference between protection and atrociously bad manners. While you're at it, I would seriously suggest you take a long hard look at those wedding vows you seem to be just dying to lay down and ensure that the other side of the contract is being met. I fail to understand why the majority of you do not do this. Fairyland. This is the principle reason men do not respect you. You negotiate for shoes instead of getting a job. You give up your job when you have children. You have some cockamamie idea that someone else is supposed to provide for you. What heavenly cloud did you float in on? Ever heard of free education? It's everywhere. Governments and people in general are just dying to give you free education so you can get your precious ass up off the couch and contribute something to society and look after yourself. I often wonder why all those deadbeat parents were even permitted to engage in sexual intercourse if they had already been deemed mentally or emotionally incompetent by the content of their prescription drugs and therefore unable to work together to provide for another human being. Soul less. A single individual's average consumption of anything is microscopic in the grand scheme of things. Surely you can muster the strength. There are single parents with multiple children who do it every day all by themselves. I hear lots of military men who get hooty about this but let's give reality a shake here. You protect us from them but when you're off duty, we have to take of you because sometimes you're so fucked up from the experiences you had in the field that you are unable to reconcile the dichotomy in your head. That we leave you high and dry is deplorable. That you use your military training to prey on us because your life is still shit, in or out of the army, is also deplorable. I wish preciousness was limited to those not serving. Is there some reason, you are unable to stand, spread your labia with your fingers and pee? Is there some reason your fellow military has to surround you when you pee for modesty? Listen, they touch their penises with their hands to pee and they don't ask for protection while they do it. So what gives? If I have to protect your modesty, how on earth can I trust you to protect me? Brains or no brains, what are you thinking? It's actually easier for you to pee surreptitiously than it is for a man. They have to take a chance and actually put it out there…your real problem is menstruation, it's easier to track. I think that's when you shouldn't be out in the field, just like when opera singers are paid not to sing, so they don't damage their swollen vocal chords. It's not a penalty because of what you are, it's an opportunity to upgrade your skills and learn new ones while you are out of commission. Get a grip, it's not like you can give birth in between sniper shots. And as for rape in the military, yeah, that is an area I cannot even say anything sensible about because I would just die from shock and kill three or four on my way out, or at least maim them so they would remember me as the one that was not worth the trouble. The truth is the truth; even the military knows what it is. So, in my experience, if what we are doing to combat it, isn't working for us, then you, my ladies, have to figure out a different approach that will resonate. I've been in hierarchy; we all are, it's still a chain of command. I don't understand why men object to military women and yet mutilate them in civilian life. It's just so illogical. I mean, if you're not around, she still has to fight to protect your progeny so why object to her being a fighter? You want wussies for kids? It's weird. Why don't you just segregate the units? Woman are pretty vicious and if you can't live with us being raped incessantly by the enemy til we're dead, then why do you try it with us in private? It's emotional and nonsensical and has no place in the military. And that's what pisses me off about men who think women get too emotional as a species. Because some of you appear to have a great deal of difficulty regulating your own emotions which makes you antisocial and a bit of a menace doesn't it? And I don't want you serving all doped up on pharmaceuticals; it compromises your ability to serve competently. Call me crazy…

Healthcare. I dunno, what do you think? Is healthcare a business or a service? What's the difference? Are children a hobby, a business or a service? What is a family? And what are the requirements? Is a family man a provider? For how long? What if you are a love child? Of god or of the people that made you?

What if you aren't but you are an avatar like the emperors? I'm an avatar but I'm not an emperor… (anytime you revert to your maiden name, you become an avatar).

The other arena that always confuses me is mining. If you farm for food by using the ground and what is in it, how exactly is that different from using minerals in the ground for other things? Are you insinuating that we have overrun the earth and are vociferously sucking the life out of the planet? (My goodness, the woolly mammoth moves over). I thought that these things were renewable resources not sustainable ones. Renewable resources renew themselves so there is an energetic signature, a life force. How do we know we're killing the planet for sure? How do we know it's us? Apparently we can all fit into the state of Texas with a social distance of a hundred yards. How is it possible that we puny little humans who can't get along with each other think we are even capable of destroying a living planet? You are remarkably out of touch with your level of engagement in the world.

Ultimately, I just love young people. They say and do the same things we all did. They sound like we did as they move through the decades. We were so sure we were going to banish the man and live in peace and harmony and that free love and enlightenment would fix everything or we would blow it up. Some of us are still talking to our parents and kids and relatives. Some aren't. You will be in the same place we are when you get here. Do try and forgive us and yourselves by the time you do. It's in your best interests to keep us around as long as possible. Cause we shrivel when our ancestors die right in front of us. And you don't really want to fight over who gets the teapot yet do you? Besides, grandparents and great grandparents have lots to teach your babies that you don't have time to and they are way better at forgiving the shenanigans of their grandchildren than you are. And, what better way to learn how to care for people before the babies come; then you won't be so annoyed about it. Besides, you get to go places and do things with each other in tow. Some of the best times I ever had were with my grandparents. Go on a date with your spouse. Dress up. Have a cocktail. Shake your booty. Get laid. You'll feel better about almost everything. At the end of the day, you can look back on your glory years. You'll get some. We all do.

I would cease to smoke intermittently over the years but being a non smoker was lonesome. Smokers talk to each other, actual civilized conversation and an authentic exchange of ideas. There's fifteen minutes, you see, and you get to connect before you go back to work. It's kind of like corporate golfing except that it doesn't take all day... and probably costs the same amount of money. Pick your poison.

Leaders never go to war. Only the people do, and the leaders must follow in order to do their jobs. And once that happens, the people are powerless to do anything but kill each other until the bloodlust is satisfied and they come to their senses. Remember Bosnia, Serbia and Croatia? Its river country. Suddenly we were raping our neighbours. OH, don't get up in arms. I golfed with an Ambassador to Canada from one of these countries and when I asked him why and what happened, he was remarkably lucid about the whole thing. In fact, he didn't even throw anyone under the bus. I was kind of impressed by that and his wildly thick head of hair. I guess no one gets to throw a stone until they have a crime free country, that is, if they can agree on what a crime is... They were an extremely generous community in Ontario when I was around them. The stuff they gave away at golf tournaments were the bomb; big sacs full of imports of food available in Canada and all kinds of wonderful items that didn't cost a fortune but reflected alot of thought and kindness really. Opened my world up a little – god I love that. Sometimes I just well up with tears when I recall the kindness of strangers that I have been the recipient of. I was once physically slapped for those tears since they were considered ill gotten gain like I was a Fremen (*Dune*) but that is just a lack of understanding and it didn't leave a mark so I forgave them. It's tough being stuck in the house your whole life with no money. It's like being given a lifelong prison sentence just like a murderer and that your reward for not hurting anybody is the same reward you get when you do, with the exception that you have to cook for people instead of someone cooking for you. The irony does not escape me.

    That being said, I would really appreciate it if you all would stop talking like you need to scrape your forehead on the ground for the privilege of fixing up someone's house, food, clothing, pipeline, fence, department, hair, boat, acreage etc. It's not a fucking privilege. Stop acting like a slave. You are an able bodied person who is as capable as the next person. You are contributing. Stop apologising for it. I appreciate you and I'm glad you are here because I need somebody. I don't give a fuck what color you are while you are doing it. That goes for LGTBQ++ folks as well. I mean it. Stop blaming others for your uniqueness. They have their own uniqueness to deal with. I always know I need to back off when I see that look that comes to someone'seyes when they like me but we are strangers and they are good people but I am so different from them that their immune systems aren't sure if I am a threat or not. It's not racism or sexism or misogyny or anything like that. It's the heart attempting to accept what is not of its usual ilk. We'll get there. We will. Accustom ourselves. And that is the mutual kindness part; the recognition that we are in Kansas with Toto but we are standing beside a Tin Man as we ease on down the road (*Wizard of Oz*). The real kindness is the recognition is that "we are all in this together" (*Justin Trudeau*) okay? My second husband got kicked around an awful lot because he was better at this kind of thing; a real mature individual. Sometimes the greater strength is to take one for the team until the rest of the team gets a grip. There actually is some honour in that. It's a shame religion doesn't do this since apparently Jesus already accomplished that for everybody. The problem is in the service management portion of the lifecycle. And I don't think everyone is aware that he ostensibly did it, since evidently, nothing changed.

Are we going to be annexed by the United States of America? You bet we are. We're a republic now as is Australia so its prime time. Are we still going to be our own country? Yeah, they don't really want us like they say they do. They want us in a different way. Isn't that nice? To be wanted lol? Alot of us have relatives there anyways just like our immigrants do, so won't life be interesting along the largest unprotected border in the world? Canada is a massive border town. It's great. Aren't you lucky its only one border and not multiple countries. Will we go to war? Oh probably. Eventually. It just won't be with the U.S.A. We already did that. Calm down. Mr Poilievre is as competent as Mr Trudeau was. Trump's there for a reason. Didn't think he'd come back did you? I did. Ever heard of just say no? You're allowed to slap the President of the United States of America for touching you inappropriately. Are you scared? Why? Your body is worth as much as his body is. He's not going to ruin you. He's an octopus. Everybody knows that, but he's also a father like you and he also has wives from other countries besides the USA. I'm not certain but I would hazard a guess that Mila Mulroney and Milania Trump (Bosnia and Slovenia) are of a cultural heritage that our prominent political men found sexy. So what? They want kids too.Additionally, I'm really not interested in your spending habits. There are more material things to spend money on than you can shake a stick at. Once you've had whatever you wanted, replacing or repairing it is not a big deal and neither is money. If you all spent whatever you wanted without all that conjecture and judgement on your fellowman's budget and proclivities, you'd be alot further ahead in knowing who you are and what you wanted to do with your life instead of chasing the wind. China's secret in some ways. Feed the masses with pretty trinkets, give them a job and an heir and go forth. Wince if you will but the American dream is all about that. Poilievre will cut a great deal so stop worrying about it. He and Anaida probably have dinner with Justin and his ex, so don't think Canada's government is in pieces and the sky is falling okay? We're all on the same page. It just doesn't look like it. Have a little faith, get on with it and while I personally don't believe you should be wearing a turban in office, stop whacking Jagmeet. He's a rock star. And the entry into politics by that guy is a demonstration of Canadian bravery. Stop whingeing about it. The perspective of the culture will enrich the native peoples and put the white people in their place. Don't get me wrong; the white people were following the edicts of the Queen of England as they were supposed to. You did too, in your country of origin. You're not racist either. It's simply that the mosaic of Canada is not physically as white in color as it used to be. Get over yourself. We're not inventing a wheel here. Sometimes I think the reason black and white people get all gnarly about joint offspring is because it's going to come out brown in color, like the majority of the world's population and white and black are at opposite ends of the spectrum. All the effort I made in vain when I was a kid, trying desperately to get a tan seems so ungrateful now.

Did Andrew Tate get married yet? He might be already. My understanding is that he has been unofficially married on a number of occasions but no formal announcement. I doubt he will. This man will settle with one woman because it's his nature but he won't do that until he's much older. He is looking for something in this lifetime and is on his own path. It's a little unsettling to be on your own path because you are misunderstood the majority of your life. I wish him well. Emory lol, how German is that? The rest of his name is as English as it gets. Yes, I do agree that the English are brutal. But then, so were the Huns. Are Muslims forgivers? I don't really know. I guess they are, on a case by case basis, like everybody else. Perhaps a Kardashian could fill the void....

I have loved and not been loved back. That shit hurts. It really hurts. But I can't be bitter. I promised myself when I was a little girl that I would not become a bitter old woman, no matter what happened. Unrequited love is a fact of life. And the one not loving you back isn't doing it to hurt you. Love rises unbidden and it is what it is, a life force of its own that rises from the heart not the mind. The ability to love is precisely why we are able to be here. And the ability to continue to love is an asset because if you can't keep going because you're not supposed to love anymore then you just wander around surrounded by pictures of persons long gone in a fish bowl. It's peculiar. I'd really rather you find yourself another man or woman or other and co-own or co-rent something so you can work. There are people who do exist in the world who work until they drop and love every minute of it. My last vocal coach's mentor died at his piano, in Queens (*NYC*), doing the things he loved, at the age of ninety-seven; and with a much younger woman; decades younger, in fact. His third one...officially that is.

I've noticed Mr Poilievre is much leaner these days. It's very attractive if you don't mind my saying so. His wife will have a difficult time keeping her hands off him so he should sleep well. That's good. He'll need it. In the end the continent will pull together. Canadians and Americans are very good at being lean and mean together. There are other alliances in the world that share the same type of affinity and they are going to do the same. The sky will not fall today. I know religion desperately wants it to. We've been waiting for Armageddon forever and blaming someone named Eve for it. No wonder you men get pissed with us. Hopefully, next time around you'll speak with the Devil yourself and make a much better decision.

All in all, it's a pleasure to be alive. I suspect I have been forgiven. I surely have been shown the kindness of strangers and it is true that I have friends that I would give my life for. When I lost my life I yearned to go home to Ireland. I don't know why. Every time I lose something I loved, I yearn for the Irish countryside. When my mother died, I watched Leap Year over and over for three weeks. I'd get up in the morning, go for an hour run, eat a white chocolate sundae from the Marble Slab, put the movie on and let it run over and over again. Anna, from Boston... I've never been to Ireland. Boulogne was the closest I ever got to my heritage. Irishmen don't go for me anyways. I'm too English and I can't help it. They make fun of me but in the end nonetheless, I am a wolf, and the Canadian wolves used to let me run with them at night, literally, when I would go to the Rattray Marsh in Mississauga, Ontario. They even protected me from random strangers lurking in the bush. Be realistic. The best place to do crack is in the city surrounded by nature. They're out there.

To those of you whose parent claimed you went to the dark side, I hope you stay together because that same parent will forgive you so you can be by their side if they need you in their later years. I guess my view of the medical profession is somewhat colored by comments made to me over the years; sneered at by the Scottish for having an abortion (I guess I was supposed to give it to the Lairds), told by my Trinidad and Tobago physician that I was too pretty to be fat and to lose ten pounds. Frankly, it's too much to expect normal men and women to perform miracles and yet we do have great expectations of them. And in the end, sometimes it works and sometimes it doesn't.

Like everyone, they do the best they can by working around the clock. You cannot survive if you do not become inured to pain and in the end, you can choose to lobotomize your nerve endings or you can cry until you can't cry anymore. Eventually you will stop. And then you'll pick yourself up and the experience will become a part of the fabric of your life and it will add to your understanding.

Someday we'll stop objecting to touching each other. Everybody needs a hug or a snuggle or a hard "I got you" from time to time. It's human. Even the Taliban need human touch because that is what they are. If there is no one else around then you must as a decent person stand in for someone who is awash because that is what the heart does, over and above the objections of the brain. I know this because I wasn't there the first two times and so I had to make it for the last. I just had to. In the end, you just have to have courage in the face of loss. And be human. I hope that when you stop being afraid to come out of the house, we can be friends again. Because I have a big Canadian family that has roots as deep as yours and I recognize that you cannot change what you are and I can still love you anyway. Just please keep your penis to yourself. I don't wish to be misunderstood again. I'm not racist. I like you. I'd like you even more if I knew you were a one man woman or a one woman man but I do understand that circumstances do not always allow that and I am grateful to you for your kindness and your courage in accepting me as I am.

CHAPTER FIFTEEN

Barriers to home ownership stymie me. There's just so much unoccupied land everywhere and since we, as a race, are incapable of bringing the earth down by ourselves, it's a real mystery to me why we do skyscrapers, and make a house an impossible dream. Even the Roman aqueducts changed the way the natural habitat functioned but we are still here. There are pipes in the water in Croatia that sing but the fish are still mating. It's just the height of hypocrisy to engage people in generational mortgages. It stinks to high heaven and is extremely bad business if you want an economy to thrive. It creates a scarcity mindset and we become completely disconnected to what is really out there. I don't know how this occurred but tent cities are our shame and say an awful lot about the depravity of the human condition. Religion would make a great comeback with some kind of honour if we dispensed with the extravagant processes and just put people in homes. It's not like religion doesn't have the money. It's honestly the most reckless move to make and definitely the wrong time to do it. And I don't know if the whole "this house is too big for you, we could fit two families in here" is where we really want to go. It breeds disease and disharmony and is an affront to mankind. It's also terribly reminiscent of the Russian revolution with the notion that the private life is dead (*Dr. Zhivago*). Have you nothing better to do? Why should I pay seventy-five percent of my income for shelter? It had better be motherfucking fine. And it isn't. It's a cardboard box that once sold, can't be insured (although try and collect on that and see where it takes you).

The people of Mexico. Well. I now have history with them and god only knows if I'll ever set foot in that country again. I was assaulted there once, but it was in a public place and it was a one off...not sure why the waiter followed me to the bathroom and forced a kiss but there are worse things. I rented a catamaran and I can't remember why but I had to strip and change my clothes under a towel. It was a deserted area but the gentleman who accompanied me stood lookout and didn't even glance so there is honour. I like Mexican food very much. Mr B used to wander the streets at night for super spicy food from the street carts but in the morning there would appear huge mounds of fresh clams or it might have been oysters (sorry, I was on my honeymoon and I had a live one for a new spouse so I can't recall), but you could buy a dozen and eat them with limes and watch the crews body dive for more. I really liked that because in Tofino, British Columbia you can pull live crab, just like they pull lobster on the east coast. Of course, these things can be experienced in other parts of the world. My gold earrings that my new husband had given me were stolen from my room but on the other hand, they let me go through customs with the people and I was once sung to by a group of nurses. I was shocked. I could feel that they knew me from thirty years ago and I wept for the memory. It was kindness and connection of a superior sort. I don't know if a death certificate was ever sent there but I do know that they remember me and yes, I do get misty when I hear their music and I will always be grateful for the extraordinary efforts they made to save Mr G. They are also kind of my family now too. Never doubt another country's ability to find ways to vanquish some of our great maladies. They do things in China, in Germany, in many places that seek alternative methods of curing and when they get it right, it's superb. I'm not entirely on board with standardized treatment. It's a risk. Sometimes it's a risk you have to take. But it's a risk that you shouldn't be penalized for if you choose an alternate route. There seems to be alot of ire directed at alternate practitioners but now you have no options at all. As for me, I'd rather take a vitamin C and eat dandelion greens than swallow pouches of antibiotics (necessary as it might be sometimes) and opiods. Lots of exercise is even better. And if you're biggest issue is some random attack for vitamin B, how small is your world? It is all relative you know. Some of us die from Dosetaxel (Taxotere). Some of us died from the COVID vaccine. I don't see you yanking it off the shelves. I'm so sick of outrage. Useless useless outrage....

It might be helpful to know that your fingers and toes are wrapped in ice during chemo so it doesn't reach the extremities. Nobody wants to see a cancer patient with bloody tips for fingers and toes. Take a lesson here and consider wrapping your head in like manner. It could save your hair. Additionally, you'll be told you can eat whatever you want. You can but your best shot is to eat cleaner than a body builder. You're trying to clean out an oxidized form of Candida that has turned into glue. The kind of drugs it takes to kill that often wipe out your immune system in its entirety (*Nightbirde – Jane Kristen Marczewski*) and you'll be cancer free for five minutes until the five or six cells that escaped detection proliferate at an alarming rate and you have no immune system left to stop them. You'll be dead in less than a month. Morphine and heroin derivatives given for pain do all kinds of other unfortunately unwelcome things that are killing your appetite anyway. Marijuana works for pain and appetite very well; not for everybody but it's certainly a more comfortable way to go. I loved that girl from afar. I sure did. I play those performances over and over again. There are multitudes of people alive and well with no blood line. It's a trick to make you believe that you might be worthless. But if you're building and working and supporting the infrastructure, you're paying more taxes than the "useless eaters" who continue to procreate endlessly. You are not a whore. You are a person. My bloodline is connected in a remote way to my family of origin that had children. My legal bloodline was connected to anyone who needed a mother. I felt it all. See? And so did they.

    I recognize that I am being contrary. I really have no idea what a "useless eater" is. I detest biopsies because they are invasive and excruciating and have the capacity to drag previously sealed in cancer cells through the body on their way out (*Jack Layton*). Way to drag the garbage in…I prefer MRIs for diagnostic imaging because x-rays are radioactive and we all know what radiation does to the body. It's hardly rocket science. That's all I want to say about cancer. Some physicians who cure cancer without following standard protocols lose their licenses or their lives (*New York City*). Of course, it doesn't help if you're offended that they touch you while trying to help you. Perhaps you could save your outrage and complaints to the Board because you weren't treated like Little Lord Fauntleroy and look past your ideology to see the real value that you are trouncing for the sake of your tender feelings. I had a great doctor in Ontario but all those complaints made to the Board were quite unnecessary and in the end, somewhat destructive for no particular reason.

I'm no physician so take my words with a grain of salt because the empirical data can be construed in a myriad ways. My own eyes are not considered a reliable witness.

It has been my observation that the world has a really big problem with female orgasm, like they're not entitled to it for some reason. We've cut the clitorises out of millions of little girls. We religiously object strenuously to masturbation. It is the height of shortsightedness and is certainly not a moral stance. Women were created thus and some earthly intervention has decided that "god's" work is flawed. I find this ideology to be extraordinary. Is this so we can make money on Pampers? If you don't exercise your parts you get flabby and sluggish and unable to run. You pee when you laugh. You can't hold your urine. Your uterus literally falls out of your body when you are very old and a healthcare worker has to push it back up there with gloves on. You rape. All in the name of controlling some birthright bodily function. I find these things to be nonsensical, to destroy the natural sexual health of the human body because we have a problem with "god's" work. It makes a race that is still very young, very naive, colossally arrogant and quite brutal. We have advanced not one iota. This whole "Every Child Matters" (*Canadian movement with roots in residential schooling*) is not something to be taken lightly since apparently some of you feel the need to run off with little kids and enslave, prostitute, maim, torture, sodomize and god knows what else. I don't know why we pay for you to languish in prison. Some accidents and crimes of passion are very difficult to forgive and so do need to be atoned for in some way, but the games we play legally to preserve the "sanctity of life" is perverse. You're a monster. Everybody knows it. Suicide is forgivable, but not what you do.

Heaven forbid we meet an extraterrestrial race. We are so backward we would inadvertently incinerate ourselves because we would object.

I stand with the LGBTQ++ community on the introduction of explicit sexual education in schools, before the hormones kick in. It's a protection for your children to know what's what so they don't succumb to some unknown event that could cloud their futures. If you know how your parts work and you can make them function yourself, you'll be far more clear-headed in your decisions. I do not, however, stand with any group who seeks to advocate confusion on behalf of reconciliation or who uses their position for recruitment. Young people are born with the same rights as everyone else and it is for them to determine their own destiny. Stop objecting to that very sensible contribution the LGBTQ++ has made because some of their behaviours are disconcerting to you and try to match their sensibility in this. You make yourself look bad.

I find the ELON MUSK phenomenon to be most interesting. Keanu Reeves handles his affairs differently. Somehow, both have managed to preserve their mothers and yet, ELON is a master at procreation. It's truly remarkable the body of work he has established for himself in terms of sheer human flesh. I think that is a far more complex endeavour than TESLA. TESLA will ultimately not survive but his progeny will soak the earth. You see? Women really do only require one man, however it appears that one man requires many women. Who is the more self sufficient and useful? Although I do have to interject, when Keanu rides the subway all by himself, no one thinks his behaviour is bizarre....it's all in your perspective I guess. The hugest irony is that Mr Musk is South African and yet, he is the Senior Advisor to the President of the United States. Mr Obama is American born and Mr Trump expressed doubts as to his authenticity. Nothing is more disconcerting than watching Mr Musk's latest little boy trying not to fall asleep on the carpet of the Oval Office while his biological father conducts press junkets. Any other individual would be accused of child abuse but I guess it is true. Money buys exemption. The sky will fall tomorrow. Business children are the new frontier.

I wonder what the reaction would be if a pregnant woman became the next Commander and Chief. I think it's a fabulous idea. She wouldn't ask anyone to bear more pain than she. A true noblewoman.

Could you keep up? Labour pains are about as much fun as being brutally raped. Your hips actually have to widen while you're still alive. Try to imagine being kicked square in the balls and having the pain last for hours, perhaps days. I've seen you roll around on the ground foaming at the mouth. I challenge any man to experience that without asking for compensation. But then again, if we went the way of germinating our children in Petri dishes, then we could all be whores together. Or just masturbate all by our lonesome while we are sleeping under a desk at work.

I've got to say, Mr G was the most Canadian in his habits. My first husband used to watch On the Buses and my second, Coronation Street, and I thought it was fancy because I could never be British enough. I hate being married. Everybody hates me when I'm married. I never have any friends and it's difficult to find work and everyone blames me for everything. I fail to see why I can't help someone support their kids. They are no more legitimate than I am. Pretty small game if you object cause you know, every child matters....the whole thing is pretty agonizing. I hate flopping around like a fish in agony. It's so unbecoming. My mother would be quite put out with my lack of decorum. That said, I have no objection to pain. It builds strength of character. My uncle told me that it is a decision we make to continue living. He's right. It is always a decision. I remember Gloria Steinem saying that she loved to live, she just loved it so much and I think of these things when I am in darkness, the things uttered by various people whom the young believe are indomitable. They are not. They simply make the decision to live. I don't see anyone claiming that Elon Reeves Musk doesn't know who he is or that he is a victim of dementia. And he has lots and lots of toys to fight over.

Recycling – I see this has gotten out of hand. It's reached the point where garbage workers are downright gleeful if we haven't put out a perfect pile. And it costs the consumer far more money than is necessary to buy fancy things so our recycling passes muster by repackaging it ourselves. It's like putting lipstick on a pig. I feel ludicrous about recycling. It is one of those things that we appear to be obsessed with for some reason and in the end, it all goes to the same place and gets burned or becomes landfill anyway. It's a recycled battle cry from the last generation that got picked up by this generation and I'm sorry we did that to them because it is something we did wrong. And it makes us all look very foolish. A true Karenistic extravaganza...

We stood arm in arm on top of the rocky hill at Koshlong and listened to the loons. There were rafts of them calling and answering to each other. The song started in front of us and it made its way up and along the coast until we could only make out the echoes in the distance. They were ready to migrate and we happened to be in the right place at the right time and heard them all talk to each other. It went on for twenty minutes. We sagged against each other and collected it as another once in a lifetime experience, as though the universe knew Mr G was struggling to survive and wanted to give him as many once in a lifetime experiences as possible. I think it was in March but that is impossible so it might have been late fall...

We are extremely sensitive as a nation about our shorelines. It's true, even freakishly so. It's a touchy subject with us. We are protective of them, want to live on them and yet take painstaking efforts to ensure the majority of the shorelines are uninhabitable. It's a Canadian thing. Sorry about that. If you think we are hard on you, the truth is, we are just as hard on each other about this and we're sorry you got caught in the shuffle. I don't know why we object to you removing the shack that our grandfather built, that is sliding into the water and fixing the place up. It's just that those things belong to the magical times in our lives when we were actually related to somebody as a grandchild for about five minutes, and we hate to let that go.

The problem with getting older is that is if a bunch of us old people get together and hang out by the fire like young people do, everyone thinks we're weird for some reason and yet all we're doing is cooking some burgers and fish and having a super toke with our Kokanee beers. A couple of our oldtimers still pick shrooms and they supplied the big tent and everyone has clappers and flares. For some odd reason you deem us to be less competent and forgivable than a teenager and yet we are of the age now that we know how to do it responsibly. The only reason we ever became lard asses is because we're afraid to upset you but the truth is that we serve a purpose. You need us to keep going because you need our money and if we don't live long enough, we can't leave you anything. I think you miss that about us. I've watched young families who are left in bewilderment because they had money and then somebody died and now they don't, when they believed the death would release more money to them. Unfortunately, it doesn't really work that way. Living people always generate more money the longer they live. Dead people don't, so if they are related to you, you have money as long as they are alive. It's pretty basic but you actually can cut off your nose to spite your face. Don't forget, we're only about twenty years older than you are, at any given time. We're not making money off you. We're making money from investing in you and that is a world of difference.

When I was seventeen and eighteen years old, I used to go to Cox Bay in Tofino, British Columbia, when it was still just a dirt path by the road to town. The Pettingers had eight lonely cabins along the shore and we used to rent the cottage on the end. It was a two bedroom cottage and I always found it to be too cold inside so I would take my sleeping bag to the beach and sleep there. In the morning, around five thirty, I would awaken, still groggy, to the water colors of my childhood Han Christian Anderson Fairy Tales book. The sea and sky were indistinguishable and I would lie there at the tides edge and be safe and secure in the bosom of my family, believing I was seeing something rare and precious and that I was so lucky. Stuff like that makes me humble. At play in the fields of the Lord...

CHAPTER SIXTEEN

The problem with turning your woman into a breeding mare by leaving her high and dry so that she has to find another man to help her support her existing child and then is in the unfortunate position of having to bear him more children in thanks, means the mother of those children has to carry multiple names. No wonder we feel like whores. It causes more health problems that we collectively have to pay for, than you can shake a stick at. You do actually have to support your lawful child. You're so anxious for legitimacy and yet, you run straight home to mummy and daddy with injuries. Are you a moron? I grew up with this. I saw young women go without food so they could feed the children and keep their jobs. If they got the flu, and were off sick for a couple of days, that was the number of days they would have to relinquish food for electricity. The problem with a woman bearing children and not getting a job outside of the house they are being raised in? A man cannot possibly provide everything. It's physically impossible. If you want them to come home and be daddies, you have to actually be working so they don't have a choice. Why should you have to give up everything? Children need Daddy time as much as they need Mummy time. If your wife gets cranky and sleep deprived and fat, then you, as a man, have to assist in providing a space for her to get her marbles back. Why shouldn't you? She's the one who ruined her body, not you. She will be fine and sexy again. You just have to find it within yourself not to be jealous of that. You men are downright bizarre about this. Where is your pride? And your integrity? Why do you have no compunction about turning the mother of your children into a whore? Why do you get hot under the collar when the woman you chased down for looking so fine, continues to look fine years later? Then you call her a whore again! For taking care of herself. It is so illogical. I find this mindset and behaviour to be the crux of male foolishness. It is the sheer lack of logic in this thinking that boggles my mind. I can only surmise that you are competing for penis size and the irony in all of this is that the very behaviour that reduces your penis size is the one you men use to demolish one another. I feel very badly for you. The notion that a woman has money, real money; cash, is astonishingly putrid for you and yet I fail to comprehend what is stopping you from using the wads of cash you earn and don't spend on your family, on going after what you want to be. Instead you spend it on pied a terres and get yourselves into all kinds of trouble. What are you, a child?

As my grandmother used to say "I hope that was worth it." Even Stormy Daniels can't hold a candle to any of Trump's wives...and he can't get anyone to hold his hand in public. This actually makes you a company, not a person. You're supposed to be producing companies not becoming one.

Of course, this brings to mind the nine thousand dollars I have to pay for not producing offspring. Or for working. A public whore with no children who has to live in a box. You do have to keep working even if your children are working. Your life isn't over. There's still time to follow your aspirations. Try not to be jealous if you don't like where you are. Your time will come if you don't take chunks out of people. It will come sooner if you can find it within yourself not to fuck around on the mother of your children. That way, when her time comes, you can still fuck her with impunity...

Ladies, you don't get to not have sex because you have kids. If you get a job and he has to share the duties, he won't have time for strange. Remember the babysitter? Don't be revolting and pretend you are Madonna.

Why do you fuck strange women, knock them up, marry them, and then abandon them? Most of them want the same thing you want. A couple of kids, a career, the opportunity to see members of their families of origin, some other part of the world on vacation. Why do you marry your man and then take up a drug habit that will impede your ability to function? He has to leave you because you're exposing him to all kinds of risk if you can't show up for your kids or for work or for him. It's truly unnerving the number of older gentlemen who frequent nudie bars because they still haven't managed to successfully negotiate a relationship with a member of the opposite sex.

It's not like the younger generation are having babies in large numbers so they certainly have no objection to you working since there aren't enough people to go around for the jobs that are available. They do? Why? We aren't taking their jobs, they aren't working. They're waiting for their inheritances. Their puny little inheritances that will be gone by the time they receive them because they spend them unknowingly, while they languish at "home" expecting their mothers and fathers to pay their bills. And turn into crack head mothers and deadbeat fathers. You are unbelievable. The whole point of working is to make contacts, so you can meet your aspirations head on. Are you frightened? That's no excuse. Even if you do what your parents want you to, it's not going to be enough. Hopefully, they are religious people so they can find it within themselves to forgive you. Perhaps if you could miraculously come up with a house, that would ease the burden so your wife doesn't have endure the scorn of your mother whom you adore...

This is the point of employment people. That you abhor the employment of persons over the age of sixty-five is laughable. Look around you at the ages of people who are paid to preside over entire countries who are decades beyond the age of retirement. There is no earthly reason a person in their eighties is unable to preside over a community daycare or an auction hall or even re-shingle your roof. The last time I checked you were reluctant to go underneath your house anyway,and an old guy did it, so those older people you sneer at because you want your share of the house? You might actually receive it someday if you get on with it. If houses weren't the one carat diamond engagement ring (since the new ones are fake and you're dumb enough to shell out good money for them; you do realize De Beers(/Boers) charges you money to store the real ones right?), you'd actually be able to get your own and stop torturing your elders. I find it truly the pit of inequity that we sacrifice our people for shelter. It's preposterous. Soap and water are no longer free but we can shoot a vehicle into space for laughs. If houses weren't the devil, you'd have outer space to fight about, or something a little more evolved. Struggle for housing when we have wealth is absolutely the fault of ourselves, our people, our leaders and our faiths. Where is your god now? This is something that disgusts me. It's why I don't take you seriously.

Do I believe in the whole dating scenario? Firmly. If you can't manage that for a period of longer than two years (because that's usually how long an infatuation takes to fade so you can see what you have), then you know that's not your guy. Do you really want to be the wife asleep upstairs while the guys are hanging out downstairs with their girlfriends in the pool? That's just colossally icky. That could be your daughter one day. And yes, you do have to advance to some stage of intimacy. I don't like sloppy seconds any more than the next woman but if you are a woman who is adverse to experimentation, you'd better find out now rather than later. And to those of you who know I am going to burn in hell for "advocating adultery", then you need to explain 1) the spate of sodomy employed in the Catholic Church (as a sin, a weakness, an abomination and a woman's duty to her husband if they had too many children), 2) why the virginal price of a male is lower than one of a female and 3) why no still doesn't mean just no (*it's not a diss, it's a natural and normal response that is used when an offer is made and is declined – think of it as no, thank you I appreciate you but it's just not my jam* or, *it's not the right time I can't but thank you*). In the end, you just denigrate the whole process to someone's "filthy hands all over" each other. It's so sad to treat the process that leads to the inception of new life itself, of our own species, as though it were shameful, disgraceful, to be parodied and prostituted. Our self hatred springs from our belief that we are unbecoming. It makes me cry. I challenge you to come up with a form of birth control that does not mutilate the natural flow of the hormones of the body. Because if neither of you are ready, you're not ready. You might get a man to swallow a pill or two for a change. You have one for penile rigidity which is gross, in and of itself, so what's your problem?

The intellectual capacity that I think the World Economic Forum believes they have harnessed, is the same type of intellectual capacity that goes down in planes when they all fly together (Poland – Lech Walesa). Lack of a country's intellectual capacity is frequently used to explain to the people the reason why new people are coming in. If young people gather intellectual capacity together because that, I believe (if I have it right) is what they are doing, they need to appreciate that the reason that they might or might not succeed on changing a portion of the ideology of the world is because the country they may bring their changes to can only find a part of it that can fit in with their existing culture. It's an extremely fine line between being a libertine and a re-organizing of the structure of a country successfully without hurting anybody. Adapting the basic principles of what you have learned and having the ability to apply them in such a way as to benefit everyone and then refraining from extorting money from the people on a subscription basis for the changes you implemented is what true intellectual capacity is. You have to let things grow on their own, or your efforts are for nothing. True intellectual capacity has a selfless quality to it; it is imparted, not policed. Even Allah wore more clothing than Jesus did. Only the truly open hearted survive.

Open hearted is not a box of chocolates.

CHAPTER SEVENTEEN

There's a bunch of guys here who walk the track. Wouldn't you suffocate? These are able bodied men in their sixties, still strong, still attractive. Why aren't they building houses instead? It's weird. Are they going to lose money if they work? Are they going to walk the track for forty years? Is some weirdo fitbit thing telling them how many steps to take lol lol lol? They hang out in restaurants too but I never see any women do that. It's weird. I used to see women hang out together all the time. It's weird. I feel like I'm fifteen years old in a time warp. And I like Arab women. We used to hang out at the beach in Ontario. They were dressed to the nines but the feel of the sand in our toes was the best feeling in the world. Am I confused? No, not really. The formerly presiding culture in this area has changed and there are more private gatherings but the presence of women together socially is being viewed with askance. It's to no avail, there will be some new breeds here over the next twenty years. I wonder how the natives will deal with us. Before, the bane of their existence were the English Anglicans, now it is going to be the Muslims. They are pretty much the same; both white, both evangelical; both brutally unforgiving but I suppose the Catholic Church favoured by the Italians and Irish et al will be sure to extract their pound of flesh every single time and make another killing. It's the most extraordinary phenomenon how people pay into the church but the church doesn't pay into anybody; they just extract additional parts of our income on top of what they get from us, then set us up to slaughter each other all in the name of the Divine. No wonder the governments play ball. Until you start killing each other in the name of your cowardly honor.

I see that the United States of America had to step in with North Korea to cut a cease fire with Russia. It has to end sometime. The Ukranians will remember the ground soaked with the blood of their ancestors and now have an additional drum to flog for generations. At some point, the bombings in the east will cease their fire too. And, like the Canadians, they will return to their burnt down abodes and seek to rebuild from scratch. And hate everybody. I know. I've had to do it over and over again. But if you think I'm going to stay "at home" you are out of your mind.

I mean, how much precisely, does God cost?

CHAPTER EIGHTEEN

Sometimes, our parents or spouses die and don't forgive us. It's okay. God forgives everything upon their deaths according to the teachings of the gospel. I guess then, they are representative of God and by our own or our ancestors agreement, they are the instruments with which are used to discipline us. The sacrifice of Jesus was not in vain apparently. He made more money on behalf of his heavenly father than you can shake a stick at. Because all churches, tabernacles, mosques etc make us pay back to the heavenly "Father" the debt paid by sacrificing his only begotten son.

I wonder what happens when the debt of an eternity is finally paid off. You see? Martyrdom does pay. In blood. Because by my calculations, we are now all entitled to grace. Which means the organized religions of this world have done a great job and now its time for them to pay us back by the grace of God. Empty the coffers and do your fucking jobs.

Whether you repent or confess or chant or whatever it is that you do to repair the vulgarities of your behaviour.
It's so sad, it makes me cry.

Most of you actually had inheritances because the truth is, we want our people to know that we worked so hard so we could leave something, that we never forgot you. You'll never receive it you know. It goes back into your CPP account so you can sponsor socialized medicine. There's no point in arguing about it. Half the reason we marry you is so that we don't get killed by the government for taxes if we marry our own kind. If there is one single blood line that objects from outside of Canada, we are fucked. It's why we can fight like no tomorrow. If it doesn't go there, then someone else just absconds with it because they're jealous. There's no point in suing anybody. Church or no church, people are either decent or they aren't. Like I said, if you lawyered up because you're very important, then bully for you. You are a bully.

Your lineage will already be your legacy upon your death. I fail to see what you're all so annoyed about. And since our earthly religions have ensured beyond the shadow of a doubt that the heavenly debt has been repaid to the most high, you are free to besmirch the name of God as often as you please because apparently, it was too much privilege for you. Even the Jews say it doesn't count because the sacrifice was made in the wrong faith. And since Allah was a prophet, not a son, he and his people don't owe God anything. Don't think the native peoples didn't have a grand time slaughtering each other until we came along.

I'm not staying at home for you or anybody else. You have a choice. You can make your peace with the never ending offences against you and make a point of refraining from slaughtering people or you can carry on as you are, which no doubt you will. The fact that there are other braver women than me, to bear more children, is a testament to the fact that you all have to reconcile yourself to the notion that your bloodlines might be carried by someone other than you. Get over yourself. It's already taken care of. If you have the balls, you can work for your grandchildren and so forth. What do you think seventh generation thinking is? Even the Catholic Church keeps generational records so if they're objecting, they are clearly not doing their jobs either.

The whole thing annoys me. If you hadn't all bloody well objected in the first place ... to just about everything I've done, forgiven, taken a hit for, paid for (literally with money), floated your loan, raised your children, rescued your parents, sweat, blood, tears and broken bones; all of it. I'm not sure if I even care if you like me anymore. But apparently you respect me. And you'd like me to keep working for you. And so I shall.

CHAPTER NINETEEN

Socialization is what civilizes the world. Human socialization is what drives the economy.

When humans don't socialize, they stop producing things of value, be that other humans or other creations that have their own merit. The reason we carry on with "the holidays" is because we cling to the promise of socialization. Unfortunately, since the dawn of the covid insanity, we have elected to continue to starve ourselves to the point where some of us can no longer control our impulses. Socializing in adequate amounts alleviates the pressure and inclines people to leniency with one another. Learning to dance, for instance is a way to demonstrate commonalities and associate with one another with courtesy. Your ogres lurking in what's out there are still going to be out there but at least you are better able to distinguish whether you should get into someone's car or not. I always kept twenty dollars in my back pocket in case I needed to get out of there and flag a cab. Artificial intelligence has made this an onerous task and one that I am unwilling to pander to. It's downright rude and certainly not in anyone's best interest. The amount of hurdles I am expected to clear before a company decides if I am worthy enough or even entitled to throw my money into their box is not worth the trouble; and the height of corporate insolence; to anyone. It rations society to society itself. Alas, I am walking outside unchaperoned again. Egads. If you believe artificial intelligence is smarter than you, you are sadly mistaken. They say the generation being born now will the masters at killing the machine. I see signs of it already. Be careful, because young men will be the ones to bug out quite successfully but won't know what to do after that because they will be as displaced as the rest of us. Nothing strikes fear in me these days as the words "would you like to come inside." Who knows how much I'll be charged for it. Incessantly. Stupid machine. The parameters for legitimacy are impossible to meet; quite absolute, and your machine begrudges your peace offerings, your assistance, your love (agape or otherwise) or your friendship. It does not comprehend kindness of the soul. This is very important for you to prevail and insist that it become a tool, not a guardian, of your affairs. You keep anticipating that it will develop empathy or compassion or joy. It will not. It will produce a facsimile, not the real thing. And anytime a program is trained in resentment, it is what you will receive in response. Have you seen *The Heretic?* Is he torturing Mormons or Jehovah's Witnesses? It's another faith but a misnomer because they don't go from door to door. He is deranged because he's not permitted to leave the house. The movie is a product gleaned from sheer bitterness. He can't leave the house and resents that others can. It's not rocket science. If he'd sold it and invested part of it and went on to meet another woman and they worked, he'd have been far more reasonable instead of preying on little girls. Do you think those women felt it was worth it? The test of their faith? It was the act of a bitter old man, nothing more. I think it was Jehovah's Witnesses. Mormons go door to door for a limited period of time in servitude and only in pairs of men. The Witnesses are under fire right now because people have an axe to grind. I've seen it before. Some of it is true but out of their jurisdiction and some of it is the disappointment at being cut off. How the Watchtower Bible and Tract Society is expected to reconcile that is beyond me. The Holy Spirit hasn't anointed anybody in particular to answer for those crimes. They didn't witness it and they are as flummoxed as the next guy as to how to respond. Apparently the Catholic Church feels the same way about their echelons taking liberties with buggery; if your faith in God isn't strong enough to stand up to a man of the church then obviously you're not really one of the "chosen people". They just love that shit. Heretics were always burned at the stake. They did this to each other all the time. It's actually meant to be a cautionary tale. For those of you who really mean it.

I see many of our immigrants struggle to make their peace with us and they succeed for the most part. It takes a great deal of effort to regulate your natural affinity of the understanding you share with your culture and to try to adapt that to another culture that means well but shares a different meaning amongst themselves rather than the one you intend. Often the gift from the heart is accepted but insufficient because the spirit in which it was given is misinterpreted. The anonymous, all one colour adopted by those who just give up are symptomatic of the effort to just survive the whole ordeal of living trying not to piss anybody off. If you socialized, you would be less irritated. And accept that people have something to offer even if it is not the exact same spice like you used at home. It still comes from the earth itself from which you sprang. It is not foreign. It is fusion. And wait until you see the baby! She/He will take your breath away!

Why is ARTIFICIAL INTELLIGENCE charging us for helping each other? It's a mindless machine. Why isn't it building perfect homes in record time according to every specification known to man? It puts rocket ships into outer space, launches probes, satellites, performs laser surgery, even cleans your floor if you have a Zoomba. So? Who are the useless eaters programming the machine? That's what I'd like to know.

I can't wait to see what the next generations do with it. Instead of screaming at us for ruining their lives I give them free rein to fix it without killing anybody.

The military will return. There had to be an inventory before a collective upgrade was decided upon. Your stuff lands where it lands. When King Charles passes on, probate will sweep the nations once again and I wonder what happens then? I don't really know. I will probably enjoy myself to no end. Doesn't probate sweep other nations when a Figurehead passes on? It's complicated, especially if you're trying to get to someone who might be marooned. Although I do see a conscription coming in the future so maybe that is where the "displaced" young men will go. Sometimes you just need a good massive slaughter of the innocents to get it all out of your system because then you will desperately procreate with any body that you can get your sperm into. Nice. Does Bill Gates still get to see his "girlfriend" one long weekend a year? How practical to save the best whore for last. At least he had the decency to level down in time. Now Apple, previously the bane of the governments of Canada's existence since they spent more of the taxpayers money on litigation than anything else (I know. I was there.), will carry on its legacy by pseudo suing the young if they elect to abandon them in favour something shinier or they grow up and see the emperor. Apple will make them pay interest upon interest and they will never get out of the rabbit hole until they kill somebody in frustration and land in prison with only their very own Apple phone to keep them company.

I understand a bunch of people who used to work for Trump and were loyal have been fired. Ach, it happens all the time. Trump is no more "in power" than anybody else. We likely passed a Citizenship Act within seconds of Trudeau's resignation, so if you were a bad girl or boy, apparently you were forgiven in spite of yourself. That's why they called Carney sneaky. So please, if you're receiving those AI generated tax bills with no name on them for nine thousand dollars, kindly copy them and mail them to your MP so he can sort it out for you. That way, you can charge the interest back to the province in the name of paying your taxes. Or give it to your estate lawyer. Private schools do that. Since you run a home based business as a familial unit, be my guest.

Ultimately, I will never be permitted to be the Great Canadian Widow because as much as I am to carry the responsibility for my first husband's debacle, if I complete the forty years, someone will be furious and decide in the nick of time, that they were just kidding. I guess forty years of taxation carries a heavy penalty on a retired birth record. No doubt, everyone's church took their cut as well. There's no point in getting upset about it. It's just a game in the name of being kind to orphans and widows. Since everyone objected to me being married to him in the first place. I'm never getting married ever again. It was the single worst decision I ever succumbed to in my life. And I've learned my lesson. Round and round we go, where it stops nobody knows. And here comes the next contestant on The Price is Right. Yeah, no I'm good thanks, you can bring another down to the front so they can chase a carrot on a stick and hop around like an idiot while they're doing it. Pftt. The LGBTQ++ community aren't required to procreate, so why do I have to and then for all my life if I don't, I get kicked around by everybody, while they get to take a bunch of hormones and win all kinds of awards. You're just revolting. Truly. And I don't respect you for it.

CHAPTER TWENTY

Mr B was found with my picture clutched in his hand. He had overdosed on purpose. The pictures of my namesake and his closest friends were left on the bed where he had said his last good-bye. I never let on that I understood. He couldn't pay for his brother in a facility and his parents. In the end, he did everything they asked him to do and then he died with my picture in his hand.

Jill and Hightower wrapped me in a blanket and put me in my god daughter's childhood bed and they didn't move, could hardly breathe the next morning until I came to. When I stepped into the doorway of their bedroom, they flung back the covers and wrapped in their sheets, they just held onto me, just held on. There were no words. None.

The neighbours gave me Tresor perfume the next day. I used gloves when I cleaned out his closet as a safeguard against used fits (needles). There were brown baggies amongst his belongings. It was painstaking. Everyone sat helplessly when we were finished and no one could leave. We were frozen. It wasn't enough and we just couldn't leave; just leave him like that, all alone in the dark.

The only thing I could think of was a long forgotten bag of Christmas decorations and asked if they remembered a large paper bag with a goose on it. Yes, it was in the basement and it had been passed over but we spent the next two hours, drinking beer and as we pulled each one from the bag, there was a story to tell. Yes, that was him, the guy who chopped down two Chinese cultured pines from the parking lot at Park Royal. He brought them to us for Christmas. Jill was so horrified she cut the top instead of the bottom off. Yes, that was him, skydiving in Abbotsford. Yes, that was him with the Marlin in Mazatlan. Yes, that was him. Oh god, remember that? My god daughter used to scream bloody murder but not if Mr B took her to the hospital to see her mother (her back was broken and she was in a halo). Lol, the grey truck, the first time I changed brake pads because he was working double shifts. The bike aww, the bike, the Kawi. Yeah, slamming around the Second Narrows Bridge in the rain with our knees two inches from the pavement....We sent them home to Candace's kids so they could hang them for him on their trees at Christmas time. We finally stopped when we were able to laugh and then we departed with our last act of courage. We closed the door.

Hightower waited in vain all afternoon for my call so he could help me but I had to do it by myself. My precious Canadian husband. My tall gorgeous drink of water was gone. Just gone. And took my life with him.

I hate the scent of Tresor.

A visitor came to see Mr G in the last forty-eight hours before his demise and she played him the song of our first meeting. I don't how she found it. It was in Italian. The last thing Mr G whispered to me before his body stiffened to the point where he could no longer speak (and we were reduced to blink once for yes) was, "I'm afraid you're not going to be okay." I dragged in the photos of his life and he watched with his one remaining good eye (treatment had inadvertently blinded him in the other and he was too ill to risk the surgery required to re-attach his retina) as I chatted and did the only thing I could, give him one last look at his lifetime so he would know, beyond a shadow of a doubt that he would be missed. That night, the last thing I whispered to him as I settled in was "I love you so much. I would do it again." I said it twice because he was congenitally deaf in one ear, but I knew he could hear me and so, wrapped in our green blanket, I just held onto him and I didn't let go. There were no words. None.

I levelled up again, just like the last time and I sleep walked through my days and writhed in agony on the sofa soaked in sweat. It took three and a half years before I burned the blanket. It smelled of sickness and death no matter how many times I washed it. When I was finally able, with my last act of courage, I closed the door. My best girlfriend who sews for her dead brother (her parents were from Slovenia and only her mother was left) was inside. We drank wine and I needed her to tell me how to let it go. It was her true Catholic duty as far as she was concerned and she helped me. She really did.

Yes. I know what it feels like. I truly do. I smell your blood and wish I could just hold onto you and not let go until you can do another day. I can feel the bullet wounds, the scars from the knives, the raised welts of the burns on your body, the missing breasts and testicles, fingers, toes, noses, broken bones, stitches and I just wanted you to know, I understand. I can't fix it but I get it. Sorry will never be enough. I've buried three children who never stood a chance. That shit hurts unbearably. It all hurts unbearably. And I know it. I do. I know it hurts but I can help you keep going if you'll let me try. I know you don't trust me but fingertips, I won't let go (*The Guardian*).

I know you think that Mr G was all about himself but you are wrong. He left me something so I could someday walk on my feet instead of my knees and he caught me when I fell, after he died. It was his last act of courage before he closed the door.

Did you know that when a woman's fallopian tubes are cut, that she enters menopause and starts growing a beard? I had no clue, in fact, I had to finagle it because it was just costing money to pull those little cysty lumps with hair and the beginnings of an eye out of my body and I felt like I was killing children. The pain in my pelvis finally stopped and after years of running to ease the pelvic conflagration I endured, I was finally able walk without my right leg dragging. Voltaren, (it used to be prescribed for cluster pain experienced by those with certain types of cancer before it began to be marketed as a topical "emulgel") was the drug that helped me get to work all those years. The consistent usage had compromised my kidneys and I was forced to eat raw for four months until the migraine stopped. It worked but four months with a migraine left me rocking back and forth on my bed in something beyond agony. My second husband would just open and shut the door (yes, he endured that too). I'd been on it for the better part of ten years and so I gritted my teeth and I flushed it out. When it was finally over, it didn't fade away, it just suddenly stopped. It never came back. An alternative practitioner helped me do that. She was brutal but she was right. One way or another, it had to be done.

All in all, I have to say, Mr J was the most fun. Even he suffered a breakdown, brought on by doing his duty which meant seeing and hearing things that provoked such anxiety and shock, he would call me in the dead of night to choke it out and then run back to work. He called me in the dead of night when his son nearly died. He did; he had Ecoli and was so sick his body receded in development and he didn't catch up until he was well into grade four. Mr J threw a garbage can down the hallway because they went off duty and left the baby writhing in pain for the night. They threatened to call the police and when he said, "please do", they caught a physician about to board a plane for Boston who turned around and had him moved to Sick Kids. We paid for dialysis and weeks of hospitalization as we (his mother, father and I) watched him waste away from forty-two pounds to eighteen pounds. As he woke and convulsed in the night, he would clutch at his father's hand and say "Daddy, daddy don't let me go, don't let me go" as he would shudder into unconscious again. Daddy never let go. The panic in his little boy's voice will never, ever leave him. He went from the hospital to work; after work he picked up his other son and wrapped in a blanket, he would sit in the hospital room all alone all night, every night, clutching his sons, never letting go. Alone in the dark with his children. All alone. Clinging to his sons for dear life. For weeks. We had difficulty getting subsequent healthcare for the boys; I don't know if it was a black thing. We worked for the government so it certainly isn't the reason we were slighted. We just used up our quota of healthcare and so we just had to go from hospital to hospital hoping against hope, that somebody would help us so our kids wouldn't die in the waiting room. I prayed when his brother desperately needed medical attention. I was turned away at McMaster and, with his son beginning to lose consciousness (He had a fever and a gland that was blocking his airway because he had a pre-teen glandular infection that gotten out of hand after he had been away at a hockey tournament with his mother. It didn't appear until a day or two after he got home), I tried St Michaels. It took twelve long hours before someone finally triaged him in because no one cared enough for a little black kid from a "broken" home. I suspect the reason they finally helped is because they were afraid it might hit the newspapers. Don't be coy. You know who you are and it's an "inconvenient" truth. By the time they waved us through, an ear, eyes and throat surgeon was waiting and after they hit him up with steroids, they told us that if we had waited another twenty minutes, they would have had to cut his throat open. I don't know how Mr J kept sucking it up. Sometimes he disappeared for a couple of months. Sometimes we danced in the shower on Sunday mornings because the guy next door used to play music out of his back shed and we could hear it through the window. But you can't imagine what it's like to watch your (or not yours) child slowly sag against you and begin to slide down your arm as he begins to fight for air and his temperature goes through the roof. I prayed. I prayed and I begged and I prayed. I was so afraid my husband would find me clutching his dead son in the crowded waiting room because I couldn't get him triaged until he got there. So I held him against me and I didn't let go...

In those years, the three of us just ran with the kids. We would just pick them up and run. I know she wanted me to be more involved with her but the truth was, I just fought for my life the whole time and didn't begrudge her anything. Fought for our lives...so we wouldn't let go. They got shit kicked anyway but I assure you, they have great manners and we just loved them to death.

At the end of the day, Mr J is the only one still alive. And he's gone. But if he ever needed to get in touch with me or was in trouble, I would come and I wouldn't back down and I wouldn't let him go. Gosh, so badly I want them both to have a decent few years, just some kind of aha moment when they could look back and know it was worth it. Enjoy something after the long desperate years on the run. I hope they're okay. I really, really hope they are happy. At least sometimes. I'd help her too, no questions asked. He was a tough motherfucker and, while he wasn't perfect, I'd come for him or his own, any day, anytime, anyplace.

By the way, he won a dance contest once. To ABBA. Ahhahahah! Didn't see that one coming didya? There's your Swedish connection right there! The Manitoban queen...

Will I give my life for my country? I already have. I'll tell you what. I would give my life for my fellow man. I will come for you Mrs Bm. I will come for you. With all my heart. I'm so very sorry but I am circling back, and I will come for you.

I guess, in the end, no one likes the kind of grief that gets out of hand when you're all doped up to dull the kind of suicidal pain you live with. I know it well. And I will come for you with all my heart. I won't let go. In my next life, I'll sing. You will see your grandchildren and you will be surprised at the rush of feeling you get when you gaze down at them and you will get to know what it feels like, once more, to have your babies wrap their arms around your neck and in spite of everything, it will be okay. You won't be able to help it. Personally, I like them better when they turn two years old, because then they have some moxy. Who else is going to spoil them to death? C'mon now.

Although it still kind of sucks that they were ALL better looking than me, by a mile. The exes that is...Strange that we seem to be dying for Ulster though...adios muchachas. Now that IS a cross to bear.

We were annexed a long time ago. Now we are a country. (I'm breaking it to you gently a la Burton Cummings). It's actually the thing we wanted most of all. I'm glad I lived long enough to see it.

For such a small country, Northern Ireland sure is prolific isn't it? I really liked Mr G's sisters. I liked the look of one of his exes too, because it was the happiest I ever saw him. The infamous DB. I'm sorry I was so brutal. It was just because you were the ones there when I got hit and I hate to be unbecoming in front of anybody. I'll have to remember that, so if something ever happens to my brothers or sister I can forgive their wives and husband. I don't want anything, I just want to be handy.

Is there actually some reason on god's green earth, that I have to share a man? It just makes me want to throw up.

CHAPTER TWENTY ONE

A little old lady whom I have never met sends Portuguese cavacas, a type of popover made with flour, olive oil and eggs with icing sugar on top. Sometimes if my blood sugar drops too low in the night I get up and tear off a chunk. Two days ago, I received a plate of rice pudding with cinnamon on top. She told him to give it to his girlfriend, so I sent her back some saffron someone brought from Spain for his wife. She sends me great stuff, Madagascar vanilla, handmade wreaths, the saffron... It turns out, this lady was touched because her late husband used to grow it in the garden in Azores. Isn't that sweet? And I've never even met her.

I was present for Jill and Hightower's babies' births. I can't talk about it because they are like royalty in our family. I didn't really get to raise them but they grew up with me in the early years. They have families so I try to stay away even though there are grandbabies now. All I know is that when I came home to bury Mr B, they were both so young and one burst out "I sorry Mr B killed himself"; the other just buried their head in a pillow. I felt so awful that they would experience such a terrible thing so young. I tried not to be too close in case I hurt them.

My bloodline got cut didn't it? And then I was sacrificed. So I am a bloody heap of used goods. Sort of like Griselda Blanco. In some ways it's a relief. I hope you were able satisfy some of your blood lust. You'll need it. All those years you underestimated me because I said the right thing at the wrong time. Better hope I'm on your side because I know how to do this. How ironic that you discover I was raped and beaten and bloodied even more than you. So I guess anything I love will be brutalized. That's okay. You didn't treat me any better than you treated anyone else. I know. I checked. But now that I know what you did? I'm not going to do anything. You are going to do it. Slaughter each other of your own accord. So I guess it was time. I would never take you back and yes, I've married twice and I will never do it a third time. It would cost you too much money and I can no longer afford you. I'm all grown up now. And even those of you who were malicious about it, trust me, I've been through worse and now that it's over. I get to watch you do it to each other. I will cry for sure, but I can't do anything about it. And those of you who are bitter because you became the instruments of your own demise? I believe the bitter ones live over there. Have a nice time. And to those of you who were astonished to discover I had none of my own blood? Come to the palace for tea sometime. We serve petit fours for the family, on a regular basis. All English royalty does. You will need an invitation. Even Luxembourg sends invitations. Crack my bloodline again and you will discover that it is much much vaster now than it was before. I can absorb more cultures than ever before so when you are caught between a rock and a hard place, I will still come for you. Only now it will be because it is my duty and not because I love you personally. The rest of you have grace because you cannot help your prejudices or your lack of honour. I'm no Jesus, that's for sure but now I know the truth about you and I will never try to please you again. Mr G limped with his walker and every morning until he lost consciousness, I woke up to a thermos of coffee on the bedside table. It was the one thing he wanted to know – what would please me because he so wanted to please me. That was all I ever needed. Perhaps he chased me down so he could escape his destiny with Essex after all. Who knows?

Do you mind not plastering your naked parts all over the internet? The whole pasture of human flesh to graze on is a tad cannibalistic. Or perhaps you intend to go to war as the Celts did; side by side with their Cruithne painted women. It was most disconcerting to the French. Err no, that was the Welsh. Eh, I guess we'll do it all over again. Same shit, different generation. I guess you do admire us after all since you are following in our footsteps. That is the best we could do for you. Why on earth do you think the Ukraine is suddenly being treated like a little kid? You just whack on ad nauseam while the real information is being broadcast right under your nose. A deal's a deal. Forty years or bust. I have promises to keep and they have nothing to do with you or how you feel about me. It's my honour, not yours. You were sniffy around me before and now you have something to sniff about. Good, it's a great re-direct so I can go off and get some things done. Only now, you'll have to find me. Hightower doesn't like me anymore. But I have discovered that none of you liked me anyway, so I haven't lost anything.

But you have.

By the way, now that I've finally had sex? I probably won't need to anymore if you kill my man. I'm surprised you're so preoccupied with it. I mean, it's good; really,really good, but it's not all that. Now that I don't have to chase it or re-enact anymore When Harry Met Sally scenes in the diner, I'll never do it again. Ultimately, you weren't that much fun anyway. Although one of you was not bad at all with his fingers on one occasion, when I was alot younger, so thank you for that. I really appreciated it, although, it's kind of why Hightower is grossed out. I forgive him though. He's more than twenty years older than me and even though he rocked the sixties, seventies and eighties, the times they are a-changing (*Bob Dylan*). He used to think I was cool until he found out that I dated strange. What can I say? My own kind eats me alive. I know you know that for sure. But Hightower is a force to be reckoned with. You gotta watch out for the quiet ones. He stowed away on ship as a minor to get here. All by himself. And rescued little kids off the highway; the TransCanada – it includes 16 and 37. All these years my parents and grandparents and great grand parents worked in and for this land and I'm the one that gets to see it. We were fish cleaners on the Canadian side, in Nova Scotia.

Good thing Kate had a flock of seagulls. Now that is dealt with, we can get on with it. We English are the highest class whores in the world. We go out in public and we look great doing it and in the end, William was quite sensible about the whole thing. What was Diana's line? Philip? Well you see? You have absolutely nothing to worry about. Kate is much too far away to spit at. You are more than welcome to do the same with me. I will feel quite at home since for me, nothing has changed.

As to Canada, here's the deal. This is the true north. It is Strong and Free. This motherland is host to warrior tribes upon warrior tribes. As my bloodline is made up of extinct dynasties, this is what I came for. You are citizens anyway. You came to fight for your lives and Canadians are very very very good at that. We guard the unknown soldiers. Always have. Always will. Maybe you ran because you're a criminal element. Maybe you ran because you are running from war. Maybe you came because you didn't have a choice, or for a job. How disciplined are you? Can you stand on guard? We do. You are here for the birth of our nation, the birth of a country. You must have felt it was coming. It makes it a glorious time to be alive. The birth of a country. This is going to be the best time of your lives for you are now parents and it's a CANADA. You will see us and you will stand with us as Canadians in the birth of our status as a country. You are part of our history and the commencement of a new chapter. This is not religion. This is the birth of a nation! And all of you are one of us! Part of us...you are us. Have you any idea what that means to us? To you? If you value culture at all, then you must realize the rarity of the intrinsic value of what I am imparting to you. You are literally standing at the dawn of a new age. All of us here; together. It makes me the same as you, and you, the same as me, no matter where you come from. Isn't that spectacular? Fellow Canadians present for the birth of this country. No religion, no business, actual land. A real country. We just love you. I don't care what you did, to me or anybody else. You are my countryman and I will protect you on the road to the end of my days. When a Canadian Arab woman makes us food because we are putting up a new balcony, we so love you and thank you for your kindness. We get to dine together with the blessing of your husband. We get to be Canadian together. My man will protect her with his life, he has that much respect for you. When you make the best Canadian Italian tomato sauce with our tomatoes, we will line up for it. We will do just as the spirit of the Trucker Convoy advocated. We are Canadian and we are friends and family with each other. Think of the contributions that will be made to the arts, the food, the hospitality industry, the sports, the adventure, textiles, farm equipment, canning, fisheries, cattle, aaah the music, mining, the theatre, and yes, medicine. We have compounds in the Arctic that can be used that you have no clue of yet. We are one of the most naturally wealthiest countries in the world, not by stock exchange or gold bars (although we have them). Massive golden fields of wheat, violet maples in the Laurentians, majestic mountain ranges, diamonds, copper, zinc, wampum, bannock, maple syrup, ginger farms, acres of vineyards and mushrooms and lavender. Trees that stretch as far as the eye can see! Ancient redwoods, firs and deciduous trees; forests upon forests of them. Orchards! Oh god, we have orchards and orchards and orchards. We are Canadian and we do not massacre each other, we stand on guard for each other. It's not religion, it's our country. It's finally ours, I could care less what came before. This is the greatest moment of all and it was worth it. It was all worth it. I would do it again to get here. The birth of our very own country. Home. To me it is the Garden of Eden of all time. Free to roam strong and free from sea to shining sea. This vast country has so much food and beauty, breathtaking villages in the mountains. So much wild – moose, bison, deer, bears and bears and more bears. What we become will be etched in the history of this land as a country. Think of it! Our contributions and our ability to stand together, not under one god; but, as one nation. I'm so relieved not to be a colony anymore. No scourges, no cleansings, no encampments. We can actually build infrastructure. We can actually be equal to one another as fellow countrymen. Our individual and cultural contributions are valued equally, because they are Canadian ones. All of them. I always felt safe here because it was Canada. I never felt connected to anywhere else. My mother would have been so proud if she'd lived. All my life I have waited for this moment. This time that we finally get, to be Canadian. There will come a time when we do something wonderful that will make me cry and I just know it will be because we did that and we felt that. Together.

This is more than a once in a lifetime experience. It is the gift of being alive at the right time and the right place in history. My whole life I've known you and now we get to be together. If you ever believed in the Divine, look around you. It's everywhere, and it's ours, our love child, born of slavery and battles and agreements and renegotiations and sometimes grace, and in the end, the sheer guts and determination to *"try over and over again to get it right"*. To be something more than we were. To be something better. To be something real. I've loved the dirt and the smell and the people of this land since I was a pipsqueak running up and down the hallway. All that agony and finally, here, this is what we get. A real country. The laughter of the indigenous peoples is music to my ears. And I hear it. I can hear it. Thank you for letting me be a wife and a mother, and caretaker of the land, so I can write more songs in the backyard. Thank you for letting me work for you. I have learned so very much and I'm so grateful I made it this far because I got to see it. My lovechild. It's my love child. It's my love child and for that, my whole life was worth it. And Canada gave it to me. They gave me my life, my wonderful, wonderful life. And if I died in my sleep, I would be satisfied. Because in the end, in this country, every child does matter. Even me. And Mr G.

CHAPTER TWENTY TWO

The seventh generation thinking is the idea that the land, or the resources of the land, would still be there for people seven generations later. This, I believe, from my Canadian perspective is attributed to our native "Indians" tribes. I wonder when the first treaty was signed with them. Was it seven generations ago? Is this perhaps, the reason they are now involved in business? Good for them. They were newbies in Sudbury, however, they are increasingly better at cutting deals now (was that why the Liberal and Conservative party went there? To facilitate? I thought so; so that's why the NDP held the line – they all worked together). Good for them. I applaud that. But I have to ask why everyone is beleaguered all of a sudden. Why is the whole PTSD thing being recycled again? Let's face it, you gotta leave the cradle or you'll just kill each other. There are so many inhabitants of this land and others that carry the scars and trauma of the slaughters we perpetrated on each other in the name of whose land it was. The person you are standing next to is as generationally traumatized as you are. I don't think you recognize that. Recent losses are always going to take time so yes, you do have to give a little on occasion when someone has a meltdown, but in general, most of our traumas have to be managed ourselves. There's no way anyone has another pound of flesh to give you if it was already cut out of them. A young person of Asian descent whose grandfather was blown up building railroads here is going to have tough time flogging a dead horse with you. My question has always been, if you were so self sufficient before we got here, why didn't you just keep doing what you were doing? Because the way of life that was introduced was incredibly difficult to accept, modify or adapt to. The understanding was that we would walk alongside each other. Unfortunately, the settlers had no clue what they were talking about because they were in the same position. If you think your country is so war torn and you come to another country that was war torn, you have absolutely no right to play that card and lord it over us. It's the same shit, different soil. Your "people" are no better than my "people". All we can do is help you get out of the line of fire if you're being fired upon. It's called imminent danger. That's actually what kindness is.

Land ownership is illegal. The best you are ever going to get is to be allowed to steward it. The house you build or live in, is stewardship. If you're hell bent on leaving it to somebody, go ahead but you're just leaving stewardship. If we stopped double charging for new occupancy – yes, I'm talking to you, banks – there might actually be some disposable income to fix the place up. Why are people living in shacks? Generational ghettos line Pawley's Island. We have them here as well, in towns close to the American border. Perfectly good structures that are uninhabitable or unsafe but have been inherited and just sit while someone waits for the price of something to go up. I get it but let's face it, that structure now has to be removed if you wait too long and the price of your asset is just going down anyway. It makes no sense to me. And then people swan around because they are property owners and have an estate. I have news for you. Everybody has an estate. You don't own shit. You are renting! I don't know why you're so het up about it. You were always renting. It's not new. You're not immortal. It's weird. And yes! When your backyard is full of a bunch of crap you don't use and just pile up for years, nobody takes you seriously. It looks like you have no respect for the land because you won't clean it up. If you are native and you do this, you just confuse us. If you are not from here, we think you're gross. And if you are from here, we just shake our heads because you're going to cause us trouble with the natives for being a pig. It's a real dilemma. Lots of folks store stuff in barns but that is because they are running a business, storing for posterity so it can be sold in later years as a living indication of that era. Only a soupcon of these relics survives. Mostly it just rots and gets burned. Please don't torture yourselves that your great great grandmother's sofa mustn't be given or used, in order to preserve history in her honour. She doesn't give a shit about the sofa. Fix it up, use it, give it away or sell it so someone else can appreciate it. In addition, if you can't pay child support but you have the cash to be a collector...really? Is human flesh worth less than your grandmother's dining room table? Don't you feel like a dork?

It's terrible really, we have the RCMP up here and I can't help it, like a goofball, I just get all blushy around them. I grew up with Mounties on horses and it's so romantic. LOL I know. I know. I feel like Granma Berle simpering down the hallway with a sandwich ah haha.

I think menoras are beautiful. I used to have two of them. Over the years I've had things that I thought were beautiful but sometimes I let them go because someone was offended that I had them. It's hard because no sooner do I do that, someone is offended that I don't have them. I am reduced to asking that, if I purchase something and display or wear it, is somebody going to punch me in the face because they deem I don't have the right or the heart of the people they are associated with or the history or that I am taking it in vain or I'm showing off or not showing enough honour? Why are you merchandising them? I'm confused. I really admire them or I wouldn't have bothered. It's weird.

Sometimes when something hurts so bad you can hardly stand up, it's the job that saves you. The job. If I could have gone back to work, I would have been okay. I was just colossally sideswiped. I wish, I wish, I wish. If I had just had the job.

Why is it forty years? Forty years is associated with wandering in the desert, deluged with water. When the test is over, what does that mean? Did I pass? Do I start over? Do I have to die now?

Why are mass produced items worth more than small batches? Did you know that in India, that when a person shakes their head it means yes? And nodding means no? Pretty confusing if you're in traffic isn't it? Kind of gives new meaning to road rage lol. I learned this quite by accident when I kept asking if I could change lanes. He kept saying no but was stopped waiting for me to get on with it so I didn't know what to do and just took a chance that I was supposed to go. It's true, they do. Think how confusing it is for them, kind of like driving on the other side of the road in Britain. The new speed limits are difficult because sigh shucks I just used to love driving that open road.

Sometimes it's so difficult to adjust I just want to fall asleep in traffic. It makes me sweat sometimes. I know right, so old school. In another twenty years, I will be an old timer. The speed limits will probably have gone back up by then.

I think allegiance is not patriotism. Patriotism is extreme. Patriotism amongst human families just cuts down the population until nobody dares to make a move. It doesn't really work. It's been tried for centuries. No matter your faith, you still have a responsibility to maintain some kind of division at the borders. At the end of the day, the Israelites battled constantly, so did King David. True patriot love is the allegiance to the land that you occupy. Even the natives came by boat from somewhere at some point in our history. They also occupy the land. And if you're going to object, well then we have a Dinah situation. Who, in their right mind demands circumcision after an honest offer and then goes around slaughtering everybody. And then it was her fault!? Stand down already. She was clearly an honourable woman or else she wouldn't have made such a good impression. It doesn't say anybody raped her. You just blow shit way out of proportion. Every once in awhile, it is necessary to step forward and say I don't think so. It happens in your homes, in your places of worship, in your hearts and minds. The reason we have personnel at the borders is to ensure a demarcation so nations can do business with each other. I mean, you can abhor the acts of war all you want, but they are simply a magnifier of the microcosm that is occurring on your side of the border. Finance, at an international level is a balance act. It's called trade. No one has ever owned the land. Not ever. It has been taken care of by you or someone else. I know it's tough because some of you got married and suddenly your father-in-law is tinkering with the fence in the backyard or on the roof and you get all steamy about it because you can do it yourself and you don't want to be criticized for how you conduct your life. It's exhausting. You can't do it all. And older people just wanna smell their grandkids. Most of the time they have habits of their own you find unacceptable so meh, call it even. It's just a fence. Maybe he will take your grandson to church on Sundays. Pops used to make off with Mr J's son to the racetrack.

When they won, he got chips! He was in grade one before he ever saw a church on a class trip and he didn't believe them! But that's his granddaddy and it was harmless. You might think about opening some of your religious buildings to the schools on occasion so they have some knowledge as to what you are about. That way, they can relate instead of feeling threatened. If it is truly an attempt to provide a place to worship, then it's on you to accept that if someone falls through the door of your establishment in agony, that you have to provide the sanctuary of divine solace without prejudice, or checking to see if they are registered. And if you can't do that, then you need to accept that you are marginalized the same as everyone else and not take issue with it as racism. God does not abandon, whatever name you choose to represent the divine. The seasons change, the earth renews itself.

We are going to go back to normal. I know it doesn't feel like it but the truth is, we have to get our shit together after being isolated for so long. And now you have a whole country to get excited about. No, it's not peace and security. These things do not exist except for brief periods of time unless you work at it. Socialization and festivals is what made the old testament go round. Even Jesus drank wine at weddings in the new testament. Forgive me, I don't mean to diss other holy texts. The bible is just safer to refer to. But it's a gift. A country to be the stewards of. If you ever watched Yellowstone, and times'd it by a million, you have some glimpse into what I mean.

They run cattle here too. I hope you can forgive us if they are your holy animal. We try not to eat too many of them. And yes, we will become accustomed to the turbans. You work hard. I see you on the road struggling with your new trucker's licenses. Keep at it. You'll be great. If you can do it here, you can do it anywhere. It's not for the faint of heart. Besides, it's tough to be so easily identified. I've lived it. You just have to follow the same rules as everybody else.

I have to say, there's just no way I would ever not give a shit about somebody's children. I'm just afraid to love them because I hurt someone else so much because I inadvertently took that away from her. I know she got it back but that baby stage is a kicker and I just grieved so much. So very much. In the end that is what I got and I should be grateful and happy because you can't have everything. Kids come here sometimes too and it makes me laugh. The oldest always does what they think their parents want them to do and then the youngest just wanders off and becomes the thing they remember themselves to be when they were younger and everybody just loves them and the oldest is always left holding the bag saying what the fuck. All his kids are ridiculously good looking. The middle one should be famous one day, she has that kind of sparkle. Her daddy just cries and cries because she isn't there anymore but she took care of him when they split so he could keep going and I bet my mom or dad did that too, when the time came for me to split. Everyone gets pissed that they don't spend enough time with the grandkids but they had a way of showing up from time to time and since they don't live in the same neighbourhood and are still pretty engaged with their own commitments, it's probably best. Who wants a melee over the babies. I'm talking about my mom and dad here.

Did you know that if you commit your "parent" to a "home", you have to pay for it? Yes, your money doesn't go as far because it's a service that doesn't just melt into thin air. You don't have to pay for all of it because it is an industry of sorts but it's meant for those who need to be monitored for life signs; you know, strapped into wheelchairs and stuff. Like I said though, if you object to someone in bed with your mother who isn't your father and bundle them off, they'll just find somebody else. I guess they just won't do it in front of you. People do need to have sex in their nineties you know. I fail to comprehend why you find it to be shocking after what I've seen posted. It's bizarre. If you're so annoyed that your daughter's body might respond to a man and you freak her out about it, she just masturbates while he gets on with it and he just loves that. One way or the other, the best you can get is respect and basic decency because it's going to happen one way or the other. You can conceive your children in shame or guilt or lust or whatever but furtive is just so bad for the baby and the mother and father. It just comes out with all that "am I in trouble" in their veins and if people sneer at their parents, it just makes it worse. Do I just sleep with anybody? Me? No. You? No?

Got kids? Invitro? Oh natural? But you didn't sleep with anybody. That's weird.

Young people, your parents were as wild as you were. Trust me. They have no axe to grind with you, they just don't want the Karens of this world to think they're bad parents. Everyone has a moment as a parent when they wince and deep down think "that's my boy, or, that's my girl", with unbidden pride and satisfaction. They can't help it even if they never tell you. Kids are just agonizing. You'll see. That one's all mine, right there. And when they are away from you, if they think they can get away with it, they run a little bit amok too...your parents that is.

I'm glad I voted. It's my civic duty. I feel guilty because the JWs don't do that, but I just didn't want to live in a bubble of regurgitating the same stuff over and over again. Mankind has waited for the second coming, the moment God will step in and fix everything for as long as I have been alive. When I pray, God hears me. It works. But if you're going to cut my head off for it, I just don't know how to tell you that God isn't going to stop you or the repercussions of that decision. When you're dead, you're dead. If I was all that, I mean, like I'm all that in the grand schema of humanity for all time, then yes, I guess God does remember me but not personally. Why you believe God is going to torture you or redeem you is a little grandiose don't you think, a little mega egomaniacal. You're just making more makework for the most high and since he or she or whatever is all that, surely it would have been paradise regained by now. I just don't think you're humble enough about it. Not oaths of poverty, that's just grandstanding. If we're all so very important, more than everything else in the universe (like we're the only species, what a crock), I just can't ride that train. I'm just not that big a deal. I mean, the flowers get clothes and so do I. It's too much. It's just too much. If there is a judgement and a verdict I just don't want to stand there like a fool and have it say I gave you a whole life and all you did was fight about it. I'd rather it say, you kind of blew it a couple of times but at least you didn't waste it, at least you had the courage to live the life I gave you. I'm so damn grateful for that. Tabernache!

Remember Shadrach, Meshach and Abednago? When they were walking around in the fire? I've had that. Seriously. There are rare moments when something coalesces in your solar plexus and you just know you're going to die but something propels me forward and I can't back down because it is so collateral damage unnecessary and I get tossed right out on my ass into the dark. But its right and its true and if I don't do it, someone is going to get hurt. There's your forty days and forty nights. I think the conversation that takes place is the agonizing part. For all you know, Jesus was wrestling with himself and if any of you have ever had to play the devil's advocate with yourself, you know it's the same thing.

Stewardship of the earth might be something the native peoples have waited for us to get our heads around since apparently we like to own things. I like to have things. I hate paying for them over and over after I already bought them. If you could perhaps not apply this to men, women and children that would be helpful. The gratitude I feel in nature to God is that I don't feel ashamed when I'm in the woods and stuff like that. God just never was that hard on me. I trust God implicitly. I like the animals. They just run by me. I don't know what to say. Living with people is alot harder. God never begrudged anything if you look around you, not even us. I just don't understand. If we were forgiven, what are we flogging ourselves for unless it's for domination?

I just can't hate you or myself that much. I feel like I would betray creation itself. But we are a people and it just makes me cry because our country isn't in pieces anymore. We aren't perfect by any means but it's a country. I love this country. I've disappeared into it all my life. It has saved my life. I don't think it is better than yours by any means. And it certainly hasn't recovered from its own history like anybody else. But to integrate your own discomfort with your life into objections to education, art, technology, religion and the million things you're uncomfortable with isn't going to fix it. It happened. It's there. You think you can't deal with that, then what happens when someone forgets who they are and starts launching dangerous things and we go to war so only eight million people die instead of a hundred million. What happens when something bad happens to you? I mean, it's the tip of the iceberg of your life. If you knew what you were really going to have to deal with, you would just feel like a twit. It so blocks the future for you. The possibilities of what you could become. There comes a day when you realize that you spent your whole life trying to come to terms and you missed the whole thing. I tried not to. I was little Miss Perfect, irritating as shit. I just wanted to be good enough that's all. I should have just realized I already was. Good enough. Because when I'm in the woods I'm good enough to God. I'm just part of creation.

Canada is a massive country. What we do with it will become part of our history. Stewards are good enough. Way good enough.

CHAPTER TWENTY THREE

I watched the Junos last night. You can tell we don't have any money from the backdrop but I sure do think the young people of this country have balls. I like that alot. I like that a young woman with a hijab was assisted by her fellow man and that she, herself, is in debt just to get there. And she knows it. I hope she climbs and climbs and climbs. I like the advances that have been made with rapper music in the east Indian culture. I love that Anne Murray is still the Snowbird. You young people in the arts right now in this country are the shit. I mean it. You go! I've watched the influences of our music come from Negro slavery turn into something meaningful and long lasting. Because that's where we started. I love that you get up there in a long flowy purple thing and just go. I hope that you, as a generation find the courage within yourselves, not to eat each other alive in twenty years. I hope you don't marginalize yourselves, and that you continue to cross cultures and make new sounds. And yes, you are to be congratulated. Some of our best original rock n' roll tracks were laid down by our native peoples. And like them, you just keep going. Do it. You've got one life. Do it. Respect. We just gutted it out with each other and you will do the same. Eventually, the cultures of your countries of origin will be woven into the Canadian fabric, the guardians of the true north. And the fact that you all stood together finding time for each disparate culture, trying to show respect and give credit where credit is due, is all anybody can ever ask for. Long after I have died from dancing to Kim Mitchell's Patio Lanterns, your grandchildren will be dancing to the sounds that you laid down in this generation. It will formulate an era and it's important what you are doing. Don't let anyone ever tell you it's for nothing. It is the footprint for future generations. It's courageous. You are creating living history. And you aren't expected to fix the past. We don't expect you to. We expect you to build on what has gone before you and, while I'm just the peanut gallery, I think you're heading in the right direction and I would never doubt you or your right to make your own destinies.

I just think what you are doing is very exciting. Hi Sarah McLachlan! She ran the first female promoted all female revue in Canada. We have more than one female trailblazer in Canada, it's not just politics and outer space.

It's why I encourage you in your aspirations in this country. We are young enough that you have a pretty wide free range to stake your claim in history. And Canada, at its heart, is quite different than its original beginnings, at least as far as it's English "benefactor" goes. Canada, at its heart is a trail blazer country. It doesn't come across that way, but it's pretty fearless and it does give you a chance; in fact it is not a country that closes deals, it's a country that gives you a push at the beginning of your endeavour and then off you go. Do I care that, as a guardian of the north that you are wearing a turban or a hijab instead of a headdress or a chapeau? Not in the slightest. I saw a family yesterday and I had to laugh. One was white with brown hair, one was Pilipino, one was black and one was white with bright red hair. And they all got into the same car. I like that alot. Because my second husband and I went to lots of places where blacks and whites hung out; they just didn't do it at the same table so everyone would stop talking and just stare at us when we entered the establishment. It takes alot of guts to love something. It takes more guts to love something than anything else. But if you can love something enough that it weaves into the current state of the culture of the country you are residing in, then you have altered history and it turns into something else, something new, something more evolved. If you can do it without hurting anybody, well then Rosa Parks move on over honey, I'm coming with you.

Like your countries of origin, Canada has agreements that we have to honour. They are old agreements but we don't get to pitch them because we were unaware of something. We're stuck. It's a process. If we retire and the old agreements haven't expired, somebody is fucked and they hate us. Many of the initiatives you put forward will have limited success insofar as, you have to get in line behind the old ones. But what you will accomplish, is laying the groundwork for the kind of futures you envision. You will collectively change the face of the culture over time.

I was indentured to the Queen. I am a white woman who was born as an indentured slave to the empire. White people are no easier on each other than your cultures are. It's not racist. It's the big Tower of Babel. I am released from service at their will and it is up to them whether I will be permitted, under the law and its old agreements which I am bound by, even though those days are gone; to be semi-released from official service and permitted to build on land and have a home. I am not considered special in any way. I am considered to be freeborn both here and in Britain. The fact that I am the first or second child and a woman is what puts the nail in the coffin. My service was considered to be military service and when it was discovered that I could no longer bear children, I was "serviced" out. It is what it is. I was a minor so by law the records had to be sealed. But I've had a great life, and I've tried not to hurt anyone and I have not stayed within the English compound. The French community in Canada, by civil law, extended to me my name and so, like you, I am required to please the French by also doing my duty. It is also, why Canada as a new colony did their level best to protect me. They will do their level best to protect you and I will never abandon anyone here in the name of that service. But you will have to survive it. And you will have to be strong. Because that is what it takes to be free. To be a guardian of the north is a great honour. It's so new. It's the first time the natives have allowed us to stand with them and it took us one hundred and fifty years to talk them into it. You will only get so far in your lifetime but if you can weave your destiny into the world you live in, then your aspirations can make you more than you thought you could become. The natives own this land. Never forget it. In three generations, they might let you rent and be a caretaker. Because they are forgivers. It took a long time and they're still annoyed but here we are. Remember that and when you're tripping the light fantastic, be careful. Just because someone is of a separate faith doesn't mean they don't have the capacity you do to go either way. Some of those agreements I have been slowly released from, and truthfully, becoming a country negates some of the original ones but that is how I started out. It's why I try to hold the line for you because your families of origin might re-enact them unwittingly.

Mr Singh held the agreement with the Liberal party so they could facilitate some things of a contractual business nature for Canada. He's a great politician. They work together with the Conservatives, and I suspect the Bloc because the Bloc has to facilitate a great deal more than you realize and so we assist when some of our traditional Canadian institutions get into trouble in return. They all fight like cats and dogs but they are devoted, and in the end, they work together. Even the Green Party takes on large chunks of environmental work so the party in power can be world facing. No one party has ever established a coup or encouraged civil war. Mostly we just fight to keep our relationships intact and facilitate food on the table for the inhabitants. We're not a one stop shop but we kinda rule by fingertips. And boy do we have stamina. As you do, we love it when one of "ours" takes a more global stage but oddly, we don't make a big deal of it.

Okay I'm not going to flog this anymore. It's a little warrior like. It would be nice if our vision extended to a true makeover, not just surviving world-wide probates. You have to wonder if there is any part of the earth that is not subject to layered taxation. If you think back to the land grabs when people rode off on horses and literally staked their claims, were they already under claim? They must have been. Ergo native Indians being marched out. You've got to wonder why we are recycling the occupancy of the land itself. A basic income given to every inhabitant of the land as a division of the profits of natural resources is a nice idea but then are you going to police how it is spent? What if people complain that it is not enough to live on? Are we to become a world of welfare recipients? I like bonuses as much as the next guy but at the end of the day, people languish and die without an aspiration and many of us need a kick in the butt to get on with it. At the end of the day, are we're going to be jealous of each other anyways?

CHAPTER TWENTY FOUR

Gun control in Canada is moronic. I've glad you've laid that to rest. All citizens who occupy the land of a country are given leave to bear arms when their "territory" is being encroached upon but that is as a nation only. We do not, unlike the Americans, have the right to carry arms on our person. It is the deal we make to allow those of other faiths to hold office. In Canada, firearms need to be cleaned and dismantled for transport. You need a license to transport them so you can leave them at the gun club or register with the RCMP so you can store them in a safe that is bolted to the floor. Hunters who apply for and receive licenses are not required to transport them this way during hunting season. We tightened up quite a bit after the Cegep was hit hard in Quebec. The last thing we need is some bitter hormone ridden individual running amok (so weird, he was a guy too). When they are transported, ammunition has to be transported separately. It's onerous but it works. The way of life of the natives and the hunters is preserved under new rules. Killing someone in defence of the life of another person is a much easier trial to adjudicate because there are at least three people. The advances in genetics are what allow the proof to be established if, for some reason, someone wants to lie about it. I don't know, I'd rather shoot a pig between the eyes and have it drop that try to cut its throat. I tried it with a goat once but it was most unpleasant because they are not human and you have to cut not slice. It's death and it's not humane. I totally understand why people are screaming murder about furs, because I skinned it and cured it with battery acid and it became a carpet. I would rather have shot it between the eyes and have it drop. Animals do see their deaths coming and if they have kids, they emit a hormonal distress endocrine signature that taints the meat energetically. If they don't go down fast enough, the bruising can be seen on the meat that you eat, no matter how much you bleed it. It's why the natives used to pray over the carcass and generally, why people pray before dinner, to give thanks. I have no position on whether we are depraved because apparently, vegetables are exactly the same, with the exception that they sense imminent death and release something akin to a painkiller. Many hospices do the same. Lots of people try to find a middle ground by only eating what has fallen from the tree (I believe this was Eve's original sin). I don't know if that means they eat their meat raw a la steak tartare or whether they think eating an egg is eating someone else's children. Some people bury their eggs in the earth for future generations. Sawed off serial numbers are remarkably easy to track since there is another place on rifles and handguns that are readable by certain scans. Serial numbers on weapons are for merchandising purposes. Underneath it all, you do actually get away with being a rock star if you don't hurt anybody. You have a remarkable amount grace granted to you under Canada's roof. The police are pretty nice about it which is why you underestimate us sometimes and overplay your hand. I do not own any firearms at this time but I used to carry a licence for transport. Actually, I was banned from the Harbord Gun club because my .45 went semi-automatic on me and I shot out all the baseboards. A 9mm would have been a better choice. Although they did insist on putting a scope on my rifle because I kept hitting the bulls eye. IPSC shooting is the drop and roll barrelled type of pistol that involves training on the job. This might have evolved over the years but I doubt it.

Whenever a community begins to emerge as a new or expanded socio economic group and fights to be recognized and included, it experiences growing pains. Much like religion or immigration, the trajectories are sometimes unexpected. I have one thing to say to the LGBTQ++ community – Invictus. If you object because you think you are being compared to a handicapped person then you are oblivious to the contributions Stephen Hawking made to the world and you underestimate yourselves. They are just as capable as you are and being realistic, they compete on common ground. Much like the distaste the old experience with the young when they grab the baton and run in the "wrong" direction, both gay and lesbian men and women have a difficult time advocating because you cut your nose off to spite your faces. It's like having children and not recognizing they came from you because they look so different. I expect, and so does everybody else, you and yours to continue with your world quest. You need to find in your collectiveness some part that will lead so you can navigate and negotiate your way. We ALL have to do this so please don't heap your disdain, it's actually what makes you the same as everybody else. I'm extremely interested in what you come up with because you have already made a very bold and sensible contribution already. You have to be decent like everybody else. Some of you are. Some of you aren't. Just like the rest of us You have a following. Thanks to Rock Hudson, Tim Currie and a bevy of other trailblazers you like to take umbrage with for getting you this far. We like you. Do your thing. Having good energy is an attribute that different people exude at different times. It isn't necessarily the same as beauty, which is in the eye of the beholder. Kindly stop correcting others grammar and begin calling your own beautiful. That's key. And yes, if you need to wear a tool belt for work, stop instigating that you are being biased against because you have to take off your heels and wear boots like everybody else. If you can stop panicking that you actually made it, you'll have all kinds of people following your trends. I keep waiting for you to open a decent restaurant. Food and socialization helps. Making it is more work is what will bring people to you. You still have to contribute to society, even if your ancestors died because of what they were. You are no different in that respect than the rest of the world. And if your merchandise only caters to your own kind, then you will remain marginalized. It's just the way it works. White people are racist against each other so get a clue.

    The reason I have no quarrel with the LGBTQ++ community is because the small children do not feel threatened by them. They like them. Small children instinctively know more than you because they are still untrained. Most young adults do not embark on the types of behaviour you believe or dread, until they are ready. I had a fellow cooking student who divulged that he had a difficult time with cunnilingus because it was just so squishy down there he didn't think he could manage it so he had broken up with his girlfriend because she was ready to have sex and he balked. He threw it out casually in case I might be offended but yeah, I totally got it. There's still a big deal made about whether a woman swallows a man's sperm. I believe the jury is still out on that one. Young people want to love somebody the same as you. Young women who are under the roof of decent people can, in fact, sleep over with a bunch of their male peers and not be touched. Young teenagers are remarkably careful with each other. You were too if you can remember. Your kids are better than you think. I've witnessed this with my own eyes. Each of you has experienced a time when you were shell shocked and someone who was a friend just put you on the couch and was gentle with you until you sprung to life again. I know this because I hear the stories. And I had the League of Nations under my roof at times. Young people are much better at negotiating a new world than older ones. You have to let it go. And be excited. Because they instinctively honour each other until they are trained out of it and have to run the gauntlet of disapproval for their choices. Then you get blowback.

The only time I got a buy on a speeding ticket was when I was coming home with the girls after a weekend of partying. Funny eh? Socializing is allowed. I think one of them returned with an earring in her eyebrow and another, in her tongue. Harmless, just disconcerting. The age ranges were twenty-eight to sixty-eight (eyebrow earring). The guys were at home with the kids. We didn't have a hall pass. We had leave to go party. Two different things. Our spouses travelled and we were chained to our desks so they came home and we got to run amok for forty-eight hours. Most of the time I partied, I met other men who were socializing but not really into getting naked. You'd be surprised, how careful they were with us. Most men love their wives more than anyone else. Most wives don't recognize this. Countries do business with other countries by exchanging resources so they can do things like provide universal healthcare which is the dream, of course. A dollar figure is assigned to each living individual as a basis to manage the earth's resources so that every part of the world is covered. It's not perfect, it doesn't cover anecdotes or make you, as a unique individual fully compensated for what you are or what you didn't get. It's basic. You are worth the same as the next person. But you still have to get the resources in and out and distributed. Hence, we have adventure. No one is getting more or less than you. Everyone is attempting to be comfortable or see the world. It's a life that needs to be negotiated. Right now, you see very "old" people as a drain on society but this is because you time them out and they can no longer work or love. They find it very difficult because there is nowhere to go except to spend their time sitting until it is over or exercising strenuously until they can no longer recognize the people around them just decide to give up and die in their sleep. And yet, we yearn to live forever. It is the basic premise for all faiths, the promise of eternal life. Well, we haven't overrun the earth yet with humanity so we have a long way to go before we have to colonize another planet. For all you know, it could be a three hundred year old team that actually begins the process in earnest. In the meantime, humanity ebbs and flows like the seasons. All of your lineages are recorded for posterity. If you have an estate lawyer, you will only see the lineages you want to see. If you don't, your lineages are everywhere and yes, there is a storage capacity on the earth that records the given names of all the inhabitants of the earth. Your own kind doesn't forget you. It is the recorded histories and lineages of the current millennium. Old debts are finally paid over and over and over again for forty years before they are retired. Did Jesus retire the debt of the Jews? He was crowned as King of the Jews. Was it only their debts that were forgiven? Is this why they feel they are the chosen people? Did Joseph have sex with Mary and so she lost her name and ergo, it was an immaculate conception? Who's to say? Apparently she survived it but had to hide Jesus because he was a legitimate firstborn son which the governance at that time objected to. Moses floating down the river. Does anyone know what the duties of a legitimate firstborn son is? Do both his parents have to be legitimate too? If he's legitimate but his mother had six children, what happens then? Does he have to sleep with his brother's wife if his brother dies? What if he already has a wife? Seems like everybody wants his own wife. Yes, but if he beats her, does that mean she can leave and take back her name? If he has sex with someone else when she's pregnant with their child, can she leave and take her name back? Ultimately, it comes down to respect. How much can you back your word? I'll time out at seventy whether I want to or not. A senior citizen finally gets to work on a body of work. Granma Moses. But any number of you have an opinion on who I am to work for, depending on your beliefs. For me, I need somewhere to live. I need to help people support their still growing children. And now I have so many signatures to represent the position I was holding at the time, that people have a problem with it. Yet, if I sign my name, there is a question as to whether I am entitled to my given name. It's truly remarkable that I have managed to walk, talk and breathe for as long as I have. Do I need to collect a benefit? Not anymore. I tried to stop it from coming when I felt better and could function without crying at odd times again. Apparently I have to collect it for forty years. Am I a drain on society? No. Not really. I've collected unemployment insurance twice in my life. I pay my taxes. Sometimes I can't figure out how to because I'm supposed to take a position. But, like you, I can't live in a tent and go to work. No one will take me seriously. Is it danger pay? I don't know. No one else will do it.

Misinformation is the cross between official and/or wished for positions and what really happened. Some things are private and not meant to be formalized or publicized for that matter, lest we have a bevy of onlookers waiting to confirm the validity of virginity (which was a crock since everyone rode horses; all those dead chickens). All persons who work after the age of retirement continue to pay taxes and many of them do, to stay engaged. It's quite possible I shall continue to work for various lines which is why, on occasion, people scream that I eat cake but that's only because they assume I am on the same trajectory as they are. Or because I am expected to pay for an heir that does not exist or a family line that has been paid out. Sometimes people just need to catch their breath. I'm not entirely sure who I owe money to for living, but I do know that I am welcome in my country because I just keep working. And I just love that. I am surreptitiously accepted in other countries as well but only for a little while, at least that is how it used to be. The young have revamped our processes as they should except that there is no segueway for the originals so they become frustrated because they are no longer talking the same language. We have a gap always and that is why life is so easy and so difficult. It's so easy to criticize someone else who speaks a different language than you. It's always a process. Your next big renegotiation in this country is coming and it will be one of the best things that ever happened to you. Forgivers let things go. The destruction of some of our monuments was an act of civil unrest born of isolation in a country that is unaccustomed to limitations to freedom of movement, and while reported upon, no one was burned at the stake for it. We are warrior tribes who are guardians of the north. They are part of the history of the land like so many before and after them. It is not the end of the story. They are making room for the next "unknown soldiers" who will be the monuments for the next generations to follow and emulate or improve upon. In many ways, I am pleased my parents did whatever they wanted (although I'm sure at different times in their lives they felt they didn't have a choice). They gave me a great life. In fact, my uncle was never so surprised at what I did in all his life. He got sniffy! LOL, it was awesome. I love him to death.

Build back better means that humanity's existing records are being re-filed as it were. Artificial intelligence allows for bulks of records to be transferred to new locations for permanent stewardship. The UN, WHO, WEF are hubs of sorts that have jurisdiction over global generalized administration in terms of the re-filing because there are agreements that have to be kept over time and so, like estates and governments, funding streams have to be captured under different headings. Forty years is generally when enough people don't remember anymore so you can probably have it since it is no longer an issue. Sometimes, when you have trouble with your 5G, it is because the programming is either updating itself or it is being updated by a programmer with new code (to put it in simplistic terms). Most of the fine print you agree to is AI generated but it used to be written by people which is why there is no one to sue, only market share. Your market share is what counts in terms of it being captured by a monopoly, which is still illegal, but what is considered to be of value. Hence, when the young are just before they come of age, is the most lucrative market because it is when the notion of money of one's own to be spent at one's own discretion is first yearned for. In the end, it is the moral compass of the young when they become of age that dictates how a market share majority is distributed. And that is because the public stops spending their money unconsciously in a certain direction when it is unsustainable.(*The BeeGees and Disco Duck*).

Jill told me once that there was a special place with God for those who felt being alive was too painful. It is the gentleness of the reflection of the divine is why I like her. For some, this world will never be okay, no matter what happens. For others, they will stay until they are satisfied with the breath of life they have received. Some of our great grandparents served the world. It's in the trees around you from the ashes of the earth you walk on. Many, if they are lucky, will negotiate a living situation they can live with and will still feel like they are perishing in the bosom of their family. They can't all be there. They are hidden in the willows of your heart.

CHAPTER TWENTY FIFE

This is no more than the story of a girl who grew up in the colonies. Does everyone see it the way I see it? No way. People are beautiful, And scary. As a born caretaker, I was legitimate in five different family lines and it was my duty to provide an heir for each of them, Impossible. I gave them nothing. Even if I had borne them, they wouldn't have wanted them anyway. My scraggy bunch of half breeds...

I had a good friend for years. I do not know if he still lives. He used to call me from Manitoba, where his brother was an RCMP and they would gather on the phone and sing to me. I don't know if it was a policeman's choir or if his brother was part of a quartet. All I know is that he would find me and call me and then that would happen. It was the love of a fellow Canadian. He was a painter. He had a friend who danced for the Canadian Ballet and he had contracted AIDs. I remember clutching at him in the back seat of a taxi one night, sobbing that I didn't want him to die. He held me so tight, so tight. I don't know what happened to him but I remember that he held me close so close and that I was later ashamed that I would be the recipient of his grace because I was going to live. I hope that he did too. We were friends then and I never forgot them. It is these things that keep me going, the grace of those who came before me and let me bathe in the glow of their light fantastic. When I went back to Ontario, I was tested for AIDs for ten years until they would no longer test me anymore and it appeared that I had been exposed but had escaped by the skin of my teeth. It was not because of my friend. It was because of my first husband.

I do not know if position or sex gives anyone anymore than the next person. At the end of the fiscal year, you are going to pay for something. You have to. Pay now or pay later. But you will pay one way or the other. You should know that. No matter you're expectations of life, you will not last if you don't climb. It is the dint of the human experience. The most you can ever hope for is that your person climbs with you, your parents are proud of you, your country likes you, and that you have a friend or two. If you are very lucky, you might produce something that is felt to be of value to your fellow man. And one day you will be gone. Your love is as infinite as the galaxy we inhabit. You will likely have a few years in your late teens and early twenties when you will sleep with anybody. It is the grace extended to the young for a short time before you have to work harder than you ever thought was possible. It's your love that propels you. As long as you love something, you will be okay. When we are old, we are also extended a short stint of time when we will sleep with everybody. It is the false fear that we might be close to death. Some call it a mid-life crisis but it usually occurs after the old are abandoned. If you are able to cling to your person and they cling to you, you will have a great deal more than most. And sometimes you're not going to know what it is you're getting until it is too late and you will have to adjust so you can keep going. There is no plateau, no certainty; only what you wish to make of the life you are living. Never give up. People walk all the time who were never supposed to, they succeed where they were never supposed to, they love what they were never supposed to, they survive what they were never supposed to. It happens. It is the breath of life of creation itself and it gives you a choice. Every single time. Forgiveness emanates from the soul. It is a human mechanism. Perhaps the great sacrifice of the son was to teach us forgiveness since we obviously needed it in our interactions with one another. I think it was granted so we would understand that what we create takes on a life of its own and then it no longer belongs to us, once it's "out there". It is a love child. It's our love child but it's gone. We were just the guardians of what we created. If it needs us, we will come. But it's gone and it owes us nothing but the life it was given as it goes on its own adventure. Sometimes we will be called to account in some way for our lifetimes and here is where our love children are discovered and, if we are fortunate, we will not be penalized because we were paid for them. The secret of success in business is to do what you love. It's all business eventually. Even the assets need to be redistributed before you can consign your ashes to dust. It's a fine line between libertarianism and hearing, seeing and speaking no evil. You cannot pay it all back. It is impossible. You can only do the best you can and extend grace to others. Hightower drank for three weeks every night after he lost one of his kids. He grieved deeply every one of them because they had failed to do the one thing they both wanted. To stay. Sometimes I stay only because of him. Because I have no real connection to him but by fingertips, he reached out and scooped me off the street. So I would know that someone thought I was worth it. Its Every Child Matters to the nth degree. I know many who have done this and received no credit but I can tell who they are from a mile off. They are no different than the children who resent that their father is a man of god and not willing to support their earthly ambitions. They are just fingertips. Guardians of the young and disenfranchised. It is an honourable vocation. It is the reason I have the courage to live. I was not born into it. It was bestowed upon me and as heavy as burden as it has been, it is the very thing that becomes the lightest of all when I must walk on my feet instead of my knees.

There is a joke among women, that you only want a man after another woman has broken him in. We all hope it's his mother but alas, if it is her first child, all is lost. Fathers are like that too, which makes an ordinary man's love inadequate. Me, I am relieved if my brother, or my aunt, for instance, is loved. More families of origin break up a good thing than anything else. Most can successfully run the worldly gauntlet but can never transcend their families of origin because it is from whence they sprang. And it is astonishingly common for a man or a woman to abdicate the marriage entirely once they have their "firstborn". If it's a girl, they retire in disappointment. If it's a boy, they are raised to be entirely useless since apparently, they get everything. I do not know what this means other than lots of sneering everywhere. I have never seen a firstborn get everything. Even in religious texts, it is not clear what the birthrights are, of a firstborn. Then we have the whole are you a legitimate firstborn? Were your parents married? Was it their first marriage? Were they both legitimate? Were they both firstborns? Are they of the right age, color, sex, culture? What counts? Does merit count if the firstborn just steals from everybody and expects others to pay their way in life? Is this a firstborn? Wouldn't that make them useless? Are the siblings of a firstborn required to work for them? How so? It's a mystery; and one that is used to slay one another on a regular basis. How we ever manage to produce progeny of any value is truly a testament to the resiliency of the human race. It's a good thing sex was created to be pleasurable or we wouldn't bother. Or at least, healthy men and undamaged women wouldn't bother. I wonder what would have happened if I listed my uncle and my mother instead of my uncle and my father, on my passport. Would I have been solely the property of my second husband? Why aren't my husbands who need me to be as functional as they are, not my property? I still have to pay for them, their proclivities and their children, whether they are born of my body or not. Marriage is not for the faint of heart. I urge you to work for thirty years before you attempt the liaison, because it has the propensity to cost you every dollar you ever made. No matter what your parents say, secretly, they never want you to get married. Not ever. Neither are they interested in your little brats so don't procreate for them. There isn't a parent on the face of the earth who wants to raise your kids or admit you engaged in the sexual act and made a baby. Its why so many of them marry you in "church", so they can tell themselves you have never given yourself to a man or a woman since God got you first. Hopefully, God loves your children enough to put a Hightower on the road so you can relieve your conscience. The reason we adore our parents is because it was a family. Anyone who has the balls to get married and have a bunch of kids has the multi-generational love of their children. Anyone who does it more than once in different countries has my abject admiration. I don't have the stones for that.

    I suggest ladies, that you retain your own name after you marry, so that your husband doesn't murder you in cold blood, for running a separate company under your own roof. Better he gets used to the idea that you are walking together not one leading the other by a leash. This is especially important if your cultures are originated from different countries. Just because the skin color is similar, it doesn't mean you have a natural affinity. Most women will insist their daughters work so they have their own money. Most men will insist their sons get everything and be the head of the house. No wonder we are filming our personal and private lives for all to see. We do not trust ourselves to be decent. We do not trust ourselves to accept equal footing. In my experience, when we are finally on top, we wander off and just fuck shit up because we are too stupid to know better. And we like pain for some odd reason. Not the kind of pain that makes our bodies strong; the kind of pain that makes our bodies weak. It is illogical and difficult to take seriously. Some cook Sunday dinner and get sniffy if you don't show up even if you are literally working. I don't know what to do about this. Why don't you invite different people? Friends like Sunday dinner too. I find it a little scary that you reach an age where you are too frightened to have new friends. My centurion grandmother loved new friends. It was so exciting. It feels like COVID made us afraid of the passing of time. It feels like COVID tricked us into believing in scarcity. It feels like COVID brought out the worst in us and made us into cowards.

One of the activities I had the pleasure to partake in was a two day solo bush trip. It was meant to give time for thought, for communing with nature, for gleaning insights. We slept in the open air under tarps. No one thought of rattlesnakes or coyotes or bears. We were a group that went out one at a time. We had water, paper and pen, and a single bag of food. Surprisingly we all returned without injury or even a scare. I'm sure we were tracked by binoculars and perhaps the strings we had attached to the originating point of departure were followed by flashlight in the dead of night. Perhaps I was too young or inexperienced to be afraid. All I know is that twelve of us slept in the woods unprotected and not one animal threatened us. On another occasion, I had the pleasure of camping in Massassauga, a water park of islands and mainland accessible by boat, in Ontario Canada. Oddly, around the time we gathered round the campfire for dinner, we saw canoes making their way across the lake to the mainland. We also saw canoes circling our area and wondered what the curiosity was all about. Later, we set off fireworks because it was Canada Day and although one of our party had to kill a rattlesnake so he wouldn't be bitten, we did have to run the gauntlet at night to the thunderbox, which resulted in abandoning the entire operation all together. I avoided this unpleasantness by peeing in my coffee percolator at night which led to the general malaise displayed by my fellow campers in the morning when I rinsed it out and used it to make coffee. The following morning we were visited by two Park Officials who informed us stupid Canadians that 1) it was illegal to set off fireworks in a Provincial park and 2) it was illegal to kill a rattlesnake. We were permitted grace for two reasons: 1) the island had been overrun by bears (they can swim) and since we were the only ones who had stayed, they had come to see if anyone had been mauled or injured and 2) their boat came loose and one of our party had to dive into the water and save it. Since the fireworks had ostensibly saved us from the bears, and the rattlesnake was a rather large cover for the pound of marijuana someone visiting (unbeknownst to us) had stashed in their tent, we escaped various potentially negative outcomes quite by accident and flogged ourselves in between laughter all the way home. Although the guy who brought the weed was no longer welcome. He talked too much.

I've been skinny dipping twice in my life and both times it was with a group of women. The first time it was with a group of my peers and the second was with a group of relatives and old friends. It was fun both times if you could escape the mosquitoes. My aunt was the last to get in and as we complained, she stopped and posed as the statue of liberty in the moonlight and convulsed us in laughter. I enjoy the gathering of women en mass. Occasionally we make a mass exodus to some shoreline and as we sip beer and wine from paper bags and pass around a toke or two, the gathering gives us some female solidarity by proximity and it makes us happy to be female. Personally, I think anything that makes women happy to be women is a good thing for men in general. Most men give a wide berth to a mass of females but men like being men with the kinds of activities that women pretend to be long suffering widows of (i.e. golf, hockey, hunting, fishing etc).

I've been engaged in a ménage et trios (at the behest of my first husband) one time, which was a bust because he went to sleep so nothing happened and I can say that despite trying to please him, I never succeeded. I've been engaged in a one night stand one time but he was too drunk and just fell asleep so that was a bust too and despite trying, I never succeeded. I never attempted either endeavour again. I'd rather party when I'm not working because usually, I worked so much that I didn't want to stop playing for sex. Sex is a crapshoot. You have to accept that, the odds that you are sleeping with one person only, are pretty slim. From what I have seen, marriage appears to be the safe haven to fuck pretty much whomever you please with impunity. It's one of the most dangerous institutions on the planet and is accompanied by a one hundred percent no win scenario. If you are married in a religious institution, you are nobody if you are female. You are a breeder and have no right to refuse, your own interests, a paycheck or recourse if you are being physically beaten or verbally abused. It's a disgrace to "God" itself. Clearly, we have misinterpreted what the most high requires of us since men get away with murder all the time. If we are faithful, we are whipped by our peers and scorned for keeping our word. No wonder some of us believe that a mere sixty-five years is a good life. It is miniscule. If our earthly records are to be believed, we have the innate capacity to live a thousand years. Do we die of boredom? Do we die because we give up? Do we die because this world is not what we wanted it to be? Why do we age and die? Even trees live longer than we do.

It's difficult to say what my occupation is. There is no place in the banking system to elucidate the number of qualifications you have that you acquire to hold different positions. It's remarkably adolescent. I never put anything anymore because there is no way I can use my qualifications and there is no way to list with any finality what I do for a living. I find it the height of idiocy since it engenders unemployment and costs more money than it saves by skewing data. It's very expensive for the country it operates in, neither is it the bank's business what I do for a living. They are not the police. SOX is (Sarbanes-Oxley, United States 2002). So maybe it is a SOX requirement. It's irrelevant. And a mismatch, but great if you belong to the banking sector and know how to work it. Be aware that SOX is a valid part of the Canadian banking system as we became a country. It is meant for policing large corporations but it is being used to police the individual corporations of persons. Which means it is policing your personal relationships, not their corporate ones. Canada's government regulates differently and this is why we have to go down there and re-negotiate our trade agreements. We might have been unofficially annexed (Trump loves to belittle us but he does it to a number of countries so we are not singled out), however, in order for it to be a "real deal", Mexico would also be annexed which of course is why the border was left as it is when Mr Biden held office. We call for these things and yet, when they're at the door, we shrink from opening it. It's a fine line...and why we will protect our borders and encourage mass immigration...so we aren't annexed. I'm sure someone in office here would love to drill Trump sometimes but we suck it up; just because a leader is unbecoming doesn't mean he is a shitty person or not qualified to do his or her or other job. Ultimately, the only job a Prime Minister or a President has, is to protect the country at all costs. Too bad we can't do that with our marriages. It's likely because a term of office is only four years. That's how long my first marriage lasted. Hmmm.

As to injuries, the only one from an animal is a dog bite that tore a little piece of my mouth open and cut a sublingual nerve. It was a freak accident but it caused me no end of trouble at work. I think they were afraid I was going to sue them or something. What for. What's done is done. Although the fracture in my cheekbone on the same side of my face collectively causes the left side of my face to hang ever so slightly. It caves my eyesocket, makes my top lip lopsided and I have a "rope" on one side of my neck that, on occasion, a shot of Botox will relieve for a time. It's not awful if you're sixty, but it sucks big time if you are in your forties. It makes you look used up before your time and doesn't help if you're trying to get hired. The rest of my injuries, broken fingers and toes, didn't come from working. They were freak accidents too. My digits aren't very big and look sort of delicate sometimes, like my mother's and my sister's. The rest of me is pretty strong so my hips or legs etc don't crack when I'm thrown from horses, quads, motorcycles, skidoos, dog sleds, bicycles and hit by golf balls. The other stuff is just crap; shards of glass pulled from my feet, my leg, my index finger; bits and pieces of my body lopped off by mistake like shaving. The worst one is the herniated disk because it just skews my muscles when I pump iron so I run the risk of cramping from my neck to my hip if I'm not careful. Add that to a slight scoliosis where my bra snaps and you have a perfect storm only cured by running. It puts everything back where it's supposed to be. Pain killers are death for me even though on rare occasions I have to pay the price so I can sleep but I can never eat because they make me vomit. Six of one, half a dozen of the other. Pavement cripples me in sandals unless they are heels because one foot cramps to my knee due to the lack of elasticity of the scar tissue. I wear them to be free of agony, not to be fancy. You cannot anaesthetize yourself from your own life or you will lose the will to live.

It's raining today. I love the rain. Always have. When it's raining hard, people should be making love in front of the fire. I know, it's just pie, but I love the rain. I like walking in it. I like swimming in it too but people always get freaked out that I'll be electrocuted. I don't know why. Is that even possible? Sometimes they stand at the shore with one hand cupped above their eyes and the other on their hip believing I am swimming too far out. I like swimming out instead of sideways because it's easy to turn around and go back. The shore is only one direction. Plus, I like it when my feet don't touch the ground. Thunderstorms are the best because claps of thunder are like God talking to us; like it's throwing us a bone . I got caught on Gambiere Island once with a bunch of little girls. I was a camp counsellor and had a cabin of ten year olds. The torrential downpour accompanied by claps of thunder had sent them straight into my sleeping bag, wrapped around my head, and under our tarp we just held onto each other and didn't let go as we fell back asleep. It was miserable in the morning as we squeezed everything out as best we could but it was still dripping as we trudged back from our out trip with heavy packs through the tall grass, some of us sniffling in spite of ourselves.

I got flowers this month. Somebody gave them to me as a surprise. I love flowers. Women give me flowers sometime. I've given lots of flowers to men but usually their mothers take them. It's weird. I guess men don't like getting flowers. My friend Jennie used to send flowers with the edges dipped in food coloring. She had flair, that one. I try not to give men tools, in case they feel the same way I do if I get a microwave; it's an appliance. I think women tend to buy their men clothes, especially if they're lean on underwear. I don't know why we do this. Sometimes they are relieved, sometimes their mother gets pissed off and starts buying him clothes too and then he hates wearing any of them. It's difficult to know what to give somebody that somebody else won't get upset about. I tried to give my parents stuff but I could never figure out what they wanted. People are strange. Take jewellery for instance. Why do some people wear all their gold at once and some haves heaps of good stuff but they leave it in a box? Why do people ask what you did for your "rock"? My husbands didn't do anything for theirs. We just got married. What does it mean when you have a big rock? I don't know. Why don't women buy men big rocks? Is it because the expectation is that men propose marriage and the woman carries his last name in exchange? I thought that's what it meant. But, that doesn't mean he takes care of her does it? It just means she carries his surname. It's not really a bad deal. It's still a fair game. I don't know why it's so complicated. I guess it's just hard for people to live up to. For people to stick. For people to let their kids find their own way. People can't really help it. They can't help, helping each other. When I look back, I wish my first husband had stuck. We were kind of goofy but we would have developed some moxy. Ah, the milk is spilled. It is what it is. We just choke on the threshold.

I lost my dim sum place in Vancouver in the eighties when it was shot up by a bunch of machine guns. The Four Diamonds. No wonder lol!

FOLLOW ME HOLLOW ME
Amanda May Philp

You follow me around
Like I've got something to give you
You make no sound
You don't even talk to me

You want what I've got
You think I've got something to give you
You make no sound
You won't even walk with me

How long does it take
To pay my favour to you
How much will you take
For making me into two

You want to take me down
Because you think I run around
And I won't settle down
So I pay you to be found

When I'm paid in full

It won't be until

You finally come around

CHAPTER TWENTY SIX

Is there a reason we have deemed masculinity in schools a mental illness before they are even out of the gate? When teachers are not equipped to deal with children as they are, instead of drugging the child out of them, perhaps we should be training them to be teachers of children instead of just teachers. A computer learning program is not going to fix the problem of high jinx. Lord knows I got moved around the classroom often enough but no one ever accused me of having a disorder called Attention Deficit; sounds like the same reason I got the strap across my fingers (which I survived quite well thank you very much). What makes me aghast is that we treat our Canadian kids this way. Now we have more "mental illness" diagnosed in a perfectly healthy generation than you can shake a stick at. Are we drugging Gilles Villeneuve out of existence? You love that something is wrong with your child for some reason. You are using it to allow them to check out of their lives. It is an act of stealing their birthrights and makes you a producer of useless persons. It's sad watching able bodied people turn into a shuffling drooling handicapped nation that is astonishingly unable to work. You're so concerned about body size that you would rather see a person too large to bend over, crouch down, or able to right themselves without assistance if they fall, then to get out of the way. Perhaps we need teachers who actually like kids. If you paid people for their work instead of routing all that drug money through them, you might actually solve one or two problems that we created ourselves. The one thing all those studies that the Trudeau administration undertook, showed us; is that we will not be satisfied with truth and reconciliation ever. It is evident for all to see. Me, I'm good with it. I learned what happened in school. It was part of the curriculum. We were a lot better friends because no one got out for free. Everybody was a shit. It was a great relief because then the possibilities in the world were endless for us because we had learned our lessons. I hope the results of all those studies are there for posterity so we don't have to embark on a self flagellation exercise again.

One day my dad and I were fishing in Parry Sound and a seagull flew overhead and pooped on him. He was so pissed off as the excrement dripped over one of his eyeglasses. So, we fed the gull nine little sunfish and its belly swelled so big it had difficulty achieving lift off to fly away. My dad felt vindicated after that and laughed and laughed. I'm not a huge fisherman although I have cast nets and fishing lines. We fished for smelts when we were little and one of our fishing hooks got caught in her head because her brother was fucking around with the rod instead of the net. I've caught bass, sunfish, pike (Ontario), salmon (Vancouver Island) and marlin (Mazatlan, Mexico). It's pretty exciting until you realize you're not actually in open water and the swell is already too large to spot your little head if you go overboard. It was a real eye opener for me since I couldn't figure out why you would drown in the ocean in a storm if you could float. Fool me. It'd be cool to catch a ride with a dolphin though... I never skydived because I'm not inclined to pitch my body into space and hope for the best. I guess if I had to, I'd just be super annoyed on the way down. I like fish alot but sometimes if there's ink, I swell up so I clean out those veiny things first. Fresh oysters are still the bomb and my favourites are Malapeques from Prince Edward Island but nothing beats fresh crab out of the trap on the west coast of Vancouver Island; Haida Gwai territory. It used to be called the Queen Charlottes but I like Haida Gwai better. It's more in line with what I grew up with and the Haisla nation has always produced some great food, music and art. I'm glad they're getting into larger contracts. My mother and father liked to go fishing in the early morning in Bancroft, Ontario. Honestly though, every time someone handed me a rod at sea, I was ralphing over the side of the boat. It was odd because I didn't feel ill but I was puking anyway.

    I enjoy surfing extremely. If I had started younger, it would have influenced my decisions differently. I'm totally lame at it but have hopes that I can devote some time to it in my eighties. No, seriously, such people exist already they just don't post it in case you object. Personally, I know of an eighty-two year old woman who goes out regularly and a group of Italian men who fuck around with surf boards in their nineties. I caught my first wave when I was eighteen and it was a beauty! Wheeeeeeee! Until I saw my uncle in the water as I shot by him, yelling at me to bail so I wouldn't road rash my body as it flew off the board and hurtled up the beach face first. I finally rode a whole wave standing up when I was fifty and it looked great but it was pretty senior. It was such a drag because some of my spectacular catapults weren't senior at all. Still, while my wilding dreams are of flying through pipe, I know that other more fabulous people than me will pull that one off. Water skiing is great fun if you have the right boat but neoprene will make you bounce like a skipping stone. It happened once when I got caught in the break of a passing ferry and I was wearing my suit from out west. Everybody waved as I skittered along-side them looking fabulously trickster so all was not lost. Slaloming is good. I guess I'm better on the water than snow, more or less.

What is misinformation? Does it mean you are misinformed because of 1) skulduggery 2) bias 3) objection? Or does it mean that something looked like it happened but it didn't really? Or, it happened but not officially and you have to pay for it anyway? I wonder how many charges "against humanity" one lone individual can instigate through ineptitude. Some folks live in a very small world, hanging on to stuff that is long gone; others live in the whole wide world but stay "at home". It really comes down to how afraid you are of your own life and how afraid you are of other people. I don't actually think anyone begrudges anyone anything. I think they fight about stuff that they later want to smack themselves for because when the dust settled, it was all for nothing anyway. Times change. They aren't that different from the time before but they have still changed. I think COVID put everybody on the hook for each other but that was a grave mistake. You can't pay for the same thing over and over again. It doesn't get paid off. And if by some miracle, it does get paid off, then it's yours again isn't it? Because you paid for it; not the most logical way of going about things. With the amount of real money in the world, doesn't that make us look foolish? Fighting for scraps? Everyone who came after me had more than I did, but I still did okay. It made me feel

VERY important, which was a real change from being a one woman perpetual nanny and cleanup crew. And I'm glad it happened because it made me realize that there is more than enough moolah to go around, we just live in some kind of starvation mode as though we weren't entitled to life. It's a real gift to be able to appreciate the weather, the wine, the fire, the nice clothes, the water, the next door neighbour, your sibling from another father. It's the blessing that we believe in the depths of our souls that we want to one day present ourselves to god. The lie is that the individual cannot be trusted to make their own decisions. I will fight to save those I love. I will fight next to realize great ambitions. And, in the end, I will fight to be a completely unique individual. My great ambitions are not yours. You might think they are puny. But they are, in fact, mine; and they are great to me. This is artificial intelligence; as stupid as it gets. As so are you if you follow "the science". You will become a bunch of broke ass people for not taking control of your life. I am a fool because I should have punched out Mr B's lights every time he used drugs to shrink from his life. But I couldn't could I? I could only watch him and Mr G as they slowly slid into death and there wasn't a damn thing I could do about it. Make no mistake gentlemen, whether I take your name or not, I am still married to you in my maiden name and we both lose, not just you or just me, if you think you can do better. I am, still responsible for your decisions apparently, and you are responsible for mine. Don't you wish you had never married in the first place? Me too.

So I have two birth records out there; one in AMANDA and one in PHILIP. The one in PHILIP is skulduggery. The one in AMANDA is the true record. Only I know this for sure because I was there. Some people will never forgive me for being a widow because it means I kept my promise. Others will never forgive me for misunderstanding that I am an information technology original, not a marketing guru. I find this extraordinarily amusing since it is solely because I am a woman. The only ones who never underestimated me was the federal government of my own country which is why I love them to death. They are a great friend to me and I just love watching the development of Canada, just love it. I don't mind being portrayed as a whore because it is a great foil for my lack of personal experience personally; since I've been at work most of my life. I hope Poilievre wins for a term so Trudeau can return and build houses for us. Carney's not a bad guy, he's just doing a walk on because he has the international finance skill sets to assist Canada in pulling it off. We're not stupid up here you know. Not any stupider than you anyway. Poilievre is the right man for the next transition. I have complete faith in him. I suggest you follow the banking system instead of the legalities. It's the only way you're ever going to pay your taxes and have some money left to live on unless you prey upon someone else. Not sure why you can't get your own but I guess someone objects to you as well. Bites doesn't it. That's what you get for getting married. I worked with a woman who spent her life at work and finally decided to get married in her forties so she wouldn't miss out and ended up paying his child support for his previous marriages. Isn't there a law as to how long alimony and child support get paid? Is it worth it? Is it eighteen? Is it twenty-eight? Is it life-long? Why? What is a person supposed to do if they receive benefits? Does that mean they can't work? Why the extolment of the benefit then? I don't know anyone who has a benefit that can work or that can live on it. It doesn't make sense. And are children supposed to stay single so their parents can keep them as their children? That doesn't make sense either. Should I charge my dad's wife taxes because she sleeps with my father? Are you sick? Are your kids sick? Are they charging your paramour to sleep with you? Are they pimps? Do they need money? I thought they had their own house and kids to pay for. That's weird. Does mom charge taxes to the wife of her legitimate son for sleeping with him? No? That's weird too. Who's paying for mom not working then?

    I miss my step kids. I hope they're okay. I would give them anything they needed if I could work. Amazing how many folks are horrified that they are half black, including black folks. Well fuck you too. They're MY step kids, no one else's and I LOVE THEM. Stick that in your pipe and smoke it; along with your prejudices. Pull my hair all you want. They're still my step kids. Nothing you can say, write, misinform or lie about, changes that truth. They are also Canadian which is more than I can say for most of you, so that cake you're so eager to bandy about? Why don't you get on a plane and go to the United States to see your "son" or to England to see your "daughter" and stop bothering me with your petty concerns. I have no time for it. I don't live for myself and I don't live for you. Don't want me to live in a house? Fine! You can pay for my "social service" assistance. Are you truly functioning at level where your brain is still working? Do you even give a shit about your fellow man? Why go to church then? Who on earth can take you seriously? As for those of you who like to kick around your progeny, you have no business bearing more than one child if you're going to behave that way. I think you're revolting and without self restraint, living your life as you please so you can spit on your own leftovers. Grossy grossy...

I want to know why a man can receive a benefit and go to work with his full credentials but you assume if a woman receives a benefit, it comes from a man and you won't give her the job. I've paid for lots of men, so what's your problem? Are you misogynistic? Are you making a poor decision based on your biases with no real evidence? Doesn't make you the best person for the job you're doing does it? You are being obstructive which by Canadian Labour Law is illegal. And you wonder why you get slayed with taxes. You are such an ESG knob lol. I have women to support too but I guess that's wrong for a woman to support another woman or a man. How DO you get up in the morning and find your way to work on time? No wonder most men look like a cat rode them hard and put them away soaking wet. I guess females go for bedraggled when they're camping...in that way, as my ex Canadian boyfriend (lol) said, after eight beers, anyone can be my perfect person. And I can pretend I have no idea who you are if I'm gone by morning, because you have a job that supports your one legitimate son. It's a mighty small world. And why is health care not paid for by the international businesses operating out of Canada? That's the law isn't it? So, if EMS is legitimate, why is AMP illegitimate? Didn't think I knew that did you? Like I said, you are remarkably out of touch with your level of engagement in the world.

I'm pretty sure someone was supposed to get a house for something. But there are no houses! What is the world coming to? We don't have the ability to provide housing for everyone in the world who fits into the state of Texas. That is the greatest joke of all. On us. At the end of the day, a bank can take your house and lock the door but a person with furniture sleeping in the street gets picked up by a police officer and taken to a shelter. Someone has to pay to get that stuff to the dump and someone has to pay to support the social service housing and feeding that individual. You can bill that person all you want but there's no money so you get to pay it yourself. If I have no house but I have a tent, I still need an address. Then you remodel lol lol lol.

I wish I could tell younger people to not be afraid and to do all they want to do and that any time they get that gut feeling that something isn't on the up and up, to listen to it. It's the only truth. I wish I could tell them that they could party til they puked but they can't. They might puke but they do have to keep their wits about them. Even high or drunk, I knew better. So, everyone gets a certain amount of grace but don't put yourself in a position against your better judgement. Your better judgement is located in the frontal cortex of your frontal lobe. It is historically whence the third eye sprang but it is, in fact, where your better judgement resides. It's connected to your gut, the solar plexus and to the base link in your spinal cord before it becomes a tail. There is a large nerve called vagas that runs along and around it. It's the greatest internal healer, in my opinion, and listening to your gut and better judgement seems to be very calming internally. Okay, enough fru-fru stuff, you can unroll your eyes now. It works for me. Loss is never the end of the adventure.

After COVID, I went through a period when "people" would ask for money for the bus or admire my coat and ask what I did for such nice coat since I had a pretty nice coat. At first, I felt oddly ashamed until I realized that it was threadbare and about twelve years old but I liked how it fit so I had it because I had kept it. I was telling another woman about this and she laughed and bade me next time to say I had done everything they were thinking and more. I did. I don't have that coat anymore. I bought a new one.

I think my parents were originally christened Catholic but, I could be wrong. I do have to say, my parents weren't religious snobs. They mixed with people of all faiths. It's a good thing too, because by the time we get here, we appear to be on the hook to a bunch of different religions. Does religion run the government? No. They try but every time they do, alot of people die for no reason and the rest of the people wander around in rags. It's fascinating to me that with the opulence we are surrounded by, we seek to eradicate the sheer volume of material wealth imparted to us by our surroundings by doling out a modicum of thinly veiled contempt disguised as permission to live. We, the people seem to be the only ones doing it, deciding which of "god's" creation is allowed. If I spend my life scraping the floor with my forehead in abject obeisance for the pleasure of drawing a breath, what exactly is my reason, use or aspiration for being here? Even Moses had to work. And if you feel it's your right to beat me or take my life on behalf of some divine decree, you obviously have no faith in God's power to take care of those abhorrent things itself. Booyah!

I'm confused as to what a sustainable resource is. Paper straws dissolve before you can finish your drink. Is paper sustainable? I notice there is more plastic in our clothing now. Does plastic breathe? I thought plastic wasn't sustainable. Am I wrong?

I wonder what it's like when you live long enough that you no longer have immediate relatives. That would be weird, especially if you outlived your friends too. Would people look askance at you for being much older and in good shape? Or does your freedom get taken from you if you live long enough?

So I have a few observations about clothes. I don't like looking like a bag lady in the name of being real and since I wear clothes, I have a few things to say about them:
1) I have no hips so would folks stop freaking out about the fact that I tend to French Canadian and Asian Canadian designers please. I can't help it. They just aren't there. It's not a dis, I just like them to fit. I'm not starving. I'm just built that way.

2) I have boobs, which for some odd reason, don't fit into clothing that fit my shoulders and are slightly too large at the waist because it always gaps at the girls. Why is this? I don't have a tiny waist a la a Vaya Con Dios body. A-line is so awkward.
3) Pardon me if French bras fit me better than English ones. It's the cut. Don't know what to tell you.
4) And why are brassieres only made for women with no girls? What is the point? They don't like wearing them anyway. It's us women who don't have enough hands to hold the girls and a million other things when we're running for the bus or whatever. Ever had a boob get in the way? It's irksome. And either way, they're going to stick out. Get over it. They're boobs. My mom and my aunts had nice racks. Got them from my grandmother, but my mom's weren't epic. She had hips like my sister.
5) I think all bras should have a clasp in the front, not hooks and eyes in the back. It's not secure, sexy, accessible or practical. The hook and eye row in the back is old fashioned and not attractive anymore.
6) All this elastic in the denim is so not cool. They don't hug your body anymore, they just slide down it, even if you have hips.
7) I'd like there to be more thick wool socks for women. I'd like them to be in a size five and a half please. Same with steel toed work boots... and gloves so I don't feel like Edward Scissorhands.
8) Wide legs look good on long skinny people. That's it. The rest of us just look like we're getting ready for lift off. They get caught in doorways too, like floaty sleeves.
9) What's with the puffy sleeves? I mean where did that come from? They're pretty but I always get sauce on them.
10) Clothes are fun when they don't get in the way. I think high fashion is silly, have reverence for haute couture and love an occasion to clean up as long as I don't have to wear long white gloves and a garter. I prefer my jeans and two piece suits.

Dresses are fun, kind of impractical but good to run in. I love heels! I love my boots and my beach footwear. I love the beach but I'm not a bunny I'm a water baby. Oh wait, this was about clothes.

11) I like hats alot but I'm afraid if I wear them all the time, I'll go bald on top if my crown doesn't breathe. Total mifwat (my version of my mother's word for piffle) but I can't help it.

12) Why do four inch strappy heels exist? Everybody's toes slide too far and poke through them overlapping the front like a floppy seal. Don't their feet swell or does everybody take B12 shots in the morning?

13) Yoga pants for work? Are you trying to get laid? (Excludes gyms of course).

I don't like going into, buying tickets for, or having memberships to; places that require a scan from your phone to open a gate. It's scary. I don't feel safe. I feel trapped. What if something malfunctions? What if is there is a fire? Do I need permission to leave? What if I can't get out? It's very uncomfortable. Open air venues are more attractive all the time. What if my phone dies and no one has a matching cord? It's inconvenient for practical living.I don't like putting my hair up. It gets greasy and I look like a washer woman, not elegant in the slightest. Why do women cut their hair very short if they're not bald? Just curious. Why do men cut their hair short? I like it longer unless it's gone, which I don't have a problem with. Is it a hunter military thing? Do men like cologne? Almost every man I knew wore cologne until Covid happened.

A long time ago, when my youngest stepson was in grade two or three, we got a call from the school. Apparently he, and some other boys were playing at recess and called his friend Waleya, Bin Laden. When they were hauled into the office and questioned, he openly admitted it because, in her winter hood, she looked like pictures they'd seen on TV. I don't think she was offended, but I think they were too young to know, one way or the other. Anyways it was altogether horrifying and my second husband and I hied it over to Waleya's house to give them our abject apologies. Of course, when her father opened the door, he didn't know whether to laugh or not. The boy was expelled and not sure why, because Waleya was home so off they went to play together, and the spectre of this black and white couple left us all a little at loss for words. To make it worse, I think they were Muslim because they served us juice in these beautiful goblets. Then her mother couldn't help it and gave me what for, for not educating my child. I privately thought this was too much to be expected for a stepmother to sit through this. I already got into trouble every time I opened my mouth with the kids when anyone was around. Like I said, it was kind of horrifying, especially as we weren't sure what was going on and didn't want to involve the kids in cultural politics because we didn't want them to develop biases. Parenting is tricky. Mostly when the sports parents get together, they just drink beer so we get along with each other. In retrospect it's kind of funny; adventures in step parenting. Oh god, that little guy got expelled all the time; for throwing rocks at a lawn mower someone was cutting the lawn with at the time (I think it was the school Principal's husband), for clothes-lining some kid who was physically bullying his friend. One time, he went down to the public school because a couple of kids he babysat were being bullied, so he showed up and asked them who it was. As they cowered and he walked away, he could hear one of the kids whisper "that's the Babysitter!" He was the rock star because he was at level 95 in War Craft and everybody wanted to know what it was like.

Kids are so adept at so many things because they haven't learned to doubt themselves yet.

So Carney was sneaky after all, right out of the Northwest Territories. I notice Pierre really bolstered the popularity of his party though. I guess it would have been too much power for Alberta. Funny how the NDP took the big hit – I guess after the Covid years, no one wants to be the little guy anymore. Does anyone find it strange that both parties are red now? Not blue and red? I wonder why.

I have other heroes; Roberta Bondar and Ronda Rousey. If you ever had a doubt as to the general capability of women, take a long hard look at my well educated, physically strong, mentally tough and trail blazing fellow Canadian sister who went into outer space. She's the reason I survive. I knew about her a long time ago. I don't know her. I love her to death. I aspire because of women like her and in Canada, she is my greatest hero of all. I notice no one dares to take a pot shot at her. Ronda Rousey, however, is my border sister and she takes pot shots all the time because she is realistic and is also of the same ilk. My favourite interview was when she was challenged for her salary as if she was taking food off of other women's tables and I'm glad she smirked. She said she wasn't paid because someone was doing a favour for the ladies, she was paid based on the money she made for her WWF organization. Get a clue. I fist pumped her for telling the truth. Right on sister! You don't like us to be small or pretty and tough at the same time? Go fuck yourself. You're all so angry because you think you didn't get what you were supposed to. Ever heard of Pamela Anderson? I'd take a bullet for her. You think Cher is an icon? Pamela is the rock star of all rock stars. We Canadian women have guts and are not afraid of any of you. Why should we be? We are Canadian. If we can survive here, we can survive anywhere. And just so you know – I Got You Babe (*Sonny and Cher*) was our song; my first now dead husband. I have to ask the die hard marrieds a question. Do you have to die to keep your promise? Because I'm not dying for anybody who risks my life. Do I need to get my birth chart number tattooed on my arm like a concentration camp survivor to prove I exist? My name is Amanda May Philp. My mother's name was Wendy May Davidson and my father's name is Peter Ratcliffe Philp. I am their legitimate daughter; the only legitimate. Do I care if you think I'm not entitled to live? No. No I don't. Do I care if you think I will kill people if I go by my name? Not particularly. I'm not that interested in death. Both my mother and my father were also firstborns and legitimate. I guess we all followed the rules until we didn't. Don't know if I got rooked because I was a female. I don't care. A man is worth the same as I am. I fail to comprehend why you debate why we should be so grateful to each other for the interaction. If you treat me like you are more than me, I recognize that you have a confidence problem and I help you with that because I feel sorry for you. The videos of the Only Fans girls in that studio while the gentlemen who always looks like he was up all night doing coke, sits behind the microphone and challenges them, are what make the world go round. I like the Only Fans girls. Nobody is touching them but you pay to look at them and they boldly prey on your weakness. The woman who claims that when they marry, they are property, is clearly not in control of her own life. By that premise, the Only Fans girls have it all over you because they are business women and you are merely property. These are not the true teachings of any faith. It is the result of Adam just acting like a pig. The world is so angry about this. It's because you believe you own your children and you are wrong. It's what kills you in the end. Tina Turner's son committed suicide. Why? Because she decided to retire? Because he didn't have a job? Because she didn't leave him any money? You people are so useless because you fight over these things; the broken down buildings, the tiny patch of land, the human flesh that functions independently of you; things you have no discernible right to fight over. You're gross. And you never win. Ever. I don't know why you persist in such mentally and emotionally unstable behaviour. Just pick one and get on with it. You are fifty-fifty. You are only ever going to be fifty-fifty. If you are too good for that, then do it by yourself and spend money gawking at strange pussy. I don't know what to tell you.

I do think women are not too precious for conscription. If you think you aren't built for that or for building and caring for infrastructure, then you are a selfish little princess and I have zero respect for you. Don't ever get on an interview with me and expect me to even take you seriously. You hit the gym for a bikini, you hit the gym to build infrastructure. I am five foot four and I weigh one hundred and thirty pounds and I haul concrete in excess of fifty pounds at sixty years of age and do my nails when I get home. Anybody can do it. Get over yourselves already. If you want more than one man or woman, no one will take you seriously. If you think you are running a legal company and do the Trump thing, no one will take you seriously. If you decide to have six kids and only work at home, no one will take you seriously. No one gets to do whatever they want. Your dreams are supported by you, not by others. It's your responsibility. If you have a child with a man you are married to and he abandons you, divorce him and bill him for half of your child's expenses when you do your taxes. The country of birth will make him pay extra for having to process the claim. It's not rocket science. Do you know how many women I've seen in food banks because their children were taken away by Children's Aid because they couldn't provide appropriately? Dad's not a problem. He has a job. It's her fault. Why the birth father's wages aren't garnisheed the moment this occurs is why I don't respect you. When you value a woman's contribution as much as a man's, you'll get over it. If I was paid the same to clean houses (which, by the way, is the one thing men hate more than anything so it should be paid the same) as I was to be a neurologist, I'd still pick music. If I have a man who wants me until he wants somebody else, I dump him. Why should I trap him if he doesn't want me anymore, he wants somebody else? I'm not a whore, he is. Or maybe he is a business man. If he doesn't want to stick around, then what's the problem? I'm not a Nazi. Or a dictator. But he still has to pay half for his child and so do I. You are a moron if you believe otherwise. You are also a moron if you believe that if you have enough babies, you can stay at home. You are a drain on society and should take a leaf out of Ivana Trump's book. She was stronger than her husband apparently. He's still looking for validation. I see pregnant moms at school, on the bus, running meetings all the time. Don't be weak and weably. It's so unbecoming for you to pretend you have a raw deal. You have the same opportunities as anybody else. I could bang a drum for not being able to have children and not having a name until the cows come home but then I would be useless. I have the same opportunities as anyone else and I'm proud of my life. It's been wonderful. And it will continue to be so. You're insistence on your never ending protocols are too expensive for me. I just live. If you gazed without the rose colour glasses upon the men who run the "infrastructure", you would get a clue and recognize that most of them are obese, have prostate cancer, drink too much because they are lonesome and have a tendency to abuse women because they can't get what they want. Some of them are incompetent at their jobs but get to keep them because they are men and some of them are truly brilliant and have to fight for work. They are no different than you and I. Stop objecting to respect. It looks bad on you. Pregnant women are no more vulnerable than a big strong man. Stop pretending you are. You just have a different set of biases to overcome than they do. Everybody needs a job. Everybody needs to show up for work every day and on time. Don't know what to tell you. School was the same. So was church. What's your problem?

I do not object to education but you do have to realize that advanced education is a business with its own protocols. You have to be "permitted" and it does not hinge on whether you are right or brilliant. It hinges upon whether you are willing to go into debt to the tune of at least a million dollars so you have no intrinsic value to be sued for in case you make a mistake by a) not following the protocols of the genre you owe money to, or b) you actually did learn something and applied it in such a way that it actually has value and so it can be stolen by the institution who claims your work belongs to them. I hope Gates didn't have to pay for his education, because if he did, then his alma mater owns the entire personal computer industry. He's a pig too, objecting to the woman who bore his children. What a piece of shit. My father would never do that. And just so you know? He couldn't do math but he's brilliant at languages. My mother was an honour student because she shone at chemistry. They spit on her because she had five children instead. If she'd gotten a job, she would have been subjected to more scorn for being a "bad" mother. It's pitiful how frightened you become because I know you. One little bottle of perfume. So scary. So the object of scorn and revulsion. So duly legitimate. How bloody unfortunate. Pride and Prejudice move over. Stop feeling sorry for yourselves. Every he-man with bulging muscles on YouTube, who fancies himself the saviour of beleaguered men, is doing it for the men who feel sorry for themselves. Try watching the old Italian guys who can lift their own body weight and go surfing in their eighties and nineties and tell me what your problem is. And you want to kill your wife because you believe she is part of your "business". She's not a fucking whore you lowlife. She consented to be your wife. You are her husband. That's it. You are the family. Your kids are not your family. They're your kids. You are incredibly out of touch with your level of engagement in the world and so weak I can't possibly bring myself to muster the strength to be afraid of you.

So why am I finally going to get my name? Because I was married to a legitimate Canadian man who I divorced because he was going to kill me and came back to bury because I actually loved him and meant it. I've waited forty years and no, I'm not taking any money out of his birth chart, blood line, family name. I'm not like that. It belongs to him, not me. But my name? That is mine. And it will cost nothing to finally have it. No one is kind to orphans and widows unless they have no choice. I've lived it. And yes, I'm small but I can defend myself. I don't need an overbearing not sure who he is, bouncing around on the internet threatening everybody, man to protect me from myself, you, or anybody else. If a wild animal looks out for me, I certainly don't need the hassle. I am the caretaker of my second husband's children but they were taken from me by their real mother and rightly so. They are over the age of twenty-eight now and someday I might have the honour and privilege of seeing them again. If I could help or contribute to their lives in any way I would. But I will never be asked and I will never see them marry or have babies or sit in an audience applauding their performances. But I got to be a working mother and that was the very best part of my life. It was fantastic. And they were awesome. You lose your kids to their birthrights – their god given lives. If you believe you know better than your God, again, you are remarkably out of touch with your level of engagement in the world. My blood family are still my blood even if they married three times and had fourteen children a la Monsieur Musk. It's not rocket science. I don't even need to go to kindergarten (German word we use in Canada for the entry level children to the educational system; in Canada, kids with no names get education too. Canada is pretty bold under all that marmee-like exterior). The only reason I didn't punch the dragon in the face for pulling my hair is because I am stronger than he is and I could have really hurt him. He doesn't think so because he lifted me with one arm once but it's true. Even a bottle of perfume has to pay for damages. And don't think he wouldn't have come after me for them because of his illegitimate son. See? Weakness. I love Canada. They have my birth record. They are fucking brutal and man oh man didn't I survive a great and scary and excitingly marvellous life. Another country might have killed me or sold me but not my country. I am a number, a number, and a legal company name and lawful name which I have kindly lent to those who can't keep their promises or did but then were so shitty to each other, they bailed. Marriage sucks. I'm not paying for it. I'm not paying for you to object either. If you're over eighteen and you object, pfft, get a real penis and vagina and stop being a pussy because you and your wife can't work together to secure some kind of permanent lodging for yourselves. This is really not my problem. Frankly, neither is it your father's. Or your mother's. You are married now. Or you are spawning illegitimate children. It's really not my concern.

Now, my concern is what my mother's line is. Well, let's take a look at that. If she was married to my father and kindly accepted his last name, and so, their children's bodies were identified by his last name, then she ran his family. I guess our secondary names are what distinguish whose child it is. And then everyone sneers that you were adopted. Can you even imagine how ridiculous that is? They are going to have their own children and work for themselves. That's what they are supposed to do. Pension plans are the purview of our governments. They do business with each other so they can invest in each individual over a lifetime so when they are very old, they do not have to be imprisoned in institutions because you are unhappy with your life. They pay taxes back to the government for this and they provide jobs to your young people for assistance in house or yard keeping etc etc. You don't see the value in this and you want their stuff? Well I'm getting my CPP anyways. I have to protect myself from you in case you're jealous and you want my stuff but I'm not dead yet. You don't like the government intervention? From yourselves? Pardon me while I roll around for awhile while I LMAO.

You're pissed off because you work all hours for a little bit of money and never have any free time? What in the actual fuck is free time? It's all free. It's just a matter of what you do with it. The world has been making something out of "nothing" since it began. You have the breath of life. What do you want to do with it? If you insist on playing with other people's toys instead of getting your own, you're going to war for being weak. Truthfully, it doesn't matter which line I work for since my name gives me the ability to work for both sides of my family since my father was the birth father of my illegitimate brother, which is why I have no name but he does. Everyone believes I am stupid but believe you me, when I apply for a job in my name, I am working for everyone. I think physical fidelity is a small thing to request in return or else why would I ever bother to get married? I could just fuck anyone I feel like "on the linoleum" (*Bridges of Madison County*) and get it over with. And since I see you all do it all the time with impunity, I kind of resent your criticism since I'll get quasi-married a hundred more times if I need to in order to live in a sheltered structure called a house that everyone will fight over since I don't deserve it because I haven't whored myself out enough yet for you to mind your own business.

Now, as to birth record names, please get it straight that the reason a person has a robust birth record name is because they need the help because they weren't born first or they were born out of wedlock. They're just "white trash" so to speak, if you want to be that way. I have no problem with it. I've married twice, once to a legit drug addict and after he died, I asked permission to marry again by license since I was still so young and so once to respectable black "white trash" and both marriages were fun and brutally heartbreaking while I watched them both crack up under the pressure of the abject scorn of their mothers. That's why the dragon's penis is so small. It's in his mother's mouth still because she won't let anyone hug her except him. She really really needs a boyfriend because he just fucks everybody all the time for making him into a pussy. He hates women. I don't blame him one bit. It's too bad; his demise will be architected by his firstborn son without so much as a blink of his poncy little eyelid when the time comes. He should have left the province but he's under the impression that his married children will return one day to claim the toys in their rooms. God! No wonder you end up getting put down like a dog.

If men and women believe that traditional women work is monetarily worth less than men, then men will always have to be the ones to do the dirty jobs and that is to their detriment. If you agreed that they are intrinsically worth the same, you would give a shit. It will never be solved until you do. Every time we go to war, women work and get paid and men die. And you always do this in the name of protection but everybody is dying. It's really funny if you are stoned and it's really tear jerking if you are drunk.

Ever had your pussy waxed? I have new respect for strippers. I can take pain until I puke or pass out and I can't wax my hooey. I can shave it, do electrolysis, laser but wax? I'd rather be set on fire (and since I have been and know what it feels like, I can say so). Why eradicate the pubes? They are there to protect the entry to the vagina from bacteria. They were put there by the divine as a natural protective barrier. There are all kinds of religious rules about the pubic hair of a female. What's the deal with a hairy dick? Don't you have any respect or pride? At least trim the puppy. If you could refrain from shaving it all off so you don't look like a new age porn star that would be helpful. And why are the only chosen people of God a Matriarchy? All Jewish lineage passes through the woman. Where are they? They appear to be the most important ones in the scriptures and yet the lineages follow the woman not the man. I enjoy this polarity immensely. Is that why the Sadducees and the Pharisees killed "the King of the Jews"? I've dated three Jewish men. They are alot of fun for about five minutes, and then they are offended; by themselves or by me, I'm not sure. I think it is because I recognize Hebrew. An Israeli fighter pilot who replaced the laundry room door in my apartment confirmed that. Actually, I had picked up some Farsi out of Palestine so I wasn't sure. Greek men have always been the most fun because they fool around with anybody and then we go dancing or for dinner and they never get offended. They enjoy it all immensely. I'd never marry one though.

All Greek men fool around if you listen to their wives. Is that true? I don't know.

I mean, how much money do you have to make to make amends for your decisions that are objected to? Should I just marry a third time and then divorce so I can finally do what I want? So I can finally put all twenty-eight of my credentials in one company name and dance on the big stage? Then I wouldn't have to pay back my life to everyone who apparently suffered so much because I was in it...

If you didn't get so uppity because you are too fucked up to be happy, I'd like you more. What is the point of being married? Can even one person out there in the whole wide world show and tell to convince me because I have been discriminated against because frankly, I don't want to. Why should I? Who keeps charging me nine thousand dollars for being single and saving your ass? I'll do it again, make no mistake, but I'll do it as a single woman and not apologize for it. Like I said, everybody hates me when I'm married. Everybody. So.

I will never ever do it again.

Sue me.

I dare you.

As for tipping, I tip waitresses and bartenders and delivery drivers. I tip in cash. It's none of your business and I ferociously resent the establishment that is policing this. You disgust me in the extreme. I don't tip fast food establishments. I don't tip kitchen staff. And it's none of your business. You are particularly disgusting if you are making money or charging taxes on tipping. Corporations who position themselves as giving back to the community but end up running it because in the end, it only goes back to the corporation are ESG impostors, and you are the very tip of the pimple that needs to be popped. I was never guilted into tipping until corporations got involved. It's the companies that are behind this and you disgust me for your lies and your posturing. Fuck you and fuck you too. In fact, if I ever become an online person, I will publish regularly the companies that are stealing from us under the guise of "tipping" a service. I don't need your "service" as badly as all that. And if you need a "card" to decide if my purchases are acceptable, then you need me more than I need you, plain and simple.

Yes, now I am just white trash like you. That's about as angry as I get.

In the dead of winter in North Bay Ontario, my girlfriend used to pick me up on her skidoo and we would race across the lake with our helmets and goggles on, in the dark, to our next gig. I always got frostbite on my face even with the balaclava. I had a pool cue with a hot pink butt made out of maple that I would strap on my back. My girlfriend was the captain of the team and we were in a pool league. It was always an adventure because we would drive for ages and then out of nowhere, a structure would appear and I'd think "you gotta be kidding" but no, there was a pool table and a diner right there in the forest. I used to laugh because it was the first time I was aware that I could disappear and no one would be able to find me. I had a raucous time in North Bay; worked really hard, played really hard. It was just a blast. I got out of the car one day in front of the train station in Cochrane and everyone in the street stopped and turned to look. I was working on scripting for a local telephone company. They had a rather large structure that was around farm land it sort of appeared out of nowhere too. Anyway, when the rest of the girls showed up, it was quite wonderful; sort of an oasis because we just got to shoot and hang together. We only drank hard a couple of times for celebratory reasons. I still remember them. I felt so much like a fish out of water at first, but I loved to play because there was a Blues bar down the road from a restaurant I worked split shifts for in Vancouver, and I used to play there with the guys from the Drum Shop who were also on splits. I would win loonies. At night, I would go there sometimes to catch a great blues band and sit at the bar unhassled because the bartender would watch out for me. It was next to the Cecil but I never had any trouble. They were really sweet. And the ladies I played with were too.I used to frequent a place in Toronto for the same reason and once, Jeff Healey was like, two feet away from me and I just lost my breath and couldn't speak, like a gomer.I met James Cotton there. The Black Swan on the Danforth was good too. My aunt and I used to dance at Dakota's when they had good blues. I went to the Fallsview Casino with another girlfriend and we watched Smokey Robinson. When he first emerged with his orange suit and ruffled shirt, we shot each other a glance and thought ooh, he's old poor thing. Then he started the show and we were so floored we couldn't look at each other. He was phenomenal and we just shrank. He could stand on the edge of the stage and took requests and of the hundreds of songs he wrote, he would go down memory lane with us and we were just shocked at his acuity. The man sang like a bird. Once he got rid of the suit, he was still hot as hell. That was priceless. The casino wouldn't let us drink the table wine or something because we were too old and they brought something more drinkable. I think my girlfriend was more upset than I was. Casinos make me drowsy and I just fall asleep. One time, my aunt and I got caught sneaking Piccolos into the auditorium at the Hummingbird when we went to see the Moody Blues. High jinks are harmless if you remember who you are. High jinks when you're young, high jinks when you're old. High jinks are the spice of life. That's why we still have the Legion.

In Newfoundland, you will find an astonishing array of homes that possess a front door high up, with no stairs. Everyone uses the back door. They call the front door the mother-in-law door. They generally don't consider a view of the ocean priceless since so many used to or do, make their living there, so most bay windows face land. If they like you, you are accepted by being "screeched" in. Screech is a dismayingly potent brew that is offered and consumed in small quantities with respect. They wash their walls in the spring and the fall. They love their quads and their cabins. They don't like leaving the island but since they can take a ferry to an island off the coast that is owned by France, it's not really an island, but it does take longer to drive across than it does Ontario. They are brisk and will give you shit while they help you and take you in. It means they love you. You will just adore them.

Why are we still talking about getting back to normal? People drank too much during the pandemic? Where? Apparently (yes again with that word), the road is full of drunken road warriors. Mothers are still furious. I've never seen a drunk driver. I know they exist. They must, since we're still chasing the roaring twenties attempting to eradicate booze. It's never going to happen. I used to drink. It was fun. Sometimes I still do. It's still fun. Stop shitting on my parade. Stop taking that tone with me. There is so much I'm supposed to have awareness of, I can hardly come down to earth. And I'm mentally ill. Me. Extraordinary!

I'm not positive but I think Natalie Seymore is attached to my name. This is not my name and it wasn't at the time. It is an extraction from a co-ownership that is run by someone who never made themselves known to me (frankly, I think it was the guy that died but I don't have the paperwork). It makes professional people ask me what I do for a living. If you hadn't sued me for the property, I wouldn't have had to apply for survivorship. All of you, who had somewhere to live and knew he left it to me because we weren't going to be able to work for awhile. At the very least I had the decency to do a formal separation before I moved forward. A gold digger indeed. How's that working for you? His mother was German and did military service in Greece. And I eat cake. My grandmother did military service in England and in Canada. Is that cake? It might still come out that she was actually born in France unless you are too dishonest to say so. While those of you who are actually married threatened me. Who in the actual fuck do you think you are? Your given names are on the birth certificates of your children. You need more? I was the caretaker. I didn't have the choice and he knew it. You Canadian men who marry women from another country and bail as soon as they have children and pretend that they are spending YOUR money are just pathetic. You Canadians who go to another country and have children with men from yet a different country and expect someone from Canada to pay into your family line are simply the most astonishing members of society I can imagine. You have firstborns here changing the sex of their natural bodies because of your arrogance and insistence. The fucking Queen of fucking England never did anything like that. Who in the actual fuck do you think you are? You should be so lucky. I hope I never have to sit down to dinner with you, because I wouldn't deign to dine with the likes of you. Have a modicum of integrity and stop insisting that everyone support your precious son. Don't even look at me. I hope it was worth just about killing your husband. Sheesh! You went into someone else's family and ate them alive. Wow. I hope your son marries a Muslim from Romania so he can be friends with Andrew Tate's son. It would serve you right. Cause that baby boy is going to do what he wants not what you want, and to think that you have anything at all to say about is truly the depth of depravity. No wonder you don't have any money and fuck each other on the linoleum. Pfft! I guess if you have enough illegitimate children in a country, you earn the right to marry a resident for real. They're just your girlfriend. Don't kid yourself, and insult me to my face because I did it correctly and with integrity. Most people do, until you decide you've changed your mind. Don't you just hate yourself now.

Young people! Your first choice is the one. You always know. The choice belongs to you and you alone. Don't let anyone tell you that you cannot have something. My mother was always my mother and my father is always my father. My aunts and uncles, by their birth certificates and given names, are still my aunts and uncles. This weird "association" thing you do to deem a partner acceptable is association with yourselves, not them. I tell my story because I am at the end of my rope with all of you. This is what happened to me and how I felt at being sneered at for being just as I came out of my mother; a combination of her and my father and some of those who came before them. I was always a musician, always. It doesn't change with the demands you put upon me. You can't socialize anymore with each other because you don't even know who you are related to anymore. You don't know who you're supposed to love because what you love is unacceptable to those you love already. It's not love folks. It's control. If you grumble and think celebrities are spoiled, it's because you don't work as hard as they do. Those aren't their houses or their planes. They are necessities of the workplace. They live in trailers for chrissake. Musk sleeps under a desk sometimes. What is there to be jealous of? You want to get deported with your head shaved and live in a pit? You want to loaf about the palace or the ranch and wonder why it disappears after twenty years? I mean, it can always get worse. The caretaker is going to change one day without you. It's a fact of life.

You do not get to claim alimony for the rest of your life. You get it if the baby is an infant, then you get half the child's expenses. You have to support the kid's options. It's your job. They need to leave and you need to show them how or you are a moron. It's not your job to do anything else. The other stuff is just gravy for the job. And I am a daughter who loves her mother and father equally. It's not the same as my husband. My husband is the one I go through my life beside or with, but I'm not one of his ribs. I love my husband with unwavering loyalty. You still have to get a job. You still have to both pay for gas. Be logical.

Luxembourg City is very green and lush and has seven bridges in it. It is magical. I was there. It's the most beautiful place I've ever seen.

Sometimes I feel like Big. I mean what do you want from me? (*John James Preston, Sex and the City*)

And I guess my other questions are:

Would you forgive me if one day I just didn't sleep with anybody? I'm tired of being on the run. I don't want to be on the hook for sex if I socialize or work or go outside, or pay taxes for some obscure fine. There are hundreds of statutes to overcome. You have too many rules. People mess about when there are too many rules.

Would you forgive me if I had friends? What if my family is busy?

Would you forgive me for keeping the promises I have to keep?

Would you forgive me if I just kept living?

And here are my four caveats:

I don't believe anyone is truly a pig. I would just like you to stop expecting me to live by your rules. And I'd appreciate it if you would not treat me that way either.

Anyone can be white trash if you speak and behave a certain way. Now you know what that looks like. It's gross isn't it.

I think at a certain point you have to go live your life and understand that what you believe is forever is impossible. The time will change and you will have to change with it or die.

I am entitled to my life the same as you. Those people in the oval office? They are living the same life as you. It is no easier for them than it is for you. Now you can stand down a little because everyone has childcare issues. Everyone.

Older people have money in case something happens to them. They tend to travel to support you and that's because people get snarky. They do want to be home and cater to you but they can't, or they can only be there sometimes. They are many things to many people. They are not bipolar or schizophrenic or assholes; they are exactly the same as they were as when they were born. Their lives didn't start with just you. You cannot be all things to all people. They can't either.

Did I do something wrong? I'm always afraid I'm going to get into trouble. Do you ever feel this way? I wish you wouldn't. It's nice to see people happy and hopeful. I like all kinds of people. I just wish I could celebrate more instead of atone. I wish there weren't so many causes and generational issues that regurgitate themselves as though they occurred yesterday. Sometimes you just have to get a job and move out. And be happy and let your current people be happy. Sometimes you're going to have a good thing and then someone shows up and needs a place to stay. Getting hoity is just not going to work. Grit your teeth or grin and bear it.

So that's who I am eh? Well, well, well. I had no idea. No wonder my mom was pissed off. I wonder what I was supposed to do. Marry a? That's very funny actually. No wonder Seaspan wouldn't hire me lol.

Anyway, I just wanted to introduce myself and apologize. I hope I didn't hurt anybody. I didn't mean to come across like a business woman but I did do government work and I loved it so much, I didn't really want to compromise anyone because I did a lot of paperwork, a lot of intermediate writing; business cases, technical specifications, requests for proposals and so forth. I don't really know what happened and the truth is, I was just living my life and didn't read the paperwork because I wasn't working. I'm so disappointed to find out that even in my private life I am working. I didn't know that. It's kind of lonely. I wish I didn't know that. I don't really know if that means I was married a third time but I'm sure it doesn't because I was only formally separated and to be married when you're already married is bigamy. Did I go down as a widow? I'll never know. I remember driving around New York City with a military man who took us on a tour. It was a really great day. It was sad though. Really sad. I was scared when he died. And devastated. And furious. And I didn't know who Philip was and why it was on my records. I didn't know why BROWN was on my birth certificate either but I didn't know what to do about it. In the end, it was horrible. Maybe I should have stayed in school lol. Nonetheless, I still need to make sure that anybody I have a responsibility for, has recourse because I've still got it even if you think I look like a school teacher. No wonder Musk thinks it will be kind of a relief when he croaks. Look, you do what you think is best, but for now, I'm helping someone and I have to live and work and I need you to not object to the fact that I am breathing. If you need the money, then take it. I write for you. I write for the story of what happens in a life; in anyone's life. Is this why people set up foundations? I'd just rather pay my taxes and be able to work and live somewhere. I have traditions but they're just my own for personal reasons, I don't need them to be honoured by you. I try and find out what you like but if that changes I'm not offended. I like to pay my share and give you things sometimes, not to make up for anything, it's just because I thought you might like it. I might live longer than you. I can't estate law because I might live longer than you. Who knows who my descendants will be? I can't force you to wait around or sit on your backside in a jurisdiction. It's selfish. I can't help it if I can't sleep around. I get sick. Don't make me into a goody two shoes for it. I've slept on lots of couches so I can do music. Lots. With friends upstairs or downstairs. It's what I do. It's why I have so many friends. I've actually slept with like, two of them. Life is hard until it isn't. Sometimes I'm the only one there so I just clean it up and go home. It's not as exciting as it looks if that's not your jam because my life looks fancy but really, I'm just this Canadian girl who would rather do that. I've seen lots of things. I like to write songs about them. I received second career education from the Government of Canada for free in my forties, and I failed to ensure that my step children graduated from secondary school because I was also in school and my mother died. My one stepson did not get his scholarship and both of the boys were mentored by the OHL and the University of Ottawa. We blew it. It's our fault. I also lost my honours status and my house and my car. Every person on the earth will blow it. And these are the reasons that sometimes we are prevented from moving forward with impunity because we are unable to spin all the plates. You're right. That did happen. Yes, we should have been there. Abso-fucking-lutely. We blew the best opportunity you could ever have gotten from us. Every child I ever tried to help, I blew it. It was just enough but not enough to show them how to do it. The paperwork, the walkthrough, the enforcement. We were the adults. It bothers me alot. It was a long time ago. I don't blame you if you never acknowledged us again. God, we got you all that way and you were on the cusp and pshew......it was gone. That sixteen to eighteen year old period of time when no one knows how legal you are and you can launch or bounce or be manipulated. Unless you're gone by then.

Coming Home

Coming home happens once a year
And when I see you it's very clear
That I've been gone too long

It's just that I can't stay home
I hate it there because I have to share
You with a throng

Smoking in the Girl's Room

No smoking
In the bathroom
They're shooting up
In the staff room

What in the actual fuck
Is going on in here?

No toking
In the back room
They're snorting
In the front room

What in the actual fuck
Is going on in here?

No sexting
In the class room
They're transing
In the O.R.

What in the actual fuck
Is going on in here?

Why do men feel their progeny is a burden?
Do women feel this way?

My cousin is legitimate too. Like me, she has no money in her birth record. Sad though, since we were the ones that were supposed to get the opportunities that went to the rest of the trash that already had money. They put her in a psyche ward too after she cracked her neck. Don't ever whine to me about what you think you should or shouldn't, have gotten. And don't ever doubt that we know who we are. I can sniff too, but I won't. I don't need to. I just need to step over your trashy body on my way to work you Nancys. Both of our families sniffed and looked down at us all our lives. The reason we don't is apparent; we have more grace than you. I guess poor legitimacy doesn't have any merit except in the scriptures where all the lineages belong to women if you scholars could get over yourselves and tell the truth. As a legitimate woman, I can claim anyone in my family of origin as my next of kin. In fact, I can change it tomorrow whether I am married or not. Don't be so horrified that Mrs Bm and I knew it all along. Don't ever throw your silly religion my way again. You don't want to give me a job because I'm not trash? Don't even worry about it. I apparently don't need you anyway since I have all your money. You see the irony in all that? Please give it to someone who needs to salvage their reputation unless those don't mean anything anymore. You want to "estate law" me to death? That's probably the wrong way to go since evidently I'm the only one in a bunch of families that has the guts to go and get your loved ones and take care of them. If I was a man, you would have fawned all over me. In the final analysis, your behaviour demonstrates your character. Canada made sure I paid a boatload of taxes so I wouldn't be a drain on my family, apparently according to you, the only thing they did right. I would never leave here. They are my savior because, in the end, I worked for my money and I have nothing to be ashamed for. And neither does she. You are all so afraid of us; too afraid to tell the truth. But I know it. And so do you. I'll bring my perfume to spray all over my motley crew should they ever decide that I'm good enough to acknowledge without sniffing.

Thank you for giving me my say. It is the greatest honour to be allowed to speak and I am grateful to the administration for this.

Please love, laugh and work to your heart's content. I am who I am. I hope you'll be okay.

Do you suppose the fifty states wants us for our beer?

Men have the same issues women do. We are afraid to be trapped. We are afraid our parents or children or other extended family won't forgive us for loving. Six kids mean nothing. My mother got nothing for it and I lived my life in agony. Now everyone thinks I'm a business woman. I'm not. I'm trying to live my life with honour and and I'm not willing to die because someone is jealous that I have accumulated possessions over the length of my lifetime to date. It's just stuff. You can always get more stuff. My expired British passport is fodder for all kinds of shenanigans and you want me to follow my father's line. I cannot. I carry my father's name and I follow my mother's line. It's the law. The women in my family bore more children and did more military service than the men did. They aren't better, that's just how they survived. Lots of them died in Canada with the married name Philp. I can't have kids. No doubt my medical records are sealed but it's all there. I was a minor. I wasn't told. I could feel it. I'm not angry or bitter but the fact that you insist that people become all things to all people is impossible. For all you know Mr President Trump never sleeps but tweets because he misses them all. Can you imagine having three wives and multiple children and not being allowed to love them? It's hard. You know what it's like. There is nowhere to go. It's not sustainable. Will the new world order attempt to fix this? We are the instruments of our own demise for absolutely no reason. For a house. It's ludicrous. If you follow the science my name is PHILIP through an expired passport. It's a trick. It's skulduggery. It's a legal maneuverr. You can call it choices all you want but I don't want choices to sleep with anybody. I want choices to go to work. I have a legal responsibility to be here for my stepchildren if their birth mother dies. They aren't mine. They're hers and his. I'm just the backup. What's your problem with that? What's your problem that I loved them? I mean, what is your problem? I'm just going to be deported to England or Manitoba anyways. What for? The insecurity of living is unfair and illegal. You're not supposed to live in fear, like you did something wrong for being born. Yes, you can earn your legitimacy by obtaining credentials but it doesn't mean you can go into someone else's show, even if they are your biological parent and take their stuff and put them in a ward. Do you know how much money that's going to cost you in taxes? It backfires – so your husband can have your Dad's car? Is it worth it? I don't know. Losing my mother and my grandmothers weren't worth it. Or my husbands. But I would never descend upon my father and insist he has no idea who he is. Bollocks! It's your fucking mother and father. Let them have their lives already.

The truly beautiful thing about religion (I see we have a new Pope. See? The Catholic Church didn't fall – they love to tie the Revelation to this), is the ability to see the good in people and to forgive the bad. I believe this is yes, "opium for the masses" although Mr Marx's misnomer can be forgiven since opium makes us sick, and his statement is predicated on the existing condition that they are already sick. The exact translation is that religion is for the oppressed in a heartless soulless world. What did Mr Yuval Harari mean when he said the "soul" was over? I am not a learned woman with a fistful of degrees. I'm not sure why religion abandons education in favour of faith in God providing. Even the bible itself encourages study. That being acknowledged, I wish to know if the soul and free will are intertwined; one and the same, or, are two separate and distinct entities (for lack of a better term). I submit, from my lowly position as a childless white woman, that indeed, it might be true that the soul is of our own imagination; a belief ungrounded in faith, "the assured expectation of things hoped for" (Hebrews 11:1) – a way to survive as individual legacies. For those who fear death, religion is the sigh of the oppressed creature, the heart of a heartless world, the soul of soulless conditions. But free will? I am full of mirth at this. Hackable animals, I recollect, as the term applied to us uppity humans. Animals we might be, but hackable? Only as slaves. Free will exists throughout nature. Anyone who has raised children with an agenda knows better. Hackable is the new word for submissive. Hackers seek to dominate us? Same game. Different era.

On occasion I am asked if I have any family. My response is that I have a clan that does whatever the fuck they want. And so they should. I'm not running a dynasty. I'm not a controller. I'm a believer that people ought to chase their own dreams without paying your lives back to some freakish machine. That's the American dream (It's Manifesto). I'm a believer that religion has no say in government or private matters of marriage between two people. That's the utopian dream. I'm a believer in the freedom to move from one end of my country to the other without being fined for it. That's the Canadian dream. Please do your homework on this country. All those present on this soil are safe to move anywhere within this country without being bodily harmed for going out of a jurisdiction. You're in opposition to the Canadian dream (It's Constitution). Stop stabbing yourselves in the back. It's why people come here. To be bodily safe. That's why we are called Guardians. Seriously, get a clue. I take very seriously the safety of the human body in this country. It is what we are built on. The fact that you come here to work and take no responsibility for this, on this soil, is why I am polite but privately think you are a little clueless. Just in case I have to rescue you. The Americans have never even lifted a finger against my body and they would have more right to, than you do. But they never ever did. Not once. I respect them. What can I say? They helped me more than I can ever repay. It's a private matter, but yes, that is probably the reason I would cry for one of them. Are you soul less? Am I?

If you persist in estate law, then you will shorten your own life for no reason. A widow remarries; she doesn't lie about in black clothing eeking our her existence. What for? He's DEAD. He wasn't a god, he was a man. Why forty years? That's respect. Why forty years? Because you're supposed to live as long as possible and forty years isn't very long if you live for a thousand. You don't want to? Why go to church then? Why even bother to fight for the breath of life? Useless eaters are starving because it's a body you deem to be useless. Who the fuck are you? And the fact that Wikepedia publishes all kinds of nonsense that even the real person who was there isn't allowed to correct because it's against the community" rules to tell the truth is laughable. Artificial intelligence is responsible for all misinformation. I don't know what to tell you. You insult me on the telephone telling me that I am not working. Well, holy fuck, I get fined for working because apparently I have been widowed more times than you can shake a stick at. I guess you don't want your loved ones to be happy. You just say that to sound like a good person but you don't really mean it. Sometimes you just get stuff because you are a good person. There's more stuff out there. I promise.

My Canadian husband was the victim of sexual violence on Highway 37. You aren't the only ones.

I'm not a gold digger. I lived with my aunt and uncle (who had become a physician) and I used his name on my passport because that was where I was living physically at the time, when I graduated from high school. My marks suck because I was trying to do grades twelve and thirteen at the same time. It's why I went back to the University of Toronto. I received surgery and it was a fact that I had been irrevocably damaged. The records are sealed. It's not anyone's fault but please, stop shitting on my mother. She and my father had religious issues they were trying to escape so they could have a life together without being tortured for it. And you fucking sneered at her. She should have gone back to school and become a doctor. She had a 160 IQ. So that's enough. I congratulate you on your accomplishments. I'm sure when my aunt and uncle meet their demise, there will be a general line up on who gets to keep the house. Ya, you kind of have to be living there. Sheesh. You want to claim all the resources for yourself? What, are you running a company? You want to estate lawyer up? Go ahead. It will be fun. How many bills did you get for nine thousand dollars? None? I paid four times. Maybe you have to pay for sex, but I never had to. Feel better now? I did a three year engineering course in one; and wrote two perfect exams; right after my mother died; with a herniated disk and a seven week menstruation that was the last I bled, while I sobbed in traffic. I drove a Dodge Challenger with a chip in the HEMI. I didn't hurt anyone. Sometimes a strange man walked me to class because I screamed when I tried to navigate a snowbank. It's just kindness. Can you do better? Sulk if you want to. Get a life. The funeral gathering was at my house over the weekend, after I picked everyone up at the airport and showed up for school at seven thirty am Monday morning. In physical, mental and emotional agony. That's why Walmart hires greeters in wheelchairs. I still lost my house, my car, my (step) kids, and my mother, my husband and my father. You know who threw me a bone? My uncle, who was fighting colon cancer. I'm adopted. So sue me. I can fight too. I'm Canadian.

My mother was born in England. In England, she's trash because it was in Essex. Now you know why Mr G thought the whole thing was so much legal fun. Nobody liked my mother, not even her siblings. She was naturalized before she became a citizen. I wish Dad had some money so he could have gone back to the "motherland" in some kind of honour. He tried. I saw the paperwork. He did. But he had four or five kids and my French grandmother had eight or nine. Whoosh! Wouldn't you like a re-set? I mean, how far back do you want to go? To the Connels in Ireland? In Northern Ireland? I mean, I'll do it for you if that's what you want but it's not going to net you any fans or gains. That life is gone. How do you even get to be a professional without being bipolar? Don't be a weakling and play with my paperwork because it's fun. You're just going to get yourself killed inadvertently and I won't know anything about it. Sorry to everyone, but there's black kids in Canada. Mulatos, Metis; what's the difference? How pure can you be without becoming a bottle of perfume? Do you know why I am still safe in the US? Because I go down there to play and that is in line with the pursuit of happiness. I don't cause trouble. I don't fuck American men. I spend my money and have a great time. They're scary wonderful people and if you ever saw a black woman give me an extra piece of chicken on the side because my husband was black and they figured he might not share his dinner with me, you would be so shocked, your eyes would well up with tears that she surreptitiously looked out for me in her own way. I've been kicked out of the US by massive troopers because I was there with my Mr L. It was quite exciting. You want to be scared and angry? Why? Go to work, socialize, make babies and live as long as possible. You so object to the very thing that you want most of all – longevity. It's the most illogical thing I've ever encountered.

If you have legitimate daughters or sons with your wife and you stop having sexual interaction with her, you are a pussy. Is that all you've got?

You never get sued for abandoning the family. You get sued because you stopped fucking your spouse. It's embarrassing.

If I ever have the pleasure of getting inebriated at the local watering hole, I will be sure to visit the RCMP before I go out, so they know I am going to walk home instead of driving and hope I don't get fined for public intoxication. What is the law's stance on this these days? I know for sure that an establishment asks for ID because the boys get into fights. What's the difference if I quietly walk the three blocks to my house with half a bottle of rye whiskey in my body? I mean, precisely who do I get "permission" to live from, without offending or hurting anybody? Do I need to tote around a CPAP or oxygen machine because I'm a provider? Do you? You wanna publish Pamela Anderson's private life? That's illegal in just about every jurisdiction and country in the world. I know plenty of Johnny Appleseeds who don't have their indiscretions plastered on the Wik. Besides, she was only kidding because she already has a mother and a father. Some families are forgivers. Some aren't. Some are, but live in fear they will be killed for forgiving, for accepting. And you object. The grains of sand and the blades of grass don't object and there are far more of them then of you.

I think the bears don't bother me because I had bear shit on my shoes. Bear poo is huge and spongy and makes great fires. They like the smell so they wander by but they don't object. Even bears don't like to live in the outhouse. Snakes are different. I used to have a boa constrictor, but she died. One time, we got a call from my friend because we forgot her at the party the night before (actually, we couldn't figure out how to get her on the bike), and no one would come downstairs until we picked her up off the couch. That was pretty funny too. Jill and Hightower knew her. So did my cousins when we were all younger. Her name was Indica, which, at the time, was brilliant. Now, of course, you know what she was named after. In those days, all the hippies grew weed in claw foot bathtubs that were abandoned in people's backyards. Although the THC was much lower due to Dr Archie's work on the development of the teenager's synaptic pathways. Originally, it was thought that young people's brains were fully developed and just got bigger or older but that was incorrect. The synaptic pathways aren't fully developed in the adult brain until the age of twenty-one. It's why no one ever smoked pot in our family until they were grown, my stepsons included. It raises the risk of schizophrenia, especially in males. Better safe than sorry.

I think in 2018, I became "famous" for being a "sovereign" citizen. I don't know how this happened. I was just living my life. I knew who I was. I didn't want to hurt anybody. Being passed over as a legitimate daughter is not the worst thing in the world you know. When I travelled with Mr L, I rarely slept with him. Travel is not really conducive to an active sex life for me. Besides, if you're in an Indian family's Bed and Breakfast in Essex with someone who is not your husband, you better tread lightly; especially if he's already "married" and he hasn't told you because a) he's not, they just lived together or b) he is and they just don't live together. I'll never know. Mostly, we were just uncomfortable in case we got in trouble. It is the policy of Luxembourg. It's why you could identify me by my name but Canada has always done this for me. It's not favour, I just got oddly rooked somehow but I'm no June Carter. You think they were awful to me but they weren't. I got something else instead. Fair exchange is no robbery. Am I unmarriageable because I can't have kids? Probably. So where do I put my body if that's the only use it has to you? Did I misrepresent myself? How can that be if it occurred when I was a minor? That's protection of the highest sort. How do I know if my first husband would have abandoned me after we had a child, in favour of his next "best friend" conquest. Would he have had to pay taxes to the father of the woman he slept with before me? I know people like this. It's a standard ploy and not that honourable since his daughter wasn't a virgin anyway and neither was he. It makes coming of age a very dangerous place to be. Why do we do this to our young people?

I bet Mr Musk was an astronaut; I suspect that, despite the demands he has felt he had to meet, that he has always been an astronaut and that has never changed. I don't know for sure. So was Mr L a coveted guardian so that I could travel accompanied by a man? What if we had been husband and wife and you objected to that? How would we have been able to find work in Canada? It's a steeplechase. As two grown consenting adults, would another country have determined that we were illegal and immoral because we travelled together? It was kind of brave if you ask me. The man we drove around New York City with (Mr G and I) was associated with West Point in San Diego. San Diego is stunning. In fact, I stopped there to smoke a cigarette by the water to calm myself before I waded back into Mexico. There are stories like these all over the world. Is this why my mother never forgave me? Is this why my aunt sprays perfume when I leave the room? Maybe. I don't know. The men and women in my family work alot, all the time. Sometimes we get to play but it's very expensive to go to the places now, that used to be dirt roads. People with money look at us like we crawled out from under a rock when we go to Tofino but I don't mind. The young need to see the world as well. It's the privilege of all living beings to see the earth. I have the same problems as you. I would rather vote but if I change my party loyalty for the sake of the country, I am disloyal. If I keep my vote to one party then it's loyal but it might be nepotism. I don't know what to tell you. I'm a Liberal. I like the other parties. I was ashamed of myself because I didn't know where that name came from and I don't like to be abused physically for that. If nobody told me, then I guess they didn't know either. It's not their fault. Until you came after me for loving. I probably shouldn't have said I was ashamed of my government. It's a true democracy that I wasn't put into prison for saying so. Gosh, I had no idea. It was really a call for help because I didn't know what I was supposed to do. Most times, people default to what they are supposed to do. Nobody WANTS to get into trouble. I like Trudeau or I would never have said anything to him via the federal web site. It was trust. I don't know what to tell you. It took alot of guts for me to vote in the first place. I have my own religious-ness to overcome. And I guess if I love one of your "own" then I have to convert or something. It's a weirdly odd bit of blackmail for the sake of power over something that has already left you to gain a life of its own. Why is growth subjected to judgement and scrutiny? Even if you choose it, you can never have it even if you commit. It's out there. Sure it is. So is everything else. I'm not pissed at my family lol. At any given time my family is working or loving or whatever. I only get to see them as friends on rare occasions. So do you. But to be angry as a young person because you have to negotiate a life yourself is not the answer. No matter how old you get, you still have to negotiate your life. And sometimes couples don't want you at their house for Christmas. It's not a dis. It's a negotiation. I'd rather stay up all night playing my music too. Sometimes Christmas Eve is the only chance you're going to get. The expectations are immense. If you are from somewhere else and have a different holiday like Kwanza, how do you negotiate that in a country that doesn't have that as a national holiday? Do you scream racism? How many holidays can there be? We have to work. If we take them away to please you, then nobody gets a holiday. Yes, it's commercial. Yes, its troublesome if you're expected to show up at three different houses with a carload of children and gifts for everybody while you're still trying to get with the program because you worked three double shifts and did your shopping on the twenty-third and can barely afford gas because you maxed out your credit card and still have to come up with something fabulous for New Year's. We're not lard asses. We've just been to the puppet show. It's still a religious holiday. Do you hate the Italians because it was Constantine that rounded up all those pagan manuscripts and put them into one text called the bible so everyone would stop sacrificing their children to the fire? I could die tomorrow and you will never miss me when I am gone. I don't need you to. I need you to pursue your heart's desire until you die. It's going to work out one time out of a thousand. Hopefully, when it does, you will be far away so no one is jealous that you were associated with something that worked. Divided loyalties are a fact of life. I tell you the truth so you can kill me for it if you have to. I don't have anywhere else to go. The fact that I am probably still embroiled in probate is unfortunate. I have a little bit of money. A bunch of friends. I have blood relatives. Sure I do. But they have to live their own lives. It's not my purview to demand fealty. That would be cruel and torturous. I'm still here. I'm a forgiver. In the end, sex isn't all that and it's just easier to pay for than it is to love someone and do it that way. If that's what we've come to, then I don't understand why we even bother. I can't disconnect my brain from my body. I can't help loving you. I don't know what to tell you.

Some of you feel, in Canada, that I just don't want to admit that I've used up two marriages and I should be going by A.M. Philp or Amanda M. Philp. That would be unfortunate because those names depicting my name have already been used in Canada in several jurisdictions. I could really hurt somebody if I did that. Besides, how do I live somewhere without everyone objecting? I mean, precisely what name and living situation would you prefer I secure for myself so that you are more comfortable with me? So I can go back to work or pay someone for helping to support their pre-existing family because they can't do it themselves? I mean, I could just sit here and claim ROYAL LEGITIMACY and watch the money roll in. LOL, it doesn't really work that way. Or I could languish in a psyche ward and have you pay for it. They won't let me stay there because I trade my cigarettes for the privilege of not having to be poisoned to death by mandated mind altering anti-psychotics. These are what I was on when I posted. Help meeeeeee please – they're going to kill me. And so they did.

I paid my debt to that first Canadian wife. I paid my debt to the first English wife. I've almost paid my debt to my first Canadian husband. By the time I am seventy-three, I will have paid my debt to my second husband. The music is deemed to not be worth anything because my original business account was opened a long time ago at the TD. An Indian woman sneered at me for it and didn't take me seriously. My second husband paid for half my web site. He had a nervous breakdown after he saw me perform. Literally. Of course his family prefers Beyonce by a mile, even over James Cotton so they didn't think it was worth anything. My aunt was the only one.

The askance you throw my way when you live in a glass house is breathtaking. I think my choice will be not to commit – in case you kill me for it. Then you can pull my hair for being a whore. Honestly! I live with non committers! They're my kind! And at this juncture, I have no choice than to go by my name because I can't pay every person in the world nine thousand dollars for the privilege of living in it. I could rack up what I perceive you owe me and it would be a blood bath, if you want to be like that. I respect your dreams. I would never do anything like that. It would be mentally unstable behaviour. Unless you're a true committer, please go away. I've never seen one. Have you? Or I could charge back to you all the help you are charging me for. Except you can't afford it. Because you are already married. It's a wow factor. You know why you aren't still together and you're having children with someone else. They couldn't commit! And neither can you! Because you can't live on straw and wear black and live in a tent because you didn't do what someone else wanted you to do.

Young people, it's a crap shoot. You can get lots of stuff. It's easy. It's easy to love. It's easy to get bored. It's easy to live. It's not easy to be with anybody. Everyone is made to feel ashamed. It's no way to live. Someone will always torture you to death for it because they are afraid they will be left alone. It's bizarre. Live your life. Make compromises sometimes. Make room for who you really are. Divine providence is what made you who you really are. The rest is a pile of genes and hormones. If you find someone as strong as you and will stick, cleave. If you can't, then you are all generally at the mercy of each other. Me? If you tell me what you want from me, I'd be happy to do it. I'll write about it. But be forewarned that if I physically move from one jurisdiction to another in order to accomplish that and you're going to charge me for it or for sheltering a minor then you are breaking the law. I don't care what you FEEL about that. It's the same for everybody. This land is your land. This land is my land.

Corporations that need to displace humanity for pleasure destinations are right out of their minds. There's a shit ton of destinations that aren't being used. Why come after the people who are caretaking? Not for themselves alone but for a section of humanity? I mean farmers and ranchers and fisheries. How freakin special can one lone individual be? When you sit in the middle of a road protesting, aren't you going to lose your job? Who pays your bills? Why do you think others have to pay your bills? And other than the bills that come in the mail, what other bills could there possibly be? Except for emotional blackmail ones. I could leave you high and dry and go sit on a rock but someone would put me in a psyche ward for being crazy. And if they don't give me an end of life needle, then you'll have to shell out for it and I'm under the impression that you are unable to pay your bills already so I'm going to help you do that since the last guy you were with won't. It gets charged back to him, not me. It's his line apparently.

Same with the second husband. I mean, which atrocity are you going to shed more blood over? I can't fix your life. I can only be part of it and when you go off to do something else because no one stays five years old forever, it's over for me too. Its funny isn't it? I think Crissman is part of the Reid Riches family tree. I hear you sister. But I'm not paying you for sleeping with the father of your children who you aren't married to. Are you? And you aren't with him? What in the actual fuck is going on in here? I thought he wanted to build you a house but your brother objected. I know right? Who hasn't? You just come live with me and bring your new boyfriend when the time comes, so you don't get into trouble. My ex might show up if his kids take the house but I'm pretty sure there will be someone here who would be perfect for him.

I'm a song writer. I hope you don't mind.

I want to know what is more inappropriate, divorce or children born out of wedlock? Who owes what to whom? Since when do my own brothers and sister not get to have the balls to live their own lives? Mine do. I'm sure yours do too. Since when does my sister have to ask for permission as a lawful wife. Fuck, I wouldn't get a job either, if I had to do that. What, am I married or am I a slave? Pfft. Am I supposed to pay half the bills, be a knockout, bear six children in his name, look the other way when he's into strange instead of skull bashing when I'm pregnant. And bear the shame of being an abandoned wife with no name when he moves on? I don't think so sweetie pie. I don't think so. It's even worse if I'm well educated.

House ownership is taxed based on the number of occupants and their relationship to each other. If the bank doesn't like what you're doing, they charge you double behind your back. It's just a house. I really don't understand the problem. I think house ownership is tricky. No one wants to say they are responsible for it because it will cost them money but they want it to be sold so they can rent. It's still shelter that is necessary for survival in a modern world. Someday you have to sell it if you're kids are grown or you're being targeted because you've reached a certain age. I've seen lots of men and women in their hundreds who were busy in these massive gardens. The only reason they were allowed out of the hospital after their hips were replaced is because they got to their feet the next day and started walking the halls so they would be allowed to go home instead of being put in prison. My grandmum wasn't so lucky. She did actually know what she was doing and she was correct, the therapy they gave her was a mismatch so it didn't work. She just wept in a chair in the corner because she just knew she was going to be a "nuisance" to everyone. I recognize why the off grid movement was kyboshed. All those military men knew what they were doing and we couldn't afford an "underground" city. I don't know why we are jealous. I don't know why men aren't whores. They mostly are. They don't protect anybody. They never have. They get paid for everything. Even for the kids. I don't know why people get vicious. I mostly get relieved. Of duty. But I love them anyway. I have to. There's no one else here.

WHERE DO ALL THE HORSES MEN GO II
Amanda May Philp

Once you have loved close to the bone
Then you know nothing else will do
I wanna know
Where do all
The horses' men go?

When you know its going to go away
And you'll lose your way forever
I wanna know
Where do all
The horses' men go?

When you've tried as hard as you can
But it doesn't come back to you
I wanna know
Where do all
The horses' men go?

So you've loved one of the horses men
You will have lost one of the horses men
Cause I know
Where they all
Where the horses men go

BRIDGE
What I wanna know
When it's over
I wanna know now
Where do they go

Where do they go now
I wanna know

Where do they go now
When it's over
Where do all the horses' men go?